Published by ORO Editions
Publishers of Architecture, Art, and Design
Gordon Goff: Publisher
www.oroeditions.com
info@oroeditions.com

Cover Design: Caleb White (Cover Design), Agata Jakubowska and Shi Zhang (Cover Image)
Book Design: Caleb White and Leon Yi-Liang Ko

ORO Project Coordinator: Kirby Anderson
Color Separations and Printing: ORO Group Ltd.
Printed in China.

ORO Editions makes a continuous effort to minimize the overall carbon footprint of its publications. As part of this goal, ORO Editions, in association with Global ReLeaf, arranges to plant trees to replace those used in the manufacturing of the paper produced for its books. Global ReLeaf is an international campaign run by American Forests, one of the world's oldest nonprofit conservation organizations. Global ReLeaf is American Forests' education and action program that helps individuals, organizations, agencies, and corporations improve the local and global environment by planting and caring for trees.

10 9 8 7 6 5 4 3 2 1 First Edition
Library of Congress data available upon request. World Rights: Available
ISBN 978-1-951541-00-2

FUTURE AIRPORTS EDITED BY ALI RAHIM

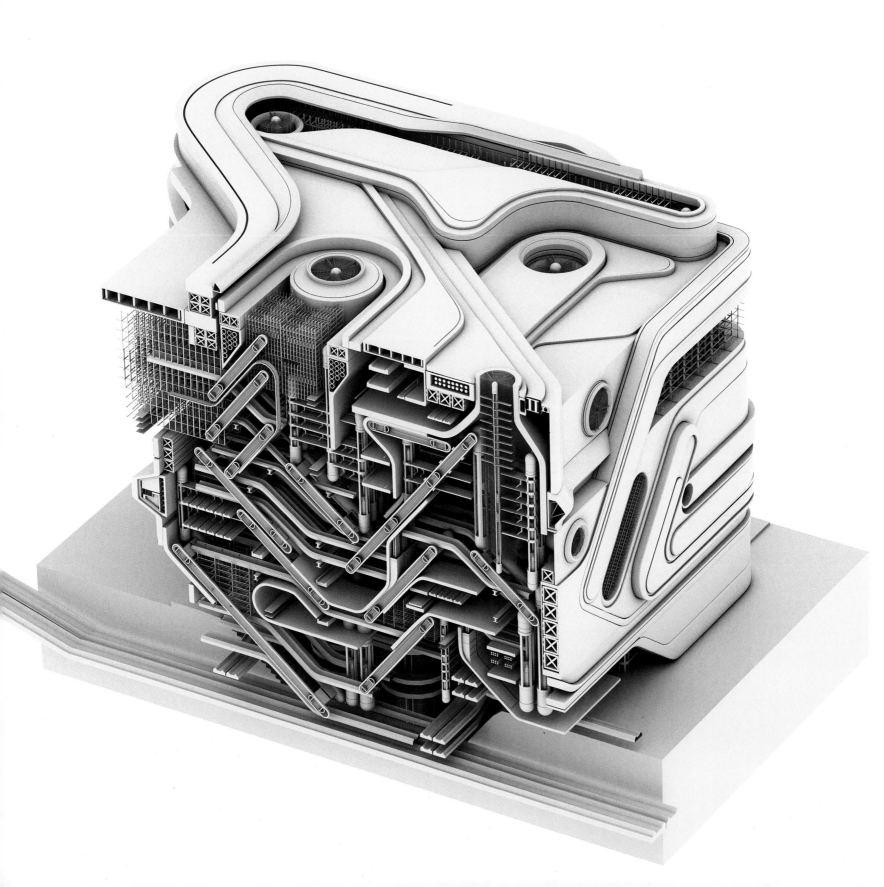

CONTENTS

Section Model Rendering. Project by Yutian Tang, Tianjian Li, and Wenlu Guo

PROJECTS

Student Work was produced at The University of Pennsylvania
Stuart Weitzman School of Design
Masters of Science in Design: Advanced Architectural Design [MSD-AAD]

One-point Perspective. Project by Rui Huang, Qi Liu, and John Dunn

00 INTRODUCTION
Ali Rahim

FUTURE AIRPORTS

Future Airports is an expansive approach to architectural design. This book explores contemporary architectural issues through texts and design research projects from across the discipline focused on the future role of the airport. The works collected here provide frameworks for understandings the complex and multifaceted nature of the future airport and aspire to influence new ways of conceiving architecture at multiple scales. The topic broadens and contributes to research on the future of air infrastructure, logistics systems, and the airport typology.

Future Airports uses New York City as a case study for speculating upon how a new airport typology can help sustain financial global leadership in the world. New York City's modern development has always been related to capital, of which architecture has been a primary form of expression. Since the establishment of Manhattan's gridded streets and parcels in the Commissioners'

Plan of 1811, land values have correlated with the densification of building mass. In the early 19th century, the grid provided a circulation/access network for people and goods and broke up farmland into smaller units. Parcels were further subdivided into building lots, and land value was multiplied vertically with the repetition of floors. In the beginning of the 20th century, land value was augmented by aesthetics, as buildings were designed to emblematize the companies that built them. Skyscrapers began to subsume whole city blocks, creating unprecedented interior urban environments. If densification responded to 20th-century desires to increase production capacity with vast implications for architectural design, can a new airport typology respond to the 21st-century desire for flow?

Airports by their nature are catalysts for local and regional economies and are conceived as containers of movement for people and goods. Today, all shipping companies move their goods through airports, and the pressure on airports to respond to the movement of increased volumes of goods is both challenging and full of potential. There are numerous new export opportunities in developing and emerging economies driven by technology and growth. There is increased demand for long haul flights and travel between Asia, South America, and Africa. At the same time, technologically driven retail giants such as Amazon and Walmart channel materials and goods to remote locations through existing delivery networks established by DHL, USPS, UPS, and FedEx. Currently, 90 percent of global trade flows through 39 airports.[1] With global trade increasing rapidly, the cities that serve as important gateways will thrive.

Despite New York City's status as a global financial capital, JFK International Airport ranks 21st worldwide in terms of the number of travelers that move through the airport each year and 20th in terms of cargo traffic.[2] Other cities vying for financial global leadership rank much higher, such as Hong Kong, Tokyo, and Dubai, which are all in the top eight for both passenger and cargo traffic. An efficient hub that deals with both passengers and cargo and is directly accessible in New York City would benefit U.S. retail and establish the city as the leader of cargo nationally and internationally. A new terminal will increase the relevance of JFK as a business and logistics hub and establish a stronger connection to global centers while strengthening local development.

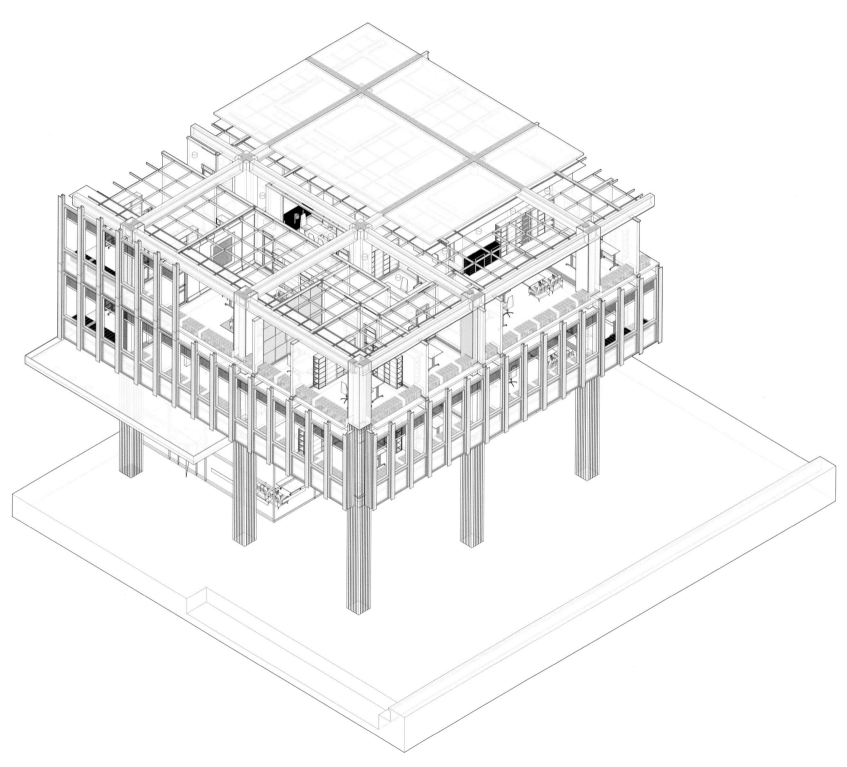

Seagram Building, Mies van der Rohe, New York, 1958. Drawing by Bingkun Deng, Yang Yang, and Jiang Ming

As such, this book posits that architecture can impact global leadership by fusing urban elements and logistics in airports in new forms of architecture while acting as a catalyst for the generation of capital. Underlying the essays and design research projects contained herein is a questioning of the heroic nature of the Modernist airport typology and its celebration of aviation. Speculating that the increased role of the airport as a logistics hub will have large-scale ramifications, the demand of increased logistics flows and systems in airports is conceptualized as a primary design engine. Logistics are the dominant material arrangement that inform inhabitation in the included design research projects. The instrumental function of logistics in these projects reconceptualizes and reconfigures airport space and experience from the normative bounds of a vacuous space for passengers. The projects develop an aesthetic that comes from the accumulation of systems themselves. Storage racks, sorting machines, and conveyor belts are all brought together in different configurations and densities to produce architectural opportunities in organization and form that contribute to the uniqueness of each project. These reflect a broader cultural need to rethink architecture's positionality and agency within the global economy.

ASSET ARCHITECTURE

In the last 25 years, there has been an immense increase in global capital due to the growth of economies in China, India, and the Middle East, including the UAE and Qatar. Global capital more than doubled between 2001 to 2011 from $37 trillion to $80 trillion.[3] While monetary capital has always played a significant role in shaping the built environment, recent shifts in the character of global finance have resulted in new relationships between investment practices and buildings, including the emergence of whole new building typologies. Traditional stable assets such as treasury and municipal bonds are yielding relatively low returns. Investors have circumvented these stable assets for real estate, which has had a direct impact on architecture and urbanism. While architecture and urbanism have functioned as assets throughout New York's history, the degree to which space functions as an asset has increased exponentially. As in the stock market, there is volatile fluctuation between growth and decay due to the amount of capital that has been channeled into real estate. Architects and architecture have not responded to this issue in any way.

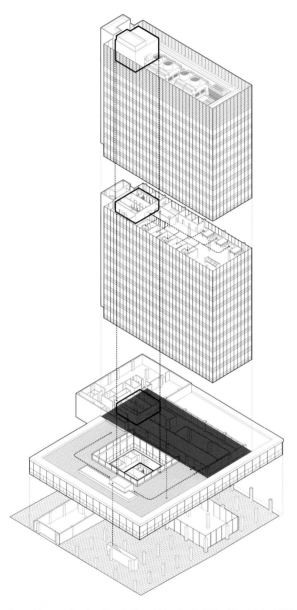

Lever House, Gordon Bunshaft and Natalie de Blois, New York, 1952.
Drawing by Zhe Zhong, Sijie Gao, and Atharva Ranade

More specifically, *Future Airports* probes the notion that the increments of architecture (units, buildings, parcels of land, etc.) increasingly operate as financial investment assets in contradistinction with the performative attributes typically associated with the art and science of building. New York City, for example, has a total of 845,000 houses and apartments, yet nearly 250,000 units or 12% of its housing market are vacant.[4] This number is predicted to double if capital growth continues to increase at the same rate in 2018. The people who own these condominiums are usually wealthy foreigners seeking financial havens and have been referred to as "Skim Milk New Yorkers" because they only spend 2% of their time in New York.[5] This trend has been epitomized in the propagation of a new building typology in Manhattan: the pencil tower.[6] Pencil towers are luxury residential buildings with base to height ratios of at least 1:7; they are extremely slender because of the exaggerated proportions that result from maximizing vertical space (read profit values) on outsized building lots. The development of the pencil tower is a major reason why so many windows dotting the facades of Fifth, Madison, and Park Avenue apartment buildings are pitch-black every evening.

This desertion reflects larger global patterns wherein speculative real estate bubbles increase in frequency and scale, inducing what David Harvey has described as a cycle in which "capital builds a physical landscape appropriate to its moment in time only to have to destroy it."[7] Cities are now globally interrelated and interconnected. Interconnectivity has caused capital flows to affect property markets and prices throughout the world, and prices in some cities have risen astronomically. Beijing, for example, has experienced an 800% increase in property values over the past eight years. Further, in China there are two examples of whole cities being left vacant: Tianducheng, Paris of the East, Zheiziang Province and Kangbashi New City, Ordos, Xaanshi province.

This points towards the future of New York real estate: New York prices will eventually decrease, and the demand for high-end condominiums will wane, decreasing the pressure on what led to the new typology of the pencil tower. To evaluate this hypothesis, one needs to look no further than the new pencil tower designed by Jean Nouvelle at 53 East 53rd Street in New York. The building went to market in September 2015, yet, currently, only 55% of its units have been sold. It is among eight pencil towers that have been designed, three of which have completed or are under construction, One57, 432 Park Avenue, and 111 West 57th Street. The other five projects have been cancelled. Now the city is exhausted with an oversupply of new condominiums. With New York's financial leadership and real estate value being challenged by other cities including London, Dubai, Hong Kong, and Tokyo, how will New York respond?

CHALLENGES TO NEW YORK CITY'S GLOBAL FINANCIAL LEADERSHIP

The fact that Manhattan has served as a receptor of global capital has maintained its status as a global leader. Financial capitals need strong economies, yet economies are rapidly changing across the world. The triumvirate of easy money, cheap imports, and strong confidence catalyze growth in Western economies, and New York City's global financial leadership has been sustained by the culmination of all three. Today these are in decline: interest rates are increasing, low cost retailers such as American Apparel and Radio Shack have filed for bankruptcy, and an uncertain political climate has shaken confidence in the U.S. economy. All three components have threatened New York City as the leading global financial capital. Looking at the state of the economy in 2019, many factors that were increasing capital in the financial system, such as the growing economies of China, Russia, and the Middle East, are now inaccessible due to sanctions and trade wars. The global network for capital has dried up, and the demand for high-end condominiums in New York City has diminished. High-end condominiums have become less desirable on 57th Street in Manhattan (also dubbed "billionaires' row") as there is little local demand for mid-town Manhattan condos. Herein lies the conundrum: New York is relying on the demand generated by foreign investors' desire to own real estate assets in the city while struggling to maintain its global status through other facets of value inherent to its real estate.

The future airport, then, addresses New York City's leadership by focusing on two specific issues that can help build a foundation for future growth: infrastructure and flow through infrastructure. The growth of air travel and logistics movement has been exacerbated by the growth of middle-class populations in other countries and their access to travel. Logistics and the movement of cargo has multiplied twenty-fold over the last five years due to the widespread success of online delivery services for the purchase of a wide range of goods. Until recently, online retailers shopped for the cheapest prices from existing shipping companies. Last year, however, Amazon launched their own logistics and shipping company, marking a new era of technology-driven retail. The integration of travel and logistics contributes to the success of any hub airport in the world. New York city's deficiencies in moving people and goods set up the challenge of the future airport in New York.

DESIGN RESEARCH: NEW YORK CITY ARCHITECTURE AND THE LONG-SPAN STRUCTURE

Through a careful study of architectural and structural precedents, this book combines knowledge sets and situates novel forms of integrating the airport hub with logistics. Design research—a method of researching through the act of designing—was used strategically to allow for the infusion of a large body of knowledge to influence the work shown in this book. The book's contributors studied the development of the tower typology in Manhattan as well as long-span structures that are commonly used to build airports.

The history of the skyscraper in New York City greatly influenced the work in this book. The Woolworth Building celebrated ornament to bring value to a company that sold very cheap products. The building's architecture exuded a greater aspiration than what the Woolworth Stores were known for. Zoning laws played a significant role in shaping the architecture of Manhattan until Gordon Bunshaft and Natalie De Blois of Skidmore Owings and Merrill lifted the podium off the street level and pushed the building envelope back to meet the 25% open area requirement for the Lever House (1952). This provided more access to public space as well as more area for corporate display. Mies van der Rohe brilliantly negotiated with the City of New York to build the Seagram Building (1958) straight up from street level by designating a large plaza for the public. In 1961, the building code was revised to emulate the success of the Seagram Building plaza and its privately owned public spaces. The Ford Foundation Building (1962), designed by Kevin Roche and John Dinkeloo while working at Eero Saarinen's office, made the most of that new building code by bringing landscape inside the office typology with the added benefit of multiplying the interior window area of the offices.

Along with the skyscraper, contributions to the book investigate four types of long-span structures that use tensile and compressive forces. These include cable and pneumatic structures, framed and slab structures, multi-dimensional splitting structures, and folded surface and shell structures. The history of such structures is extensive and starts with single-level spaces, the Pantheon (118-128) being one of the earliest, Hagia Sophia

(532-537) and St. Peters Cathedral (1506-1615) being other prime examples. The Crystal Palace (1851) used cast iron and plate glass. Later, in 1870, the first passenger elevator was used in the Equitable Life Building in New York City, which propelled the typology of the skyscraper. With the advent of the skyscraper, the long-span structure took on a different form that intersects with capital pushing the limits of engineering. In the same manner, we investigate the long-span typology as a knowledge base in order to invent new structural and spatial typologies that are appropriate for a new airport typology: the Gateway. The gateway combines movement sequences, infrastructure, and logistical flows; it connects the city to the airport and the greater world.

THE BOOK AND ITS CONTRIBUTORS

The following chapters trace the airport typology progressively through three sections that examine issues ranging from the macro-scale of planning to the micro-scale of architecture. The first section focuses on a trio of research projects that take on local and global issues of airport planning. Megan Ryerson leads off in Chapter 01 by explaining the planning implications of the airport and how it is intricately interwoven in the economy. Chapter 02, authored by an ARUP research team led by Jenny Buckley, outlines a series of development issues that pertain to airports around the world. In Chapter 03, Tom Verebes examines passenger experience while traveling through airports.

The second section examines the long-span structure commonly used in airport design. This section oscillates between the disciplinary history of long-span structures to the physical forces that flow through such structures themselves. In Chapter 04, Caleb White unpacks the disciplinary history of the long-span structure and its impact on architecture. In Chapter 05, Preetam Biswas speculates on the future of long-span structures and their effects on the future airport, while, in Chapter 06, Masoud Akbarzadeh describes vector-based structural models and contemporary design of long-span structures created specifically for airport design.

The third section of texts engage architectural issues ranging from the design of a contemporary airport to the changing aesthetics of the airport within architectural discourse. In Chapter 07, Cristiano

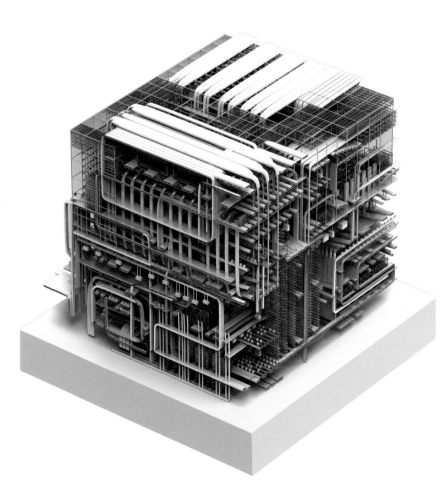

Section Model Rendering. Project by Yuan Zhang, Cai Zhang, and Yiling Zhong

Ceccato describes his recently completed design with Zaha Hadid Architects for the new Beijing Airport. In Chapter 08, Christopher Hight connects the disciplinary project that has emerged out of human and machine space to airport design, and, in Chapter 09, Nate Hume delves into detail on poche space in the discipline, questioning the clarity of figure-ground. I end the book in Chapter 10 by advocating for using aesthetics to rethink the relationship between human and logistic space.

The three sections of texts are punctuated by samples of student work developed at the University of Pennsylvania Stuart Weitzman School of Design in the Master of Science in Design Advanced Architectural Design degree program in a studio led by Ezio Blasetti, Brian Deluna, Nate Hume, and myself. Each project is presented through images and short texts. They are distributed after Chapters 03, 06, and 10, respectively, and relate generally to all the concepts presented in this book. The design research projects were developed using two precedents, one architectural and another structural, and they share the same site and scale. We selected John F. Kennedy International Airport as our site, as it connects New York City to the world. The design projects are proposals for a new Gateway Hub, which serves as the entry sequence to the airport and combines with a cargo terminal to develop a new typology for New York City's airports.

As with the authored texts, the projects have been grouped into three sections: Structured Logistics, Atmosphere, and Form. Each project section takes on a unique set of challenges that addresses the larger role and increased complexities of airports today. These categories are speculative and consider the expansion of existing logistics companies directly to the consumer. Structured Logistics enables logistics to play a role in shaping the future of long-span structures, while Atmosphere allows logistic systems to play a key role in building aesthetics and experience. Form highlights spaces that oscillate between logistics and human spaces.

We hope that by providing both texts and projects, the book is both cohesive and flexible enough to allow the reader to find their own path for negotiating the content. The aim of this book is the same as the future airport: to investigate interactions with and innovative responses from its users. As a proxy for architecture's global integration with societal systems, *Future Airports* pushes disciplinary bounds and provides frameworks for future architectures.

01 PriceWaterhouseCoopers, "Transportation & Logistics 2030 Volume 4: Securing the supply chain" in PriceWaterhouseCoopers, 2011. https://www.pwc.com/gx/en/transportation-logistics/pdf/tl2030_vol.4_web.pdf.

02 "Preliminary World Airport Traffic Rankings Released." ACI World, May 15 2019, aci.aero/news/2019/03/13/preliminary-world-airport-traffic-rankings-released/.

03 "Giant Pools of Money," from the Radio Show This American Life. Originally aired on May 9, 2008.

04 U.S. Census Bureau. "New York City Housing and Vacancy Survey (NYCHVS)." The United States Census Bureau, January 15,2019, www.census.gov/programs-surveys/nychvs.html.

05 For an overview of this trend, see Sam Roberts, "Homes Dark and Lifeless, Kept by Out-of-Towners." The New York Times, July 6, 2011. https://www.nytimes.com/2011/07/07/nyregion/more-apartments-are-empty-yet-rented-or-owned-census-finds.html.

06 See for instance Oliver Wainwright, "Super-tall, Super-skinny, Super-expensive: the 'pencil towers' of New York's super rich," The Guardian, February 5, 2019.

07 David Harvey, "The Urban Process Under Capitalism: A Framework for Analysis" International Journal of Urban and Regional Research Vol. 2 No. 1-3, p. 120, 1978.

08 Blumberg, Alex. "The Giant Pool of Money" in This American Life, episode 355.

09 Doganis, Rigas. "Trend to Airport Privatization" in The Airport Business. London, UK: Routledge, 2000.

10 Harvey, David. "The Urban Process Under Capitalism: A Framework for Analysis" in International Journal of Urban and Regional Research Vol. 2 No. 1-3, p. 120, 1978.

11 Harvey, David. "Foreword: The Urban Roots of the Financial Crisis" in Subprime Cities: The Political Economy of mortgage Markets, ed. Manuel B. Aalbers. Chichester, UK: Blackwell Publishing, 2012.

12 Levesque, Peter. "Unlocking Supply Chain Innovation" in The Shipping Point: The Rise of China and the Future of Retail Supply Chain Management. Chichester, UK: John Wiley and Sons, 2011.

13 Levesque, Peter. "The Innovative Retail Supply Chain" ed. Chris Robeson, in The Shipping Point: The Rise of China and the Future of Retail Supply Chain Management. Chichester, UK: John Wiley and Sons, 2011.

14 Levesque, Peter. "The Role of People and Technology in Dynamic Supply Chains" in The Shipping Point: The Rise of China and the Future of Retail Supply Chain Management. Chichester, UK: John Wiley and Sons, 2011.

15 JFK Air Cargo Study. NYCEDC. www.nycedc.com/resource/jfk-air-carg-study.

16 Kolomatsky, Michael. "Slicing New York's Housing Pie" in The New York Times, February 28, 2019. www.nytimes.com/2019/02/28/realestate/slicing-new-yorks-housing-pie.html.

17 "Preliminary World Airport Traffic Rankings Released" from ACI World, May 15, 2019. aci.aero/news/2019/03/13/preliminary-world-airport-traffic-rankings-released/.

18 Roberts, Sam. "Homes Dark and Lifeless, Kept by Out-of-Towners" in The New York Times, July 6, 2011. https://www.nytimes.com/2011/07/07/nyregion/more-apartments-are-empty-yet-rented-or-owned-census-finds.html.

19 U.S. Census Bureau. "New York City Housing and Vacancy Survey (NYCHVS)" from The United States Census Bureau, January 15,. 2019. www.census.gov/programs-surveys/nychvs.html.

20 Wainwright, Oliver. "Super-tall, Super-skinny, Super-expensive: the 'Pencil Towers' of New York's Super Rich" in The Guardian, February 5, 2019.

01 THE URBAN AIRPORT:
History, Contemporary Development Issues, and the Future

Megan S. Ryerson

An airport is, by its very nature, an intermodal terminal that consolidates local, interregional, national, and global flows comprised of large numbers of passengers and high value cargo and thus, influences the urban environment. Urban airports serve as "antecedents for planning" which have significant urban impacts because of airports and air traffic; these impacts are often in direct conflict in terms of the goals of city planners.[1] Consider that airports are both generators of urban economic development and also are Locally Unwanted Land Uses (LULU) with complex environmental and social impacts.[2] Moreover, airports have become the landscape through which urban competition is playing out, rendering some airports oversubscribed while others are scrambling to build air service. Altogether, the future of airport development both in the U.S. and abroad is highly uncertain. In the following chapter, we explore the challenges facing airport managers today and how they shape the future of airport systems.

BRIEF HISTORY OF AIRPORT DEVELOPMENT: MOTIVATIONS AND PRACTICE

Large-scale airport development by U.S. cities and municipalities and the growth of the commercial airline industry began in the 1920s. Congress enabled the creation and growth of commercial airlines by giving airlines the responsibility of carrying mail under contract by the Post Office through the Air Mail Act (called the Kelly Act).[3] The following year the Air Commerce Act established the "dock concept" for airport funding: funding for docks, compared with harbors, occurs at the local level. The following year, the final piece of the puzzle—aircraft technology that could support commercial flights—was realized by Charles Lindbergh's solo flight across the Atlantic.[4] While the federal government initiated legislation that enabled large-scale airport development, airports were mostly municipally owned and operated, a structure preferred by the public. Bednarek[5] describes that the public believed municipal airports would "treat all users fairly and equally" and would be less likely to sell off the land to a higher bidder compared with a private owner.

Cities and sub-state jurisdictions began building airports to own and operate with an unbridled enthusiasm. Cities were encouraged to do so by the U.S. Post Office and Military; both organizations needed airports for training and transport but lacked funding to support this need.[6] While cities shouldered the burden, many were eager to do so: underlying urban boosterism and urban competition drove development. Cities were driven by the "Winged Gospel," or the worship-like enthusiasm Americans had for aviation, to build airports; similar aviation boosterism was experienced around the world.[7] Cities maintained a "build it and they will come" mentality which largely persists today.[8]

In support of building airports and enabling flight operations, city planners actively acquired land and proactively zoned the land around airports to protect the airport from any hazards to aerial navigation. In the early days of airport development, the land acquired was modest. Large airports with multiple runways were not considered necessary. As airlines were regulated, and a single entity optimized airline service, capacity at a large scale was unnecessary. Furthermore, available aircrafts were sensitive to winds and had a limited range. City planners sought airport

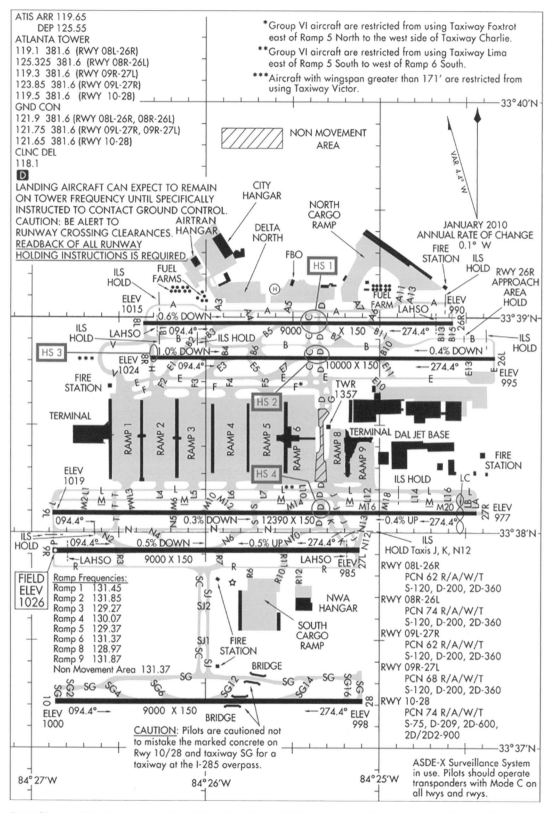

ATIS ARR 119.65
         DEP 125.55
ATLANTA TOWER
119.1 381.6 (RWY 08L-26R)
125.325 381.6 (RWY 08R-26L)
119.3 381.6 (RWY 09R-27L)
123.85 381.6 (RWY 09L-27R)
119.5 381.6 (RWY 10-28)
GND CON
121.9 381.6 (RWY 08L-26R, 08R-26L)
121.75 381.6 (RWY 09L-27R, 09R-27L)
121.65 381.6 (RWY 10-28)
CLNC DEL
118.1
D
LANDING AIRCRAFT CAN EXPECT TO REMAIN
ON TOWER FREQUENCY UNTIL SPECIFICALLY
INSTRUCTED TO CONTACT GROUND CONTROL.
CAUTION: BE ALERT TO
RUNWAY CROSSING CLEARANCES.
READBACK OF ALL RUNWAY
HOLDING INSTRUCTIONS IS REQUIRED.

*Group VI aircraft are restricted from using Taxiway Foxtrot
east of Ramp 5 North to the west side of Taxiway Charlie.

**Group VI aircraft are restricted from using Taxiway Lima
east of Ramp 5 South to west of Ramp 6 South.

***Aircraft with wingspan greater than 171' are restricted from
using Taxiway Victor.

NON MOVEMENT
AREA

33°40'N

VAR 4.4° W

JANUARY 2010
ANNUAL RATE OF CHANGE
0.1° W

CITY
HANGAR

NORTH
CARGO
RAMP

AIRTRAN
HANGAR

DELTA
NORTH

FBO

FUEL
FARMS

ILS
HOLD

HS 1

FIRE
STATION

ILS
HOLD

RWY 26R
APPROACH
AREA
HOLD

FUEL
FARM

A11
A13

LAHSO

ELEV
990

33°39'N

ELEV
1015

0.6% DOWN

ILS
HOLD

LAHSO

094.4°

ILS HOLD

9000   X 150

274.4°

ILS
HOLD

HS 3   ***

1.0% DOWN

0.4% DOWN

ELEV
1024

094.4°

10000 X 150

274.4°

ELEV
995

FIRE
STATION

TWR
1357

TERMINAL

HS 2

RAMP 1   RAMP 2   RAMP 3   RAMP 4   RAMP 5   RAMP 6   RAMP 8   RAMP 9

TERMINAL   DAL JET BASE

FIRE
STATION

ELEV
1019

HS 4

ILS HOLD

LC

094.4°

0.3% DOWN

12390 X 150

0.4% UP   274.4°

27R   ELEV
977

33°38'N

ILS
HOLD

094.4°

0.5% DOWN

0.5% UP

274.4°

ILS
HOLD Taxis J, K, N12

LAHSO

9000 X 150

LAHSO   ELEV
985

RWY 08L-26R
PCN 62 R/A/W/T
S-120, D-200, 2D-360

FIELD
ELEV
1026

Ramp Frequencies:
Ramp 1   131.45
Ramp 2   131.85
Ramp 3   129.27
Ramp 4   130.07
Ramp 5   129.37
Ramp 6   131.37
Ramp 8   128.97
Ramp 9   131.87
Non Movement Area 131.37

FIRE
STATION

NWA
HANGAR

SOUTH
CARGO
RAMP

RWY 08R-26L
PCN 74 R/A/W/T
S-120, D-200, 2D-360

RWY 09L-27R
PCN 62 R/A/W/T
S-120, D-200, 2D-360

RWY 09R-27L
PCN 68 R/A/W/T
S-120, D-200, 2D-360

BRIDGE

RWY 10-28
PCN 74 R/A/W/T
S-75, D-209, 2D-600,
2D/2D2-900

ELEV
1000

094.4°

9000   X 150

BRIDGE

274.4°   ELEV
998

CAUTION: Pilots are cautioned not
to mistake the marked concrete on
Rwy 10/28 and taxiway SG for a
taxiway at the I-285 overpass.

33°37'N

ASDE-X Surveillance System
in use. Pilots should operate
transponders with Mode C on
all twys and rwys.

84°27'W   84°26'W   84°25'W

Airport Diagram of Hartsfield-Jackson Atlanta International Airport, 2015. Drawing by National Aeronautical Charting Office (NACO)

sites that, ideally, allowed for 3,000- to 5,000-foot runways, were located along waterways to permit seaplane access, and were close to the urban core.[9] Consider that, for modern day jets, 12,000-foot runways are required.

By the late 1930s, U.S. Post Office contracts became less critical with new, lower-cost and higher-load aircraft technology paving the way for profitable passenger service.[10] The 1938 Civil Aeronautics Act removed the ban on federal airport aid and designed a funding program for municipal airports. The funding came with stipulations, namely, formalizing that a municipal airport must not prohibit certain flights.[11] The Civil Aeronautics Administration (CAA) (a portion of which soon became the Civil Aeronautics Board, or CAB) and airlines together established routes that were viable considering both passengers and mail. The CAB set airline routes and their fares and flight frequencies. The result was a high-fare aviation system where airlines competed on service only, and not fares.

In the late 1970s, the U.S. federal government deregulated the airlines. Airlines lowered fares and increased service, fueling public demand for air travel.[12] Newly free to establish new routes and add flight frequency to established routes, airlines—both legacy and upstarts—built their business around their key hub airports. Deregulation only intensified the practice of the hub-and-spoke model, as airlines added destinations and flights to better serve their passengers and provide more options to garner market share.[13]

The post-deregulation low fare environment, the growth of hub-and-spoke networks, and rapid increases in jet aircraft technology led to significant growth in flights and delays. Soon followed were the calls from airlines, cities, and the traveling public for more and longer runways; calls that were overwhelmingly met with federal and local support for airport infrastructure.[14] Air travel continued to grow through the 2000s, despite a downturn in air travel in the early part of the decade in the aftermath of the September 11, 2001 attacks. In fact, Ball et al.[15] estimate that the cost of delay to airlines, passengers, and the economy was $32.9 billion in 2007.

During the 2000s, when seven major U.S. network airlines merged into three, the newly merged airlines consolidated their networks:

they concentrated flights at their key hubs and reduced flights in smaller, marginally profitable markets.[16] Major airports situated in the largest cities saw their air service strengthen while airports in smaller metropolitan areas lost significant service due to reduced competition, leaving their customers with fewer flight options and higher airfares.[17] Smaller airports and secondary hubs— such as the airports of Pittsburg, Cincinnati, and Nashville—have been hurt by hubs getting stronger; airlines exploiting economies of scale and servicing small airports with their cheaper regional service.[18] Indeed, the findings of Hansen[19]—that airports with high levels of originating traffic proved to be more attractive hub airports for airlines—compared with airports situated in cities with weak local markets—which proved to be prescient.

AIRPORT DEVELOPMENT AND MANAGEMENT IN THE 21ST CENTURY

Airports and Economic Development
In the U.S. and across the globe, governments seek to develop and expand airports to support economic development, both for the immediate region in which the airport is sited and for the area. Previous research has found a direct positive relationship between airport passenger boarding and changes in employment in service-related industries in a region.[20] Non-stop transcontinental or international flights are a key factor in the quantity of economic development generated by an airport.[21] There are also instances where a runway is sought for concrete business partnerships or targeted economic development promises. Consider that the Greenville-Spartanburg Airport in South Carolina was upgraded with a runway extension in the 1990s as part of a $130 million development incentive package to encourage auto manufacturer BMW to move their assembly plant to South Carolina.[22] Airports tend to be very optimistic about the latent demand for new flights; the belief that airlines will increase their service to meet this demand should new capacity become available is deeply rooted in a city or state's economic development goals.

It is critical, however, to recognize that the linkages between economic development and air service have only been confirmed for regions for which airport capacity is a binding constraint[23]; not all airports generate economic development from growing their footprint or their air service. The literature on the link between secondary airports and economic development is less clear. Button, Doh, and Yuan[24] find a small and tenuous link between passenger flow and the per capita income for the surrounding area for 66 small airports in the south of the U.S. In addition to not being guaranteed, economic development is often undirected and diffused throughout a region while the negative externalities (such as noise and local pollutants) are localized to the proximate communities.[25]

When an airport sponsor seeks a new runway or a runway extension, economic development (growing aviation service, boosting local economic development, increasing global competitiveness, remaining a hub airport) is usually an equal or more significant goal than delay reduction.[26] Previous work by the author found that, out of the seventeen major airports that completed a plan for a runway expansion project between 2000-2013, 16 of the airports stated the project was necessary to grow aviation service while only 13 cited delay concerns.[27] The idea that governments build based on aspiration as much as they build on practicality is grounded in a broader history of megaprojects in transportation across the globe.[28]

The result of aspirational airport expansion in this volatile period for aviation is that very few airports are right-sized: some are constrained by their runways and have too much demand, while some are underutilized. While the busy airports are facing interesting debates over how to control demand while still maintaining their competitive positioning, it is the underutilized airports that are deeply struggling with what to do with an overabundance of expensive infrastructure. Currently the question facing airport managers of airports with the capacity to attract new service is: should an airport invest in attractive terminals and concessions or invest in airline incentives to lure new airline service?

The answer to this question is not well understood by researchers or airport managers alike. According to the Transportation Research Board's Airport Cooperative Research Program, the research literature does not cover the impact of amenities and modern terminals on passenger choice. The Transportation Research Board report notes that airports have placed higher value on customer experience for the purposes of improving the airport image and increasing non-aeronautical revenue (revenue raised from sources other than airlines) through terminal retail and food and beverage. Although it is clear that customer experience is important in terms of encouraging more passengers to choose the airport, the full extent is not known. In fact, research by the author using data collected from surveying passengers at the three largest airports in the New York City airport system, found that passengers continue to value flight frequency and time when choosing an airport above all else. Improved terminals and concessions might entice passengers to buy more items once they are in the airport, but what ultimately entices them to choose that airport is the quality of air service.

Many airports have turned to air service incentives as a way to build air service at their underutilized airports. Prior to the 2000s, subsidies for airline service were mostly federally-funded and targeted at the smallest of aviation markets; after air traffic dropped precipitously in the wake of three major airline mergers and the 2008 economic recession, larger airports began subsidizing airlines for new air service. Between 2012 and 2015, more than half of the top 72 airports by passenger traffic began subsidizing domestic (40 airports) and international (41 airports) service.[29] These airline subsidy programs, funded by a mix of municipal revenue and revenue generated on the airport from non-aeronautical sources, can be a powerful tool in luring air traffic, particularly new traffic away from competing airports. However, subsidy programs also increase air pollution proximate to the airport and require some city planners to choose between the gamble of airport-generated regional economic development and funding other programs and infrastructure investments.[30]

Scholars have introduced a third question: How could underutilized airport space be put to other use? How can airports become a hub of activity for non-aeronautical purposes?

On the "on-airport" research, scholars have investigated how airports could become new hubs of intermodal connectivity and centers of alternative energy distribution.[31] As cities look to be leaders in reducing climate change, airports provide examples of a wide range of sustainability practices from water to air quality to biodiversity.[32] Recently, an airport served as the demonstration space for a large-scale deployment of electric vehicles.[33] However, harkening back to history, building and running any function that is aeronautically related is forbidden by national governments and the FAA in the U.S. Given these restrictions, more airports are focused on planning around the airport, rather than developing on airport grounds.

Planning for Development Around the Airport:
Regional Airport Capacity Planning
Given the significant restrictions on developing on airport property, it is not surprising that airport sponsors and regional planning organizations are focused on developing the area around the airport. The extent to which regional planning organizations engage in airside and landside planning and their perspective on

air transportation planning is highly contextual. The role of regional planners will depend on the number of airports in their region and the state of those airports (congested/underutilized), their ability to engage in regional airport systems planning as deemed by the FAA, and their interest in coordinating transportation and land use initiatives directly related to the airport.[34] We can examine an example role by taking a deep dive into the operations of the Atlanta Hartsfield International Airport and the Atlanta Regional Commission.

Current and planned development regarding the Atlanta Hartsfield International Airport provides an example of a regional planning agency becoming actively involved in promoting both airside and landside development. The Atlanta Regional Commission[35] directly attributes the economic health of the region to the Hartsfield-Jackson Atlanta International Airport (hereafter, ATL). ATL is the busiest airport in the U.S. in terms of passengers moved; moreover, it is the hub airport with the highest concentration of flights by a single airline.[36] Due to mounting delays and a desire to accommodate a growth in flight operations, ATL completed construction of the 5th runway in 2006 and is planning for a 6th as of 2019.

The business, planning, and airport communities are currently working together to utilize the new airport capacity to harness economic growth focused on the community surrounding ATL through the Atlanta Aerotroplis Alliance. The vision is broadly to proactively plan development around the airport based on the airport city model.[37] The vision includes development on multiple fronts: the airport is currently planning for a sixth runway, while the ARC is actively promoting airport-led urban development and co-locating logistics centers with the airport.[38] Dablanc and Ross[39] discuss how the Atlanta Regional Commission, along with the Metro Atlanta Chamber of Commerce, worked to change zoning laws to allow for increased logistics activity closer to the city to promote regional economic competitiveness.

Megaregional scholars discuss how environmental impacts are generated at the megaregional level, and thus must be addressed at that level. This concept goes beyond rising megaregional congestion and the environmental impacts from long distance commutes: it is focused on the interdependent infrastructures and transportation flows across a megaregion. Within aviation alone, consider how some portions of megaregions benefit from transportation infrastructure while others bear the bulk of the environmental impacts.

Scholars have studied how populations living within five kilometers of an airport are disproportionately affected by emissions and suffer the heath impacts, while the economic development spurred on by the airport tends to flourish in the wealthier business locations.[40] Air service, and the imbalance of air service, might change the demand for parking; airport market leakage might intensify and concentrate the demand for parking infrastructure at the large hub airport which has a high environmental cost in terms of both local and global emissions and consumption of public space.[41] And, because a small or a midsized jet aircraft has lower local and global emissions per passenger compared with an auto with only one or two occupants, it is possible that overall lower fuel consumption can be had by increasing air service to reduce long surface access trips to large airports.[42]

FUTURE USE OF THE AIRPORT

The future design, function, and use of airports is highly dependent on the surrounding socio-technical and environmental system. In the following forward-looking section, we present three possible future scenarios and the resulting conceptualization of airports.

Climate Change, Inundation, and the Threat of Re-siting
Aviation networks, which are predominately hub-and-spoke, are particularly vulnerable to extreme weather and acts of terror for two reasons: they serve large volumes of flights carrying transfer passengers and they are located in climate-sensitive areas. Aviation networks are anchored by a few pieces of critical infrastructure, namely, the airports that serve as airline hubs. These pieces of critical infrastructure are often located in airports that were built and expanded over bodies of water. The reason that many airports are located in low-lying coastal areas is historical: municipal airport planners in the U.S., in the early days of airport development in the 1920s and 1930s, sought waterfront sites that could accommodate seaplanes.[43]

The result of having many airports located in climate sensitive locations is extreme vulnerability. According to the Federal Aviation Administration and the U.S. Global Change Research Program, 13 of the 47 largest airports in the U.S. have one or more runways that are at an elevation that is in the range of a "moderate to high storm surge."[44] In addition to storm surges, airports are threatened by droughts in the U.S. southwest and west that can increase wildfires and close airports, while hurricanes and extreme storms in the east and southeast are expected to intensify threaten airports with closures. Overall, the U.S. aviation system is highly dependent on a few critical airports which are increasingly threatened by sea level rise, extreme weather, and other weather impacts.

As the aviation system is vulnerable to outages, and extreme weather is only expected to increase, it follows that airports can expect inundation to increase. For example, the City of Philadelphia released a report stating that under a four-foot, sea-level-rise scenario, 19 of airport facilities and pieces of infrastructure are highly vulnerable and another 12 are moderately vulnerable. The airport could become unusable multiple times per month; as events could become more routine, unpredictable, and of uncertain duration, airlines may have to reframe their resilience strategies. The discussion ultimately leads to re-siting: the concept of moving the major airports to other, inland location. The challenge is, ultimately, the deep cost and politics of moving an airport. The last major airport in the U.S. to move to a new site was Denver International Airport in Colorado in the 1990s; the project was a protracted deeply institutional debate and an incredibly high cost. Re-siting an airport is far from an easy solution.

If our climate impacted-future is dire enough to render major U.S. airports unusable multiple times per month, the question of the future of airports becomes one of the future of transportation. If the aviation becomes that unpredictable, the entire structure of the transportation system and passenger choice will be fundamentally altered; the question stops becoming one of re-siting an airport and rather one of how to re-conceptualize mobility in an unpredictable, climate-impacted world.

Consolidated Futures

The past decade of air transportation in the U.S. has been one of volatility leading to "capacity discipline," a term used to airline industry stakeholders to encompass the practice of matching route supply to route demand. In short, airlines are reducing service to their less profitable markets and increasing service in more profitable markets. Capacity discipline is the result of a decade that saw volatile and high fuel prices. While this practice makes a lot of sense for airlines and their bottom line, it has led to decreased service at a number of airports which are not the most major. Major airports, which are situated in the most major cities, were the biggest winners. Small airports and secondary hubs have been hurt by hubs getting stronger; airlines exploiting economies of scale and servicing small airports with their cheaper regional service. These smaller cities have struggled in attracting new flights and adding new service; in short, there is a growing divide in the airports that "have" service and the airports that "have not."

In a series of studies the authors found that travelers will consider the time and cost it will take them to fly out of airports in within a 300- to 400-mile radius and evaluate their best options. In a future with new vehicle technologies it is possible that travelers will take to the ground more than the air. Scholars surmise that automation, from connected vehicles that assist drivers in finding the routes with the lowest traffic and maintain a safe distance from other vehicles to autonomous vehicles which perform the driving function, will reduce a traveler's effective value of time.[45] A long drive to access an airport with higher levels of service may be of little consequence to a traveler with an autonomous vehicle. If this is the case, and new vehicle technologies become widely available, then a logical conclusion is that more and more travelers will choose to drive instead of fly; either using their vehicle as a replacement for a connecting flight to a major hub or replacing the need for air travel all together. Such a phenomenon will further deepen the divide between the airports that have high levels of service and airports with very few flights. Ultimately, the most dramatic possible future is one with only a few very busy international airports in the entire U.S. that travelers must access themselves.

Fewer hub airports mean more competition across them for limited traffic. Airport owners of the largest airports will likely focus heavily on the passenger experience. This includes improved wayfinding and signage, quality concessioners, and wireless connectivity. In fact, 86% of the world's airlines agree that ubiquitous connectivity presents almost immediate benefits, and 33% or more have allocated budgets for facilitating connectivity through "The Internet of Things," or IoT.[46] Shortly, all components of an airport wireless system including both the airside wireless (communications for aircraft, air traffic control, caterers and mechanics, and the security devices such as cameras and perimeter security) and the terminal wireless (communication for airline employees, passengers, and between security and first responders) will be connected with one another and with the internet, and actors will connect via smartphones, tablets, wearables, traditional computers and servers.[47] As the FAA develops the Next Generation Air Transportation System, an initiative to modernize the U.S. air traffic control system,[48] to connect airports to airlines via satellite-based systems, aircraft, airports and air traffic control will all become tied to the communications networks.

Cities that find their airports underutilized might have a way to keep their airports busy and continue to collect revenue needed for airport and municipal functions: new logistics opportunities. Logistics and package delivery has increased dramatically in the U.S. and globally in the past years, and is expected to continue growing steadily. The growth in package delivery has led to new businesses looking for new hubs: namely, Amazon Inc. As of 2019, Amazon and their air logistics company, Prime Air, is seeking out new airports for hubs; interestingly, they have pinpointed de-hubbed airports like Cincinnati/Northern Kentucky International Airport (CVG)—a former Delta Airlines Hub—as the future location of their air logistics hubs. This "new use for old airports" is possible for some but not all. And, very much like the competition for new passenger air service, the future will be lined with airports saddled with excess capacity competing for logistics providers to set up shop in their airports.

These two scenarios share one common thread: vulnerability. A system with few critical airports is vulnerable than one that is more dispersed; a system with critical nodes located in climate sensitive areas is naturally vulnerable. The only way to address this going forward is to plan the system and not just the nodes: plan an integrated system with airports serving different purposes, right-sized to these purposes, and secured.

01 Handy, S., Weston, L., Song, J., Maria D. Lane, K., 2002. Education of Transportation Planning Professionals. Transp. Res. Rec. J. Transp. Res. Board 1812, pp. 151–160. https://doi.org/10.3141/1812-19; Garrison, W.L., Levinson, D.M., 2014. The Transportation Experience: Policy, Planning, and Deployment, 2 edition. ed. Oxford University Press, New York, NY, p. 221.

02 Brueckner, J.K., 2003. "Airline traffic and urban economic development." Urban Stud. 40, 1455–1469. https://doi.org/10.1080/0042098032000094388; Tittle, D., McCarthy, P., Xiao, Y., 2013. "Airport Runway Capacity and Economic Development A Panel Data Analysis of Metropolitan Statistical Areas." Econ. Dev. Q. 27, pp. 230–239. https://doi.org/10.1177/0891242412467228.

03 Vance, James E. 1986. "The Ultimate Ubiquity: The Evolution of Commercial Aviation," in: Capturing the Horizon: The Historical Geography of Transportation Since the Transportation Revolution of the Sixteenth Century. Harper & Row Publishers, New York, N.Y., pp. 529–604.

04 Bednarek, J.R.D., 2001. America's airports: airfield development, 1918-1947, 1st ed. ed. Texas A&M University Press, College Station.

05 Ibid. pp. 42.

06 Ibid.

07 Corn, P.J.J., 2002. The Winged Gospel: America's Romance with Aviation. The Johns Hopkins University Press, Baltimore, Md.; Adey, P., 2006. "Airports and air-mindedness: spacing, timing and using the Liverpool Airport," 1929–1939. Soc. Cult. Geogr. 7, pp. 343–363. https://doi.org/10.1080/14649360600714998; Makhloufi, A.E., Kaal, H., 2011. "From Airfield to Airport: An Institutionalist-Historical Approach to the Early Development of Amsterdam Airport Schiphol," 1916-1940. J. Urban Hist. 37, pp. 497–518. https://doi.org/10.1177/0096144211403083.

08 Garrison, W.L., Levinson, D.M., 2014. The Transportation Experience: Policy, Planning, and Deployment, 2 edition. ed. Oxford University Press, New York, NY.

09 Bednarek, J.R.D., 2001. America's airports: airfield development, 1918-1947, 1st ed., p. 126. Texas A&M University Press, College Station.

10 Vance, James E. 1986. "The Ultimate Ubiquity: The Evolution of Commerical Aviation," in: Capturing the Horizon: The Historical Geography of Transportation Since the Transportation Revolution of the Sixteenth Century. Harper & Row Publishers, New York, N.Y., pp. 529–604.

11 Bednarek, J.R.D., 2001. America's airports: airfield development, 1918-1947, 1st ed. ed. Texas A&M University Press, College Station.

12 GAO, 1996. Airline Deregulation: Changes in airfares, service, and safety at small, medium-sized, and large communities (No. GAO/RCED-96-79). General Accounting Office, Washington, D.C.

13 Garrison, W.L., Levinson, D.M., 2014. The Transportation Experience: Policy, Planning, and Deployment, 2 edition. ed. Oxford University Press, New York, NY.

14 Ibid.; Ryerson, M.S., Woodburn, A., 2014. "Build Airport Capacity or Manage Flight Demand? How Regional Planners Can Lead American Aviation Into a New Frontier of Demand Management." J. Am. Plann. Assoc. 80, pp. 138–152. https://doi.org/10.1080/01944363.2014.961949.

15 Ball, M., Barnhart, C., Dresner, M., Hansen, M., Neels, K., Odoni, A., Peterson, E., Sherry, L., Trani, A., Zou, B., 2010. Total delay impact study: A comprehensive assessment of the costs and impacts of flight delay in the United States. NEXTOR.

16 Fuellhart, K., Ooms, K., Derudder, B., O'Connor, K., 2016. "Patterns of U.S. air transport across the economic unevenness of 2003–2013." J. Maps 12, pp. 1253–1257. https://doi.org/10.1080/17445647.2016.1152917; Ryerson, M.S., Kim, H., 2013. "Integrating airline operational practices into passenger airline hub definition." J. Transp. Geogr. 31, pp. 84–93. https://doi.org/10.1016/j.jtrangeo.2013.05.013

17 Brueckner, J.K., Lee, D., Singer, E.S., 2013. "Airline competition and domestic U.S. airfares: A comprehensive reappraisal." Econ. Transp. 2, pp. 1–17. https://doi.org/10.1016/j.ecotra.2012.06.001.

18 Ryerson, M.S., 2016. "Incentivize It and They Will Come? How Some of the Busiest U.S. Airports Are Building Air Service With Incentive Programs." J. Am. Plann. Assoc. 82, pp. 303–315. https://doi.org/10.1080/01944363.2016.1215257

19 Hansen, M., 1990. "Airline competition in a hub-dominated environment: An application of noncooperative game theory." Transp. Res. Part B Methodol. 24, pp. 27–43. https://doi.org/10.1016/0191-2615(90)90030-3.

20 Brueckner, J.K., 2003. "Airline traffic and urban economic development." Urban Stud. 40, pp. 1455–1469. https://doi.org/10.1080/0042098032000094388; Hewings, G.J.D., Schindler, G.R., Israilevich, P.R., 1997. "Infrastructure and Economic Development: Airport Capacity in Chicago Region," 2001–18. J. Infrastruct. Syst. 3, pp. 96–102. https://doi.org/10.1061/(ASCE)1076-0342(1997)3:3(96); Tittle, D., McCarthy, P., Xiao, Y., 2013. "Airport Runway Capacity and Economic Development A Panel Data Analysis of Metropolitan Statistical Areas." Econ. Dev. Q. 27, pp. 230–239. https://doi.org/10.1177/0891242412467228.

21 Button, K., Doh, S., Yuan, J., 2010. "The Role of Small Airports in Economic Development." J. Airpt. Manag. 4.; Green, R.K., 2007. "Airports and Economic Development." Real Estate Econ. 35, pp. 91–112. https://doi.org/10.1111/j.1540-6229.2007.00183.x.

22 Kennedy, E.A., 1998. "GREENVILLE FROM BACK COUNTRY to FOREFRONT." Focus Geogr. 45, pp. 1–6. https://doi.org/10.1111/j.1949-8535.1998.tb00098.x.; Schunk, D., Woodward, D., 2003. "Incentives and Economic Development," in: White, S.B., Bingham, R.D., Hill, E.W. (Eds.), Financing Economic Development in the 21st Century. M.E. Sharpe.

23 de Neufville, R., 1995. "Management of multi-airport systems: A development strategy." J. Air Transp. Manag. 2, pp. 99–110. https://doi.org/10.1016/0969-6997(95)00035-6.

24 Button, K., Doh, S., Yuan, J., 2010. "The Role of Small Airports in Economic Development." J. Airpt. Manag. 4.

25 Goetz, A.R., Szyliowicz, J.S., 1997. "Revisiting transportation planning and decision making theory: The case of Denver International Airport." Transp. Res. Part Policy Pract. 31, pp. 263–280. https://doi.org/10.1016/S0965-8564(96)00033-X; Tomkins, J., Topham, N., Twomey, J., Ward, R., 1998. "Noise versus Access: The Impact of an Airport in an Urban Property Market." Urban Stud. 35, pp. 243–258. https://doi.org/10.1080/0042098984961.

26 Schunk, D., Woodward, D., 2003. "Incentives and Economic Development," in: White, S.B., Bingham, R.D., Hill, E.W. (Eds.), Financing Economic Development in the 21st Century. M.E. Sharpe.

27 Ryerson, M.S., Woodburn, A., 2014. "Build Airport Capacity or Manage Flight Demand? How Regional Planners Can Lead American Aviation Into a New Frontier of Demand Management." J. Am. Plann. Assoc. 80, pp. 138–152. https://doi.org/10.1080/01944363.2014.961949.

28 Flyvbjerg, B., Holm, M.S., Buhl, S., 2002. "Underestimating costs in public works projects: Error or lie?" J. Am. Plann. Assoc. 68, pp. 279–295. https://doi.org/10.1080/01944360208976273; Li, M.Z., Ryerson, M.S., 2017. "A data-driven approach to modeling high-density terminal areas: A scenario analysis of the new Beijing, China airspace." Chin. J. Aeronaut. 30, pp. 538–553. https://doi.org/10.1016/j.cja.2016.12.030.

29 Ryerson, M.S., 2016. "Incentivize It and They Will Come? How Some of the Busiest U.S. Airports Are Building Air Service With Incentive Programs." J. Am. Plann. Assoc. 82, pp. 303–315. https://doi.org/10.1080/01944363.2016.1215257.

30 Allroggen, F., Malina, R., Lenz, A.-K., 2013. "Which factors impact on the presence of incentives for route and traffic development? Econometric evidence from European airports." Transp. Res. Part E Logist. Transp. Rev. 60, pp. 49–61. https://doi.org/10.1016/j.tre.2013.09.007; Hihara, K., 2012. "An analysis of an airport–airline relationship under a risk sharing contract." Transp. Res. Part E Logist. Transp. Rev. 48, pp. 978–992. https://doi.org/10.1016/j.tre.2012.03.002; Malina, R., Albers, S., Kroll, N., 2012. "Airport Incentive Programmes: A European Perspective." Transp. Rev. 32, pp. 435–453. https://doi.org/10.1080/01441647.2012.684223; Smyth, A., Christodoulou, G., Dennis, N., AL-Azzawi, M., Campbell, J., 2012. "Is air transport a necessity for social inclusion and economic development?" J. Air Transp. Manag. 22, pp. 53–59. https://doi.org/10.1016/j.jairtraman.2012.01.009; Wittman, M.D., 2014. "Public funding of airport incentives in the United States: The efficacy of the Small Community Air Service Development Grant program." Transp. Policy 35, pp. 220–228. https://doi.org/10.1016/j.tranpol.2014.06.001.

31 Baker, D.C., Freestone, R., 2010. "The airport city : a new business model for airport development," in: Macario, R., Van de Voorde, E. (Eds.), Critical Issues in Air Transport Economics and Business. Routledge/Taylor and Francis Group, Oxon, United Kingdom, pp. 150–164.; DeVault, T.L., Belant, J.L., Blackwell, B.F., Martin, J.A., Schmidt, J.A., Jr, L.W.B., Jr, J.W.P., 2012. "Airports Offer Unrealized Potential for Alternative Energy Production." Environ. Manage. 49, pp. 517–522. https://doi.org/10.1007/s00267-011-9803-4.

32 Bassett, E., Shandas, V., 2010. "Innovation and Climate Action Planning." J. Am. Plann. Assoc. 76, pp. 435–450. https://doi.org/10.1080/01944363.2010.509703.

33 Silvester, S., Beella, S.K., van Timmeren, A., Bauer, P., Quist, J., van Dijk, S., 2013. "Exploring design scenarios for large-scale implementation of electric vehicles; the Amsterdam Airport Schiphol case." J. Clean. Prod., Environmental Management for Sustainable Universities (EMSU) 2010 European Roundtable of Sustainable Consumption and Production (ERSCP) 2010 48, pp. 211–219. https://doi.org/10.1016/j.jclepro.2012.07.053.

34 Cidell, J., 2006. "Regional cooperation and the regionalization of air travel in Central New England." J. Transp. Geogr. 14, pp. 23–34. https://doi.org/10.1016/j.jtrangeo.2004.10.003; GAO, 1996. Airline Deregulation: Changes in airfares, service, and safety at small, medium-sized, and large communities (No. GAO/RCED-96-79). General Accounting Office, Washington, D.C.

35 Atlanta Regional Commission, 2010. Atlanta Regional Plan 2040: Regional Assessment Summary.

36 Ryerson, M.S., Kim, H., 2013. "Integrating airline operational practices into passenger airline hub definition." J. Transp. Geogr. 31, pp. 84–93. https://doi.org/10.1016/j.jtrangeo.2013.05.013.

37   Baker, D.C., Freestone, R., 2010. "The airport city: a new business model for airport development," in: Macario, R., Van de Voorde, E. (Eds.), Critical Issues in Air Transport Economics and Business. Routledge/Taylor and Francis Group, Oxon, United Kingdom, pp. 150–164.; Kasarda, J.D., Lindsay, G., 2011. Aerotropolis: The Way We'll Live Next, 1st edition. ed. Farrar, Straus and Giroux, New York.

38   Hartsfield-Jackson Atlanta International Airport, 2014. MASTER PLAN: DRAFT RECOMMENDED PLAN.

39   Dablanc, L., Ross, C., 2012. "Atlanta: a mega logistics center in the Piedmont Atlantic Megaregion (PAM)." J. Transp. Geogr. 24, pp. 432–442. https://doi.org/10.1016/j.jtrangeo.2012.05.001

40   Bullard, R.D., 2007. Growing Smarter: Achieving Livable Communities, Environmental Justice, and Regional Equity. MIT Press.; Woodburn, A., 2016. Pushback In The Jet Age: Investigating Neighborhood Change, Environmental Justice, And Planning Process In Airport-Adjacent Communities. Publicly Access. Penn Diss.

41   Chester, M., Fraser, A., Matute, J., Flower, C., Pendyala, R., 2015. "Parking Infrastructure: A Constraint on or Opportunity for Urban Redevelopment? A Study of Los Angeles County Parking Supply and Growth." J. Am. Plann. Assoc. 81, pp. 268–286. https://doi.org/10.1080/01944363.2015.1092879; Chester, M., Horvath, A., Madanat, S., 2010. "Parking infrastructure: energy, emissions, and automobile life-cycle environmental accounting." Environ. Res. Lett. 5, 034001. https://doi.org/10.1088/1748-9326/5/3/034001.

42   Chester, M.V., Horvath, A., 2009. "Environmental assessment of passenger transportation should include infrastructure and supply chains." Environ. Res. Lett. 4, 024008. https://doi.org/10.1088/1748-9326/4/2/024008.

43   Bednarek, J.R.D., 2001. America's airports: airfield development, p.126, 1918-1947, 1st edition. ed. Texas A&M University Press, College Station.

44   Schwartz, H., Meyer, M., 2014. Transportation, in: Our Changing Climate. United States Global Change Research Program.

45   Krueger, R., Rashidi, T.H., Rose, J.M., 2016. "Preferences for shared autonomous vehicles." Transp. Res. Part C Emerg. Technol. 69, pp. 343–355. https://doi.org/10.1016/j.trc.2016.06.015; Van Den Berg, V.A.C., Verhoef, E.T., 2016. "Autonomous cars and dynamic bottleneck congestion: The effects on capacity, value of time and preference heterogeneity." Transp. Res. Part B Methodol. 94, pp. 43–60. https://doi.org/10.1016/j.trb.2016.08.018.

46   Nokia, 2016. "Connected Airports: How the Internet of Things will Transform Operations and Passenger Experience White Paper to Download from Nokia." Airport Technology [WWW Document]. URL http://www.airport-technology.com/downloads/whitepapers/wireless-applications/connected-airports-internet-of-things/ (accessed 2.27.17).

47   Fischer, E., 2011. "Airport Communications: The Future is Wireless [WWW Document]." Airpt. Technol. URL http://www.airport-technology.com/features/feature118643/ (accessed 2.27.17).

48   Darabi, H.R., Mansouri, M., Andalibi, N., Para, E., 2010. "A framework for decision making in extended enterprises: The FAA NextGen case," in: 2010 International Congress on Ultra Modern Telecommunications and Control Systems and Workshops (ICUMT). Presented at the 2010 International Congress on Ultra Modern Telecommunications and Control Systems and Workshops (ICUMT), pp. 662–667. https://doi.org/10.1109/ICUMT.2010.5676566; Federal Aviation Administration, 2014. NextGen: The Business Case for the Next Generation Air Transportation System.

02 FUTURE OF AIRPORTS AND REAL ESTATE OPPORTUNITIES

Arup Team[1]

INTRODUCTION

"Airports have started to understand the value generated by the vast numbers of people, vehicles, and goods that pass through their lands and buildings, and the revenue potential of developing this real estate for its highest and best use."
—Rian Burger, Associate Principal, Arup Toronto

New line of business: airports as real estate developers and strategic partners for cities. Airports present a very attractive business opportunity with significant potential for growth due to their location and connectivity to other metropolitan areas. In determining the viability of such business growth, many aspects need to be assessed in relation to the current airport market position and the alignment of aspirations between the airport and the city where it is located.

The purpose of this research is to present the case for coordinating between the city and the airport to achieve the goals of both parties. In many countries such as the U.K., Canada, Mexico, Turkey, Spain and Switzerland and Australia, airports have been privatized in varying degrees, ranging from not-for- profit companies in Canada to for-profit companies in the U.K. Entrepreneurial-focused governments in the Middle East are substantially expanding their airports. And while most U.S. airports are still state or city owned, airport authorities are trying to reduce their dependence on airline-backed funding arrangements, which frees them up to engage in business ventures other than just those related to processing passengers and cargo.

In Latin America, airports have recently engaged in capital improvements and expansion of core facilities. These opportunities can potentially bring in commercial development that is non-aeronautical related. The revenues generated from non-aeronautical business ventures may fund the growth and maintenance of the airport, while keeping landing and terminal fees to a minimum to make the airport an attractive port for airlines and passengers alike. Airports are increasingly building their teams with people from other industries to address this potential in real estate development. Airports have become more aware of their location at the nexus of regional transportation networks and have seen cities develop around them in a way that makes them not only centrally placed within surrounding metropolitan areas but gateways to the rest of the world through the air.[2]

Airports have also realized the tremendous customer base from the numbers of people, vehicles, and goods that pass through their facilities, which can potentially drive revenue by capitalizing on real estate development opportunities. Airports understand that they are significant drivers and facilitators of regional economies; therefore, improving their facilities in both aeronautical and non-aeronautical ventures will also propel the city's economic growth in the medium and long terms. There has been a shift in the way airports develop their action plans. Traditionally, such plans are more focused on a short-term and singular objective, but a more dynamic and strategic planning development is now being adopted. These forward-thinking strategic plans will provide more flexibility in accommodating future developments. This research demonstrates that some of the most successful airports in utilizing

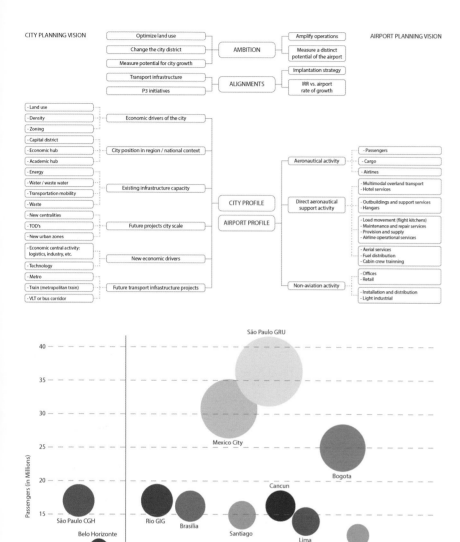

CITY PLANNING VISION / AIRPORT PLANNING VISION

Fig.1 Key drivers diagram summarizes how city and airport planning visions can align to produce an integrated vision of aviation and urban development.

Fig.2 Changes in the percentage of passengers at LatAm airports.

real estate developments have had extensive collaborations between the airport and the city to align the objectives of both parties. This creates unique opportunities and potential for significant growth for businesses located in and around the airport.

METHODOLOGY AND GLOSSARY

This research was based on a mapping exercise of certain business drivers that are generally considered significant for airport planning and real estate development. In recent years, the concepts of airport cities and airport regions have been gaining popularity. By adopting a rather flexible definition of these key terms, this research essay discusses the planning issues and different real estate offerings in, on, and around the airport.

Accessibility: The ability for people to reach goods, services, and activities. Accessibility is the ultimate goal of most transport activity.

Airport region: The region served by and economically integrated with the airport. The airport region can extend up to a perimeter of 60 miles around the airport.

Forecourt area: In aviation planning, the outdoor area adjacent to the terminal entry points.

Landside: In aviation planning, the part of an airport used for activities other than the movement of aircraft, such as vehicular access roads and parking.

Airside: In aviation planning, the part of an airport used for activities related to the movement of aircraft.

Mobility: The ability for people to move from place to place. Can also be applied to goods.

Residual land value: In real estate, a method that determines the potential profitability of a possible land investment. It is calculated from the value of the completed development minus the costs of development (including profit).

Spillovers: Economic benefits accruing to agents other than those primarily involved in a transaction or an industry.

KEY DRIVERS

Airport regions generally have either economic development drivers or technical drivers. Our research has mapped them in two tiers, ranging from direct influence on the design and business case of the airport or city planning vision down to specific businesses opportunities or projects for each of them. Airports and cities are very similar in the way that they function— infrastructure development is the building block of economic growth and a stable yet flexible framework must be implemented to facilitate such growth.

While cities have permanent residents and visitors who use the infrastructure in different ways, airport needs for infrastructure are primarily driven by efficiency in time and comfort to get in and out as quickly and directly as possible.

For both cities and airports to increase economic growth, it is fundamental to find synergies between land use optimization and infrastructure capacity. These alignments should aim to minimize the risks normally associated with these two aspects, allowing either the city or the airport, or both, to transform underutilized real estate assets into significant revenue generators.

Arup has identified key drivers in two overarching categories. While city drivers are primarily based on land use optimization and maximizing efficiencies on infrastructure capacity, airports traditionally have a single function: direct support facilities and subsequent facilities.

Drivers Based on Profile
Airport:
Aeronautical activities are those that generate the core business of the facility. These can be passengers, cargo, and airlines.

Direct aeronautical support activities are those that are driven by and support aeronautical activity and from a real estate standpoint include participants such as chain operators and sub-lessees.

Tegel Airport, Berlin

Key facts
Population: 3,400,000 (2014)
Area: 892 km² (344 sq mi)
Planning Framework: Land Use Plan (FNP)
Public Transport: S-Bahn, U-Bahn, Tram, Bus, Ferry and Cycle paths
Liveability ranking (EIU Report 2015): 20° (94.0/100)

Economic facts
Metro area GPD: USD $128 million (2013, Germany Regional Dataset)
Main production sector: Services

Airport facts
Central Activities Numbers:
– PAX: 19.6 million
– Cargo: 33,238 Tons
– Airlines: 49
Direct support: Business market
Localization within the city: Northwest

Land nearby the airport (within 5km), controlled by airport operation in partnership with private developer, currently promoting commercial development.

El Dorado Airport, Bogotá

Key facts
Population: 8,000,000 (2014)
Area: 1,587 km² (613 sq mi)
Planning Framework: Planes Maestros de Bogotá
Public Transport: Bus, TransMilenio (BRT) and Cycle paths
Liveability ranking (EIU Report 2015): 109° (59.6/100)

Economic facts
Metro area GPD: USD $94 billion (2015, IMF World Economic Outlook Database)
Main production sector: Industry

Airport facts
Central Activities Numbers:
– PAX: 25 million
– Cargo: 622,090 Tons
– Airlines: 25
Direct support: Tourism Hub + Cargo handling support + Logistics
Localization within the city: Central – West

Private land currently under transformation and development to support airport corridor business opportunities. Multiplier airport effect. It is one of the top three air-cargo airports for Latin America, as a major distribution center.

Miami International Airport, Miami

Key facts
Population: 430,300 (2014, United States Census Buerau)
Area: 143 km² (55.25 sq mi)
Planning Framework: Comprehensive Development Master Plan (CDMP)
Public Transport: Tri-Rail, Metrorail, Metromover, Metrobus and Cycle paths
Liveability ranking (EIU Report 2015): 37° (89.8/100)

Economic facts
Metro area GPD: USD $281 billion (for Miami-Ft Lauderdale-West Palm Beach – 2013, Bureau of Economic Analysis)
Main production sector: Financial services, Tourism, Trade, Medi

Airport facts
Central Activities Numbers:
– PAX: 40.6 million
– Cargo: 1,945,012 Tons
– Airlines: 52
Direct support: Tourism Hub + Cargo handling support
Localization within the city: West

Substantial land, owned by airport operator itself, being developed as a commercial cluster in close proximity with core non-aeronautical activities. It is the U.S. gateway to Latin America, as a major cargo hub and distribution center.

Schiphol Airport, Amsterdam

– 540,000 m² of airport and surrounding property areas
– 170 million Euro total revenue
– 60M EBITDA
– 350 per m²/year office prime rent

Fast facts
55 million passengers per annum
1,480,000 tons of cargo
200,000+ m² office
200,000+ m² industrial/warehouse
2nd highest office prime rent in Amsterdam

Charles de Gaulle Airport, Paris

– 1,000,000m² of properties total
(Source: wwwparisaeroport.fr)
– 241 million Euro total revenue
– 129 million EBITDA

Fast facts
62 million passengers per annum
2,400,000 tons of cargo
228,000+ m² office
600,000+ m² industrial/warehouse
2,200 hotel rooms and 3,700 in 2018
80,000+ m² retail within Aeroville Mall delivered in 2013

Non-aviation activities are business opportunities that exist in the proximity of airports. Most of these are based on ground leases by the airport operator.

City:
Economic development initiatives tend to drive policies, strategies, and pilot projects. Infrastructure capacity is key for future city planning. It drives investment to specific areas and generally seeks alignment with key economic sectors. Transport infrastructure is fundamental because all economic activities depend on good transport links.

Airport and the potential real estate development have a range of different business structures:

1. The airport owns and controls land adjacent to the airside area, and this is available for other uses related to core aviation activities according to the city urban zoning plan.

2. The airport and one or several transport infrastructure elements such as motorways, highways, metro, or train systems are located within a city urban boundary, but adjacent land owned by other public or private entities is available for future development that could be associated with the airport.

3. The airport is located within a city urban boundary and based on the expected growth forecast (PAX and cargo) will trigger economic multiplier effects that will require private land in the proximity to be purchased by the airport operator to accommodate future uses.

BENCHMARKING

Airports have become regional economic accelerators, transforming territories around them and driving business development outside of their boundaries. The benchmarking in this section showcases one example for each business structure, outlining its spatial relationship within the city urban limits as well as the economic interdependency between the city and the airport in terms of GDP, transport infrastructure requirements, and land use.

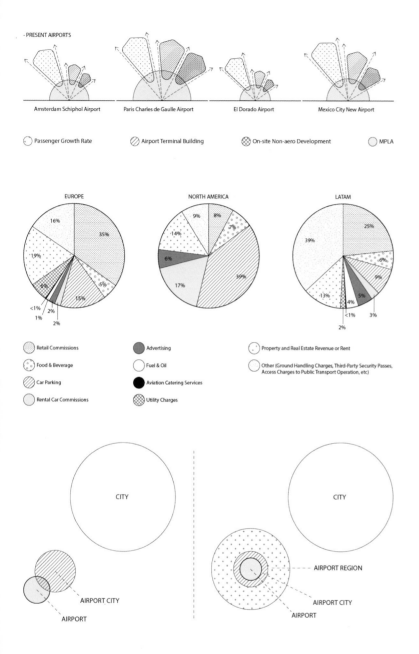

- PRESENT AIRPORTS

Amsterdam Schiphol Airport   Paris Charles de Gaulle Airport   El Dorado Airport   Mexico City New Airport

○ Passenger Growth Rate   ⬡ Airport Terminal Building   ⬡ On-site Non-aero Development   ○ MPLA

EUROPE   **NORTH AMERICA**   **LATAM**

○ Retail Commissions   ● Advertising   ⦂ Property and Real Estate Revenue or Rent

○ Food & Beverage   ○ Fuel & Oil   ○ Other (Ground Handling Charges, Third-Party Security Passes, Access Charges to Public Transport Operation, etc)

⦀ Car Parking   ● Aviation Catering Services

○ Rental Car Commissions   ⬡ Utility Charges

CITY   CITY

AIRPORT REGION

AIRPORT CITY   AIRPORT CITY

AIRPORT   AIRPORT

Fig.3 Key development variables.

Fig.4 Airport non-aeronautical revenue chart. Source: ACI, Airport Economics Report, 2014

Fig.5 Conceptual scheme of airport-based real estate. Source: Knippenber, Ute and Wall, Alex, "Airports in Cities and Regions, Research and Practise", KIT Scientific Publishing, p.115, 10th July 2009

Arup's benchmarking exercise indicates that at a regional scale (city-wide), airports seem to utilize the economic potential that brings the regional infrastructure—such as cargo rail lines and regional road infrastructure. El Dorado Airport in Bogota, Colombia, and Miami International Airport in the United States, both big cargo centers, have the potential to drive a distribution/industrial strategy.

In both cases, they have exploited their location in the perimeter of the city exactly to connect with regional infrastructure corridors. Whereas Tegel Airport in Berlin, Germany, has limited cargo but is in a suburb of a dense, well-established high-income area, so its plan is to consider different developments such as office and retail/commercial at a regional level.

The second filter to the benchmarking applies to two of the most successful airport projects with substantial nonaeronautical revenues on a local scale. Schiphol is a district within greater Amsterdam, where the property has been assigned land uses that are appropriate for a city but have synergies with the airport. Whereas Charles de Gaulle in Paris has been the catalyst to develop a "suburb" inside the developable real estate area of the airport.

BUSINESS DRIVER INTEGRATION

Technical and financial integration is key for successful airport real estate development. The concept of "airport regions" is the future of commercial airports' development plans. Because the relationship with the city's urban core will still matter—most central business district (CBDs) are still located far way from airports—investment in transport infrastructure will be shared between the airport region and the city CBD. Alternatively, airport regions could become a kind of CBD closely connected to airports. As such, a fully integrated technical and business plan would help to deliver a successful development strategy for the airport region.

Two of the most successful cases of airport regions are Paris's Charles de Gaulle and Amsterdam's Schiphol. For over 20 years, these two airports have been evolving into parts of the cities and have triggered developments for various economic activities. To understand the key variables that have helped these two cases to leverage the massive investment in transport infrastructure, Arup has quantified three key variables to measure the size of the potential of airport non-aeronautical commercial opportunities.[3]

These key variables are as follows:
• Passenger growth rate
• On-site non-aeronautical development
• Maximum private land adjacent to airport land (MPLA) with good access infrastructure
• Total size of airport terminal buildings in relation to direct jobs creation

We reviewed the Latin America region because of its strong aviation growth outlook and relatively dormant airport real estate activity.

REAL ESTATE VALUE

Throughout the world, airports are maximizing non-aeronautical revenue sources. Real-estate-based activities are key to these revenue diversification strategies, yet require a set of particular conditions—attractive location, good accessibility, and market demand.

Airports as Motors of Economic Development
During the second half of the 20th century, in a context of urban sprawl and suburbanization, airports became motors of economic development for peripheral urban regions.

The locational advantage of airports comes from their integration within regional multimodal transportation networks. As economic activities naturally concentrate around transportation nodes, airports constitute attractive locations. For instance, in the United States, employment within a 2.5-mile radius around the country's 25 largest airports is growing. Additionally, job opportunities in the airport region span across a broad range of industries—from manufacturing to service-oriented sectors.[4]

However, the size and profile of an airport primarily drive the intensity of airport-induced economic spillovers. Indeed, the larger the airport, the greater the economic impact on the hinterland. Academic research has shown that there is a strong correlation between air traffic and economic output.

Airport Revenue Diversification Strategy
Between 2008 and 2013, airport costs increased on average by 2.8% per annum.[5] To make up for rising operational costs and to mitigate losses in periods of economic downturns, airports aim at diversifying their revenue sources. Throughout the world, airports are tapping into nonaeronautical activities, which include advertising, utility

charges, fuel and oil, catering services, and real estate. In 2013, 39% of the world's airport revenue came from nonaeronautical activities. Indeed, between 2012 and 2013 non-aeronautical revenue grew by 5.5%.

Non-aeronautical revenue sources are leveraged differently throughout the globe: for instance, it represents 47% of airports' total revenue in the Middle East, but only 27% in Africa.[6] The composition of non-aeronautical revenue varies quite substantially across regions (see Fig.4). The size of the airport also plays an important role in the nonaeronautical revenue generation potential.

Real Estate Offerings in Different Geographies
From retail stores within the terminals to business parks in the airport region, there are a myriad of airport-centered real estate strategies established by airports, developers, and local governments. These real estate offerings are primarily driven by the airport's profile. Indeed, large and hub-type airports will foster more on- and off-site economic activity, and thus show greater potential for a real estate strategy.

The airport directly determines real estate offerings on the land it controls, which typically includes the terminals, the landside and airside areas, the forecourt area, and any additional buildings. The term airport city refers to all real estate offerings located outside the airport's operating space and terminals. Additionally, the airport region is the larger airport-centric economic region, which can extend up to a 60-mile radius around the gates (see Fig.5).

In-Terminal and Landside:
In-terminal and landside real estate activities include retail concessions, food and beverage concessions, parking, rental car concessions, and other property and real-estate-related revenue or rents. The composition of real estate revenue sources varies per region and airport size. For instance, as shown in Fig.4, parking accounts for almost 40% of non-aeronautical revenues of North American airports, while retail represents 35% of non-airport related activities in Europe.[7]

Airside:
Cargo is not typically considered a real estate revenue source. However, because it involves ground leases of warehouses and

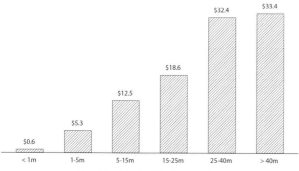

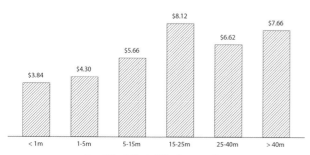

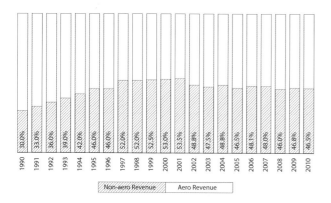

Fig.6 Retail revenue per square meter (US$ per day, 2013).

Fig.7 Operating non-aeronautical revenue per passenger (US$ per WLU, 2013).
Source: ACI, Airport Economics Report, 2014

Fig.8 Historical breakdown of airport revenues. Source: Technopak

other facilities, it should be considered a real estate product. An airport can seek to extend its portfolio of industrial land uses and warehouses, provided that it is located in an industrially relevant hinterland and convenient to multimodal transportation nodes. Indeed, regional accessibility and the local industrial basis will drive the demand for cargo.

Airport City:
Offices, hotels, and retail are typical real estate offerings in the forecourt area and the broader airport city. Users of these facilities value the close proximity to the airport terminal. In the U.S., the major real estate opportunities lie in industrial uses, parking, and hotels.[7] The optimal real estate mix in the airport city should be based on a land inventory, market analysis (see next section), and above all, the airport profile. Building a successful airport city ultimately depends on land availability, on-site mobility, and accessibility, and the airport profile (number of passengers and flight patterns, origin, destination, and/ or connections). For instance, few airports in the U.S. come with premium office space (class A) in their proximity due to unfavorable local real estate market conditions.

One of the most successful airport cities is located around Frankfurt Airport. It is one of the most valuable real estate submarkets of the Federal State of Hesse, in Germany, precisely because of its unique locational advantages. One mixed-use development, the Squaire, is a good example of the variety of uses that can be developed around airports. Inaugurated in 2011, the Squaire is the largest office building in Germany and also includes two hotels, conference spaces, and retail.

Airport Region:
The airport region integrates industries that benefit from the airport hub, such as hotels, office spaces, shopping malls, wholesale merchandise marts, and logistics parks. These real estate developments thrive along transportation networks, because accessibility and visibility from the highway are important for their businesses.

In-Terminal Retail:
While duty-free and retail stores were introduced in airport terminals long ago, airside commercial developments have been

gaining momentum. New market dynamics spearheaded by the rise of shopping-mall-like Middle Eastern airports and global economic trends have redefined advertising, retail, and services opportunities for airport operators. As a result, new marketing strategies focus not only on tailoring retail offerings to passenger profiles by introducing mid-end brands to the fashion and accessories category but also on optimizing passenger footfall by redesigning terminals around retail outlets (Sydney Airport's 3,500m² walk-through shop is a good example). Maximizing retail revenue thus supposes redesigning terminals to allow for the appropriate amount of retail concessions, providing that the airport profile and size allow for such investments. Indeed, retail revenue is highly driven by the airport size, as shown in Fig.6 and 7.

The Industrial Airport City:
While the airport city concept suggests land uses are diversified in the vicinity of airports, industrial uses are in fact largely predominant. A study by Jones Lang LaSalle revealed that 4.5% of the United States' total real estate industrial inventory is located within a three-mile radius of 12 out of the country's 13 largest cargo airports. However, it is important to acknowledge that the largest U.S. cargo airports are located in busy metropolitan areas with diverse regional industrial bases and hence naturally attract industrial land uses. The demand for warehouses in the vicinity of airports is driven by airport-dependent activities, such as import-export and perishables that need to be located within 15 and three miles of the airport gates, respectively.

Non-aeronautical revenues will continue to diversify in airports in Latin America as they evolve as regional hubs (see Fig.4).

UNLOCKING THE POTENTIAL

Implementing a real estate strategy requires significant planning. Arup developed a four-step process highlighting the key inputs, studies, and deliverables for developing a financially viable portfolio.

Airport-oriented city development timeline
Once the land phasing schedule and procurement strategies are laid out, the airport developer can start implementing its real estate strategy. While the first real estate products are reaching

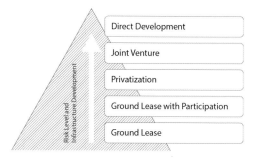

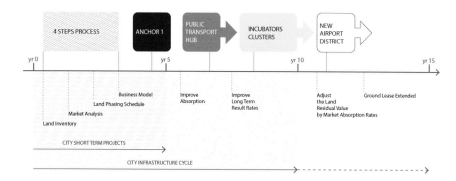

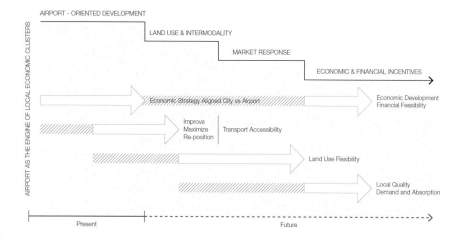

Fig.9 Procurement options for real estate developments.

Fig.10 Airport-oriented city development timeline diagram.

Fig.11 Off-airport real estate development strategy diagram.

the market, the airport needs to develop an anchor plan to better integrate the new developments with ground transportation and improve the site's overall accessibility. This anchor plan will drive market absorption and ensure that the new square footage delivered in the airport city is well received by the market. In the long term, developers also need to focus on maintaining low vacancy rates and increasing rent rates.

Once a significant portion of the real estate products have been delivered—as planned by the land phasing schedule—turning the airport into a transportation hub is crucial. Connecting the city by railway and extending the region's road network will help foster economic activity. If this strategy is successful and the airport is well integrated with the city, firms, business parks, industry clusters, and incubators will progressively recognize the airport's locational advantage and relocate closer to the airport to benefit from its enhanced accessibility. Attracting new businesses and industries will generate economic spillovers and reinforce the airport region's performance. Residents will then follow, preferring to live in proximity to their workplace. Adding residential and retail uses to the mix will lead to the creation of a new, vibrant, and lively airport district.

Step 1. Land Inventory:
Location is key for any real estate project. The feasibility of an airport-based real estate strategy is primarily driven by the land and facilities available for development. Undertaking a land inventory and an assessment of each location is key:
• Land inventory:
Which land plots, parcels, and facilities are available for redevelopment?
• Location:
Evaluate the advantages and disadvantages of each parcel with regards to the following:
  – Site accessibility: Is the location easily accessible? Which vehicles can access it (cars, trucks, etc.)? Is it well integrated with regional multimodal transportation networks?
  – Mobility: How is the location integrated to the airport site? Is it well connected to surrounding facilities?
  – Utilities: Are utilities (water, electricity, internet, etc.) already laid?

– Basic zoning and land use: Are land uses defined for each location? Are there density limitations due to the airport's flight path?

• Output: List of potential sites for real estate development.

Step 2. Market Analysis:

A market analysis is a critical step for real estate developments and informs the project's viability. It is composed of demand, supply, and marketability analyses:

• Demand analysis:

Based on local and regional economic indicators, industry statistics, consumers demographics, households characteristics, and the airport profile, what are the most desirable real estate developments (industrial, hotel, office, multifamily, or retail)?

• Supply analysis:

What are the existing real estate offerings in the region? What type of construction projects are in the pipeline? Who is the competition?

• Marketability analysis:

How do the airport's potential real estate developments differ from the existing and future offerings? Who are the target users, and how can they be approached?

• Output: Preliminary real estate product mix.

Step 3. Land Phasing Schedule:

To refine its real estate portfolio, the airport needs to research the zoning regulations. This step thus requires in depth research on the following items:

• Zoning:

What are the zoning requirements for each identified parcel? Which type of real estate can be developed?

• Environmental impacts:

What are the project-induced environmental impacts? What mitigation plans can be developed?

• Phasing schedule:

What are the projects' different phases? How many units per development type can be delivered during each phase and be efficiently absorbed by the market?

• Output: Final real estate product mix.

Step 4. Business Model:

The business model evaluates the real estate project's viability by first exploring procurement methods, assessing residual land value, and eventually developing the project's financial model:

• Procurement strategy:

What are the airport's goals, objectives, financial capacity, and risk profile? What procurement option is most appropriate from a qualitative perspective?

• Residual land value analysis:

How do the commercial and financing costs associated with each different procurement option affect residual land value? Which procurement option is most appropriate from a quantitative standpoint?

• Financial model: Is the project financially viable?

• Output: Financially viable real estate portfolio.

Residual Land Value

Residual land value is a land valuation technique in real estate analysis. Residual valuation assesses a land parcel with development potential. It is calculated by subtracting the cost of a development from the value of its completed development. Typically, development costs include land acquisition costs, building costs, professional fees (landscaping, acoustics, environmental impact assessment, etc.), marketing and sales costs, financing, contingency, and other ancillary costs. The development value is calculated by multiplying annual rent by the year purchase (i.e., the number of years required for the rent to yield the purchase price of the asset) at an appropriate yield given the property type and location. The complexity of this valuation method lies in the calculation of inflation, finance terms, interest, and cash flows against the program's timeframe.

Procurement Options for Real Estate Developments

Ground leases, ground leases with participation, joint ventures, and direct development are the most common procurement methods used for airport-based real estate developments.

• Ground lease:

The operator leases the land to a private developer who develops the property (and the infrastructure if needs be) and pays a fixed rent for a defined lease term. This structure is appropriate when the airport-sponsor is taking no risk in the project.

• Ground lease with participation:

The ground rent is reduced or eliminated in exchange for a share of building rent. This may take the form of a share of the project built into the lease rate.

• Privatization:

A private operator takes control of an asset under a 100-year lease with the airport sponsor. Typically, the long-term lease is

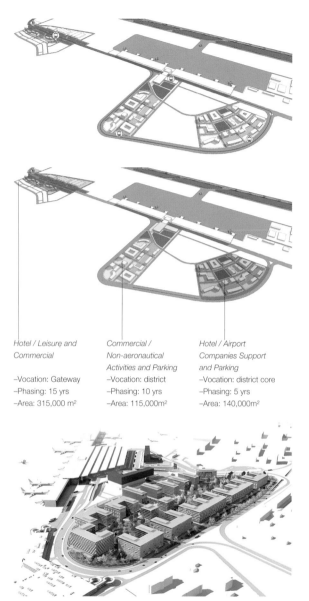

Hotel / Leisure and Commercial

–Vocation: Gateway
–Phasing: 15 yrs
–Area: 315,000 m²

Commercial / Non-aeronautical Activities and Parking

–Vocation: district
–Phasing: 10 yrs
–Area: 115,000m²

Hotel / Airport Companies Support and Parking

–Vocation: district core
–Phasing: 5 yrs
–Area: 140,000m²

Fig.12 Surface transportation infrastructure in an airport district and real estate development schematic proposal.

Fig.13 Potential land use mix and phasing in an airport district and real estate development schematic design proposal.

Fig.14 Perspective of Warsaw Chopin Airport.

based on the net present value of the asset.

• Joint venture:
If the airport operator and a private operator enter into a joint venture, the net rental income is shared based on each of the parties' contribution. Typically, the airport contributes with the value of the land.

• Direct development:
If the airport establishes a real estate agency to develop the property, the airport contributes all development costs and receives the highest returns. This is a riskier venture and requires that the airport employ adequate financial, technical, and managerial skill.

LOOKING OUTSIDE THE TERMINAL BUILDING

Explore the underutilization of land available around the airport for medium-term leases or business opportunities.

In the future, the relationship between airports and cities is bound to intensify. Inner-city airports will become more secure, efficient, and convenient for frequent flyers. Real estate developments adjacent to airports will become an urban norm, and aeronautical activities will blend with more diversified and urban land uses. More specifically, non-aeronautical revenues will continue to grow, and revenue diversification will become a mainstream strategy for airport operators across the globe.

An airport-oriented city development will be based on an efficient ground transportation system, making traveling to and from the airport area a seamless experience for passengers, visitors, and workers. Cities can begin conceptualizing specific land uses and zoning as airport-oriented development areas in some districts.

Accessibility via a reliable and efficient ground transportation network is key for the success of any airport district and airport-oriented real estate development. For the Rio de Janeiro Airport, Arup designed a masterplan maximizing land value based on local transport infrastructure.

The design of these districts within the Rio de Janeiro airport region takes into consideration a mobility system as the key variable for the success of the project. This can demonstrate to clients the best potential land use mix and phasing alternatives.

01   Co-Authored by Susan Baer (Aviation, America's Leader), Pablo Lazo (Masterplanning, America's Leader), Justin Powell (Senior Aviation Expert), Jorge Valenzuela (Senior Transaction Advice Expert), Abigail Rolon (Senior Economic Expert), Jackie Coburn (Senior Airport Planner), Gabriela Antunes (Masterplanning and Urban Design), Alix Cocude (Transaction Advice Specialist)

02   Augé, Marc (2009). Non Places: An Introduction to Supermodernity.

03   Jong, Bart de, Utrecht University, Faculty of Geosciences, "Paper 46th European Regional Science Association," 2006.

04   Kasarda, J. D., and Appold, S. J. "The Airport City Phenomenon: Evidence from Large U.S. Airports," in Urban Studies 50:1239, 2013.

05   Aviation International Council, Airport Economics Report, 2014.

06   Ibid.

07   Ibid.

08   U.S. GAO, http://www.gao.gov/assets/660/653427.pdf.

09   Airport Cooperative Research Program, 2015, "Innovative Revenue Strategies – An Airport Guide," Report 121.

10   Augé, Marc (2009). Non-Places: An introduction to supermodernity.

11   Aviation International Council, Airport Economics Report, 2014.

12   Brett, D. L and Schmitz, A. (2002). Real Estate market Analysis: A Case Study Approach. Urban Land Institute.

13   JLL, 2013, Perspectives on airport real estate portfolio, "Non-traditional revenue sources improve the financial picture."

14   JLL, 2015, United States Airport Outlook.

15   Knippenber, Ute and Wall, Alex (10th July 2009). Airports in Cities and Regions, Research and Practice. KIT Scientific Publishing, p. 115.

16   Little, Arthur D. (2009). Mastering Airport Retail: Roadmap to New Industry Standards.

03 THE DEATH AND LIFE OF GREAT AIRPORTS

Tom Verebes

Perhaps no other building type, other than the airport, has been so continuously dysfunctional as an architectural and infrastructural typology, throughout its entire history. Paradoxically, in the face of this legacy of dysfunctionality, the designers and operators of airports prop up the go-to mantra of transport engineering, and its architecture, that of the presumption of efficiency. Several questions arise. What is a well-functioning and efficient airport? Is it one in which time is minimized in the movement of people, goods and airplanes? Is an efficient airport one which minimizes delays? Or, does efficiency imply the reduction of flight-connection distance and time? Or, is it an airport that can adequately anticipate future needs and respond to indeterminate future contingencies? One cause for this conundrum in the pursuit of functionalism and efficiency is how Infrastructural planning is nearly always retrospective, rather than projective. Long durations of political and planning processes, design and construction timescales, economics, along with other uncertainties, can often lead to a new airport being the outcome of much earlier requirements and contingencies. As a result, a new airport is also most often not functionally fit for its intended purpose. In the past, successive mechanical retrofits of existing airports are demonstrative of an inability to keep up with the growth of airports. Airports tend to be hopelessly retrograde in their capacity to meet current demands and contingencies, whether increasing, or waning.

"The era of the great mechanised individuals has begun, and the rest is palaeontology...therefore we claim to be the primitives of a sensibility that has been completely overhauled."
                                                        –Tommaso Marinetti, 1914[1]

A BRIEF HISTORY OF A MOVING TARGET: THE AIRPORT

This narrative portrayal of the transitional status of airports was written in airline lounges and in flight, on a series of flight departures and delays—in the United Airways Lounge in Newark (EWR), the Cathay Pacific's Bridge Lounge in Hong Kong (HKG), and Air China Lounge in Shanghai Pudong (PVG), as well as inflight in seats 16D, 43F, 28D, and 32D, respectively.

To contextualize a set of speculations on the shape, size, role, and function of airports in the future, it may be fruitful to meander through various past productions and formulations, to present some of the problematics and predicaments of the airport in the twenty-first century. The quickly transiting typologies, scales, aesthetics and atmospheres of the changing eras of airports, from the 1950s onwards, can be encapsulated in a few examples from airports of the past. This is a history of an accelerating set of criteria, quantified by the vast increases in numbers of passengers and flights which airports were required to accommodate.

Early airfields, such as Heathrow Airport, were initially comprised of a single terminal shack during the 1940s. The airport was the architectural enclosure and vital threshold, which facilitated air travel in its embryonic era.

As air travel soon became more accessible, the typology of the airport evolved. In the heady days of when air travel was still considered to be a glamourous activity, the TWA Terminal at John F. Kennedy Airport in New York, completed in 1962,

TWA Terminal at JFK International Airport, Eero Saarinen, New York, 1962. Photo by Caleb White

remains the ultimate icon of the era of when air travel was limited to an elite socio-economic class of people. The architecture of the terminal building was as sophisticated as air travel was perceived in its time. Expressive and symbolic of the lightness and ungroundedness of the experience of lift off, the TWA terminal encapsulated the new mobility of air travel in the 1960s.

Intertwined with the optimism of post-war mobility was the harsh reality of the dangers of the Cold War between the United States and the Soviet Union. In part, the Cold War was a race to explore outer space. The cultural consequences of the Space Age, and all its science fiction infused imagery and projective imagination, implied a future in which mobility and ungroundedness was an everyday routine. Sci-fi movies, novels, and cartoons of the 1950s and 1960s portrayed a world of facility and flow, where gravity is a mere side effect of life on planet earth, which can be easily overcome. In Walt Disney's plans to build Tomorrowland, confidence in the future was at its height in the twentieth century. Tomorrowland was the prototype for what was eventually built as the Epcot Centre in Orlando, Florida, as a theme park. A remake of the 1950s Tomorrowland movie was released in 2015.

"Let's imagine... if you glimpsed the future, you were frightened by what you saw, what would you do with that information? You would go to the politicians, captains of industry? And how would you convince them? Data? Facts? Good luck!"

–Nix, Tomorrowland:
A World Beyond Walt Disney Productions, 2015[2]

As airports expanded massively in the 1970s onwards, and the airlines organized themselves to each be based in a hub, airports such as Atlanta and Chicago in the US, Heathrow and Schipol in Europe, grew, and then continued to outgrow themselves. It was no longer the airlines which the lay-traveller would share their awareness of the varying classifications of statistics from which the largest airline can be determined. The largest airports vied fiercely, in a global free-market of airport competitors, to be crowned as the world's most travelled airport, measured by the greatest numbers of passengers or planes, surface area, and gross capital spent by air travellers.

TWA Terminal at JFK International Airport, Eero Saarinen, New York, 1962.
Photo by Caleb White

In 1994–1995, I was traveling between London and Hong Kong for work. As a young architect, I tended to choose the cheaper options listed over the phone, just before the internet further democratized air travel. On my initial flight booking, my travel agent declared the cheapest fare to be via Abu Dhabi. I booked the flight, but I've often told this story as an admission that I had to consult my old-school book of world maps, for the precise location of Abu Dhabi, which I could only narrow down in my mental map of the world, of existing somewhere in the Middle East. Some months later, after flying through Abu Dhabi several times, I began to normalize Abu Dhabi International Airport's Singaporean Duty-Free staff, and the demographic make-up of its travellers due to the geo-political positioning of an airport based in the United Arab Emirates, strategically between Europe, Asia, and Africa. I took another flight some months later through Dubai, seemingly about five minutes after its new global terminal opened its doors and gates.

In fabricating a global hub, Dubai is "closed and controlled, air-conditioned and policed, connected by the highway along the coast."[3] Dubai's status as a global hub can be correlated to another City of Gold in the desert, Timbuktu, the ancient fabled city in Mali, whose obsolescence was brought on with the emergence of cargo shipping between coastal sub-Saharan Africa and North Africa during the early colonial period.[4] Dubai had dredged its harbor in the 1970s, with the ambition of becoming a major cargo shipping hub.[5] Its airport piggy-backed its lead in global shipping, and created a tourist industry, in one of the safest, and thus most trustworthy economies in the Middle East.

The global courier company, FedEx, has their global "SuperHubTM" based at the Memphis International Airport, with a fleet size of 660 aircrafts serving over 375 destinations worldwide.[6] A paradox of globalization is the relative marginality and remoteness of the location of an efficient airport hub, which is always positioned both near and far to everywhere, poised amidst each and any flight path.

As a child growing up in the 1970s, in Canada's largest city at the time, Montréal, I witnessed a new, state-of-the-art airport being built for the city, Mirabel International Airport, completed in 1974.[7] It was the largest purpose-built airport, measured in surface area, ever to be built at that time. The economic flows of globalization were rerouted elsewhere, due to the side-effects of the Québec separatist movement in the mid 1970s. Mirabel failed as a passenger airport, having its final passenger flight in 2004. It was then used as one of the airport locations in the Tom Hanks film, The Terminal (2004), before being transformed into a cargo airport, and the manufacturing base of operations for Bombardier Aerospace. The main terminal building was demolished in 2014, four decades after it opened.

It turned out that airlines in the traditional sense, were challenged, if not wholly impeded, from making a guaranteed and consistent profit. Then came the so-called budget airlines. Providing greater access to passenger air travel, cheaper flights with new budget airlines had sprung up in the 1980s and 1990s. Though democratization of air travel came with the dumbing down of its service-industry essence. At the same time as budget airlines were mushrooming well beyond their business plans, we became accustomed to going to shopping malls outside of major cities, where they also had airplanes, which you could board to fly cheaply almost anywhere. Retail was crowned as King. Serendipitously, the retail income became the primary money spinner, when airports became shopping malls. In turn, the life of airports as we knew them, was saved, by capitalism, to mitigate the inherent implosion of the airline industry, in its traditional business organization.

Networked economies and the transnational corporate mobility inherent to the model of the Global City had called on theorists in the 1990s to make sense of the ubiquity of particular architectural typologies, stripped of identity.[8] Rem Koolhaas asked in 1994, in his essay, "The Generic City," whether homogenization of urbanity, encapsulated in shopping malls and airports, was in fact an "intentional process, a conscious movement away from difference toward similarity."[9] As formulated, "The Generic City," turned out to be a celebration of mediocrity, boredom as the background to life's spectacle, and ultimately understandable as concurrently any-place and no-place.[10] In the same year, Marc Augé, published his book, Non Places: An Anthology to Supermodernity, where he lays bare a thesis on solitude and anonymity of the subject, and similitude of the globalized spaces we inhabit. Augé writes:

"…it is not surprising that it is among the solitary 'travelers' of the last century (c19)— not professional travelers or scientists, but travelers on impulse or for unexpected reasons—that we are most likely to find prophetic evocations of spaces in which neither identity, nor relations, nor history really make any sense; spaces in which solitude is experienced as an overburdening or emptying of individuality, in which the movement of the fleeting images enables the observer to hypothesise the existence of a past and glimpse the possibility of a future."[11]

The 9/11 attacks on the World Trade Centre changed almost everything about airports and air travel. Ten years before 9/11, Paul Virilio classifies the contemporary airport, "as the state's last gateway,…like the fort, the harbor and the train station of the past, the place of necessary regulation of exchange and communication."[12] The notion of an electronic threshold, in which boundaries are interfaces in transit, was replacing hard obstacles separating territories. Since 2001, the context of aviation has rendered security and the perception of safety paramount, in advance of passenger experience, whether instructions are barked by tense TSA staff, or via the invisibility of smart security sensing systems. In turn, in airports, all senses of identity relations are in abeyance, and instead, anonymity is only assured by passengers giving full disclosure of their electronic identity. The social order of airports demands from travellers, civility and collective obedience (or else), yet, in a Jane Jacobs' nightmare, without any sense of community.[13]

FROM MAGICAL TO MUNDANE

In his book, The End of Airports, Christopher Schaberg conveys how airports have gone from magical to mundane, enjoyable to tedious, joyful to grim.[14] For the rare and occasional traveller, the airport appears as a constantly spontaneous space where the seeming cacophony brings only surprise from moment to moment, and day to day. In fact, airports are dreadfully routinized and repetitious—the same flight departs at the same time each day. For the regular and frequent flyer, the airport reveals its mundane spatial order and its cyclical temporal fluxes.

Airports have become the litmus test where the immediate effects of economic downturns, terrorist attacks, natural disasters, weather events and health crises are impacted most speedily and intensely. Airlines have become money losers rather than money spinners. Airports follow the money, but never seem to get enough of it. Flows of capital are prioritized over the passenger experience, and today, the lucrative capitalism of cargo adds further challenges to passenger airports.

FUTURE

In surveying the role airports have played in society in the past, and may play in the future, perhaps in different ways than today, some provisional speculations on the future airport arise.

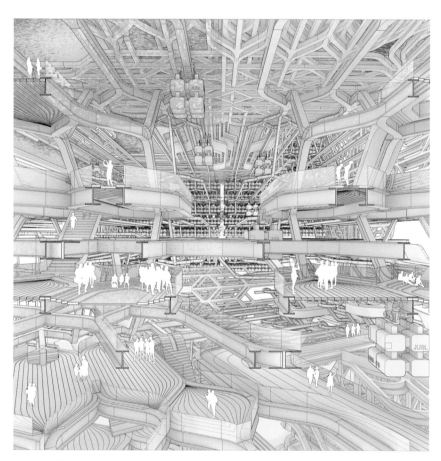

One-point Perspective. Project by Agata Jakubowska and Shi Zhang

Going back to the future, speculations on the future of airports by the Design Research Lab (DRL) at the AA in London, through post-professional masters' projects worked on between 2002–2004, focused on interventions to Heathrow Airport, as part of the DRL's three-year design research agenda, titled, Responsive Environments. Understood as a deficiency in the design of Heathrow's terminals, we focused on the resistance to different demands upon the spaces of the airport over each day, as well as questions of longer term adaptation to changing performance criteria. These projects emphasized reactive, responsive and anticipatory material systems, activated through sensors and actuators, heightening the interactivity of crowds of passengers with the material fabric of the interior of the airport, and thereby managing the expectation of both short-term and long-term change in the airport.

On the one hand, there is an increasing supply of passengers, given the rising numbers of tourists and business travellers, this latest big wave of additional travellers only helps to propel the evolution of the airport as prioritizing passenger flights. Facing future environmental and energy crises, is this supply of new passenger markets only due to increase? Is it conceivable that most short-haul flights will be replaced by high-speed railway networks? The expansion of aviation has always been dependent upon stable, if not growing economies in the future, which is also far from a certainty.

There most often exists a misfit between the latest aircraft technology and the older, inherited architectural organization of airports. Advances in aircraft technology point towards two distinct trajectories for the future of aircraft, and by implication, for airports. Firstly, much larger aircrafts are being developed and released onto the market, of which a contemporary example is the Airbus A380 double decker, which can hold 868 passengers if configured all as economy class, and 544 passengers in a three-class configuration. In addition, smaller, more lightweight and flexible aircrafts are being developed, in parallel to, and related to, drone technologies. These smaller aircrafts are currently being conceived for cargo and goods deliveries, which may also have repercussions for passenger applications. Airports are increasingly driven by priorities of logistics. The term, "logistic landscape," as coined by Charles Waldheim and Alan Berger, arises from an increasingly distributed global economy. Logistic landscapes are territories which spawn "new industrial forms based on global supply chains" and accommodate the "shipment, staging, and delivery of goods," shifting from concentrated organization, to an increasingly decentralized and distributed logic of production and flow of goods.[15] With the rise of the airports dedicated solely for logistics, no doubt some of the more practical and lucrative applications of drone crafts will be realized.

In their short history, airports have grown from small shacks alongside runways, to complex infrastructural networks. As this moving target of a transiting typology has mutated wildly, we can expect the economic and industrial context of airports in the future to veer towards information-based and automated systems, and their impact upon the logistics of airports. Regardless of the status, size, shapes and functions of future airports and aircraft, and whether they are for passengers or logistics, their conception and organization will need to be responsive and adaptive to the indeterminacies of change.

01   Banham, Reyner. "Italy: Futurist Manifestos and Projects" (1960), in Theory and Design in the First Machine Age. Cambridge, Massachusets: The MIT Press. p. 102.

02   Tomorrowland: A World Beyond (2015). Walt Disney Productions.

03   Shane, David Graham (2011). Urban Design Since 1945 – A Global Perspective. London: Wiley, p. 157.

04   Verebes, Tom (2010). "Endurance & Obsolescence: Instant Cities, Disposable Buildings, and the Construction of Culture," in 306090 Books, Issue 12. Jonathan Solomon, Joshua Bolchover Eds., New York: Princeton, p. 87.

05   Verebes, Tom (2013). Masterplanning the Adaptive City; Computational Urbanism in the Twenty-first Century. New York: Routledge, pp. 36-38.

06   www.fedex.com.

07   http://www.worldabandoned.com/montreal-mirabel.

08   Sassens, Saskia. "The Global City: Introducing a Concept and a History," in Mutations, Barcelona. Actar, p. 114.

09   Koolhaas, Rem (1995). "The Generic City," in SMLXL. Rotterdam: 010, p. 1248.

10   Verebes, Tom (2013). Masterplanning the Adaptive City; Computational Urbanism in the Twenty-first Century. New York: Routledge, p. 137.

11   Augé, Marc (1995). "Prologue" and "From Places to Non-Places," in Non-Places: Introduction to an Anthropology of Supermodernity, p. 87.

12   Virilio, Paul (1991). "The Overexposed City," in Lost Dimension. Trans. Daniel Moshenberg. New York: Semiotext (e), pp. 9–27.

13   Jacobs, Jane (1961). The Death and Life of Great American Cities. New York: Random House.

14   Schaberg, Christopher (2015). The End of Airports. London: Bloomsbury Academic.

15   Waldheim, Charles and Berger, Alan (2008). "Logistics Landscape" in Landscape Journal 27:2-08, University of Wisconsin, p. 220.

PROJECT DESCRIPTIONS   STRUCTURED LOGISTICS

The long-span structure is important in the design of the airport as is the movement of luggage and materials from check in to the plane. Generally, the structure is used to create large open spaces for the arrival and departure halls as well as shopping and waiting areas. Leaving the basement for the sorting of luggage. The long-span structure is used to make the roof enclosure of the building with few columns; however, all the ancillary spaces block the movement from space to space as each space is treated as a small building within a larger envelope. The structures are impressive and heroic but do not participate spatially in the passenger's experience. The following projects conceive of the long-span structure in a much more active capacity leveraging the long-span structures ability to create space. This strategy adds another utility to the structure of the building but also creates a novel experience for the passenger as well as opportunities for logistics systems. All three projects are critical examinations of the application of the long-span structure within the contemporary airport and speculate on a structure's relation to the creation of space and the movement of material in novel ways.

PROJECT 01   **WEAVE**

JFK Airport New Terminal Hub, Queens, New York
Han Zhang, Andi Zhang, Yanang Ding

WEAVE deals with the long-span truss as storage space for goods. The form of the structure creates volumes of spaces for logistics. Shelves of logistics storage racks are packed between the upper and bottom cord of the truss. The structural systems that support the building and creates the open spaces necessary for an airport are merged with the systems of package sorting and storage. The difference between these two systems becomes blurred as they weave around and through each other. The spaces between the truss/storage volumes becomes the passenger and support spaces for the airport terminal. The passenger then experiences these elements as spaces of different scales and their hybrid nature is revealed to passengers passing through the building. Structure, surface, and movement systems weave to create a compelling reimagination of the truss as a spatial and structural re-organization.

Top Right: Section Perspective

Bottom: Long Building Section

01   Truss Space / Cargo Storage
02   Cargo Storage
03   Cargo Control Area
04   Cargo Transportation System
05   Passenger Area

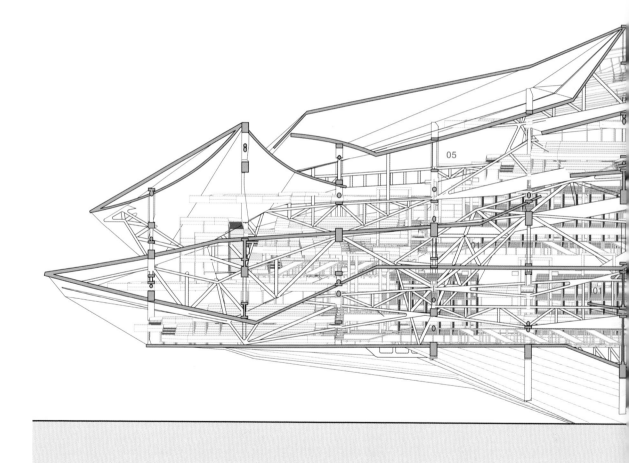

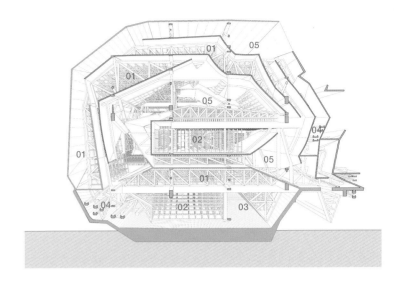

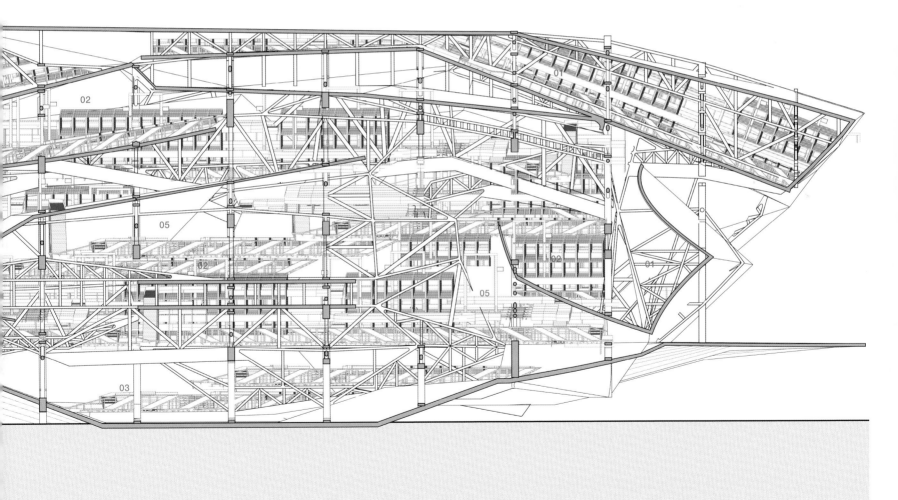

Choisey Axonometric

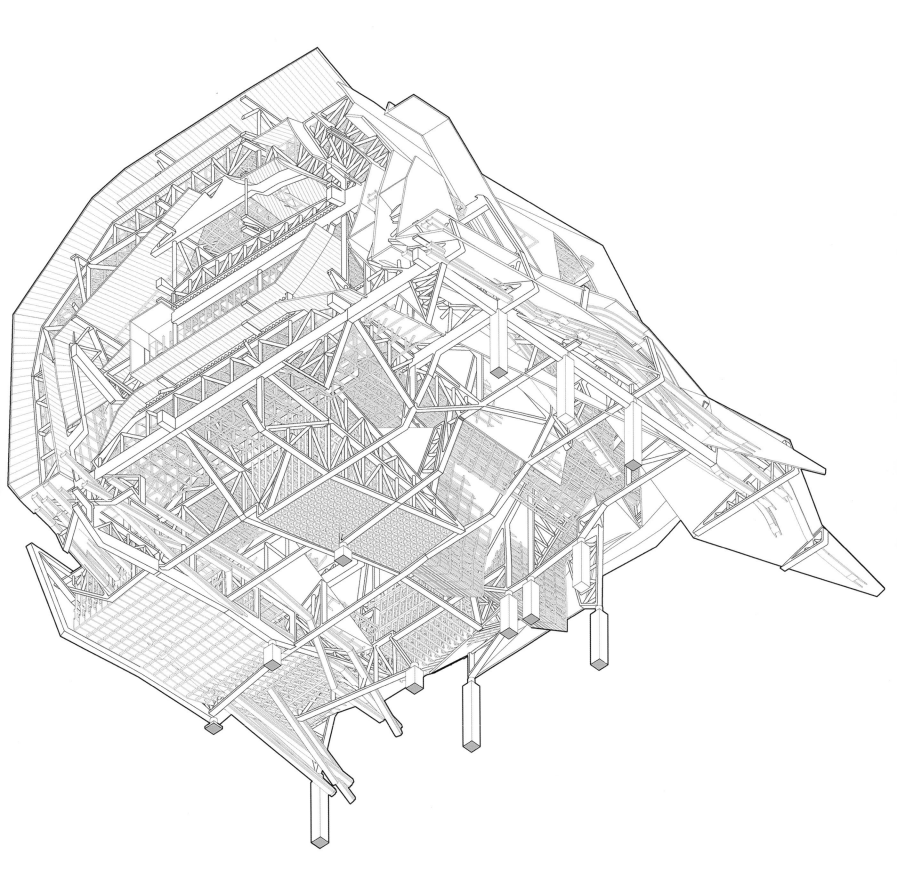

Section Model Rendering

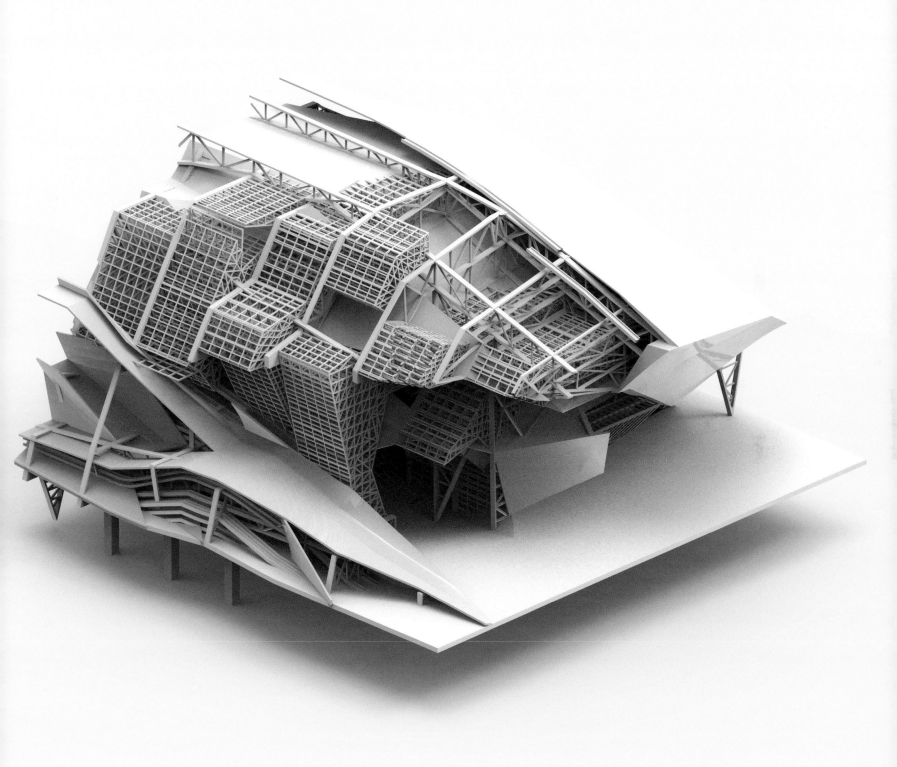

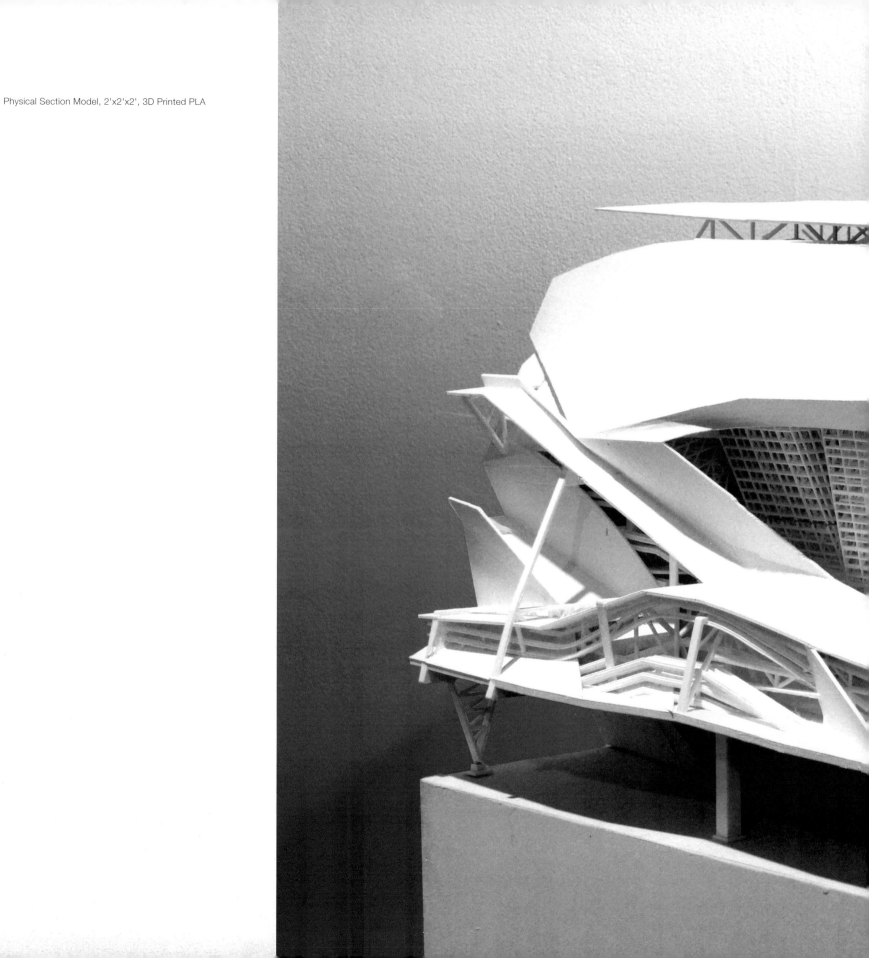

Physical Section Model, 2'x2'x2', 3D Printed PLA

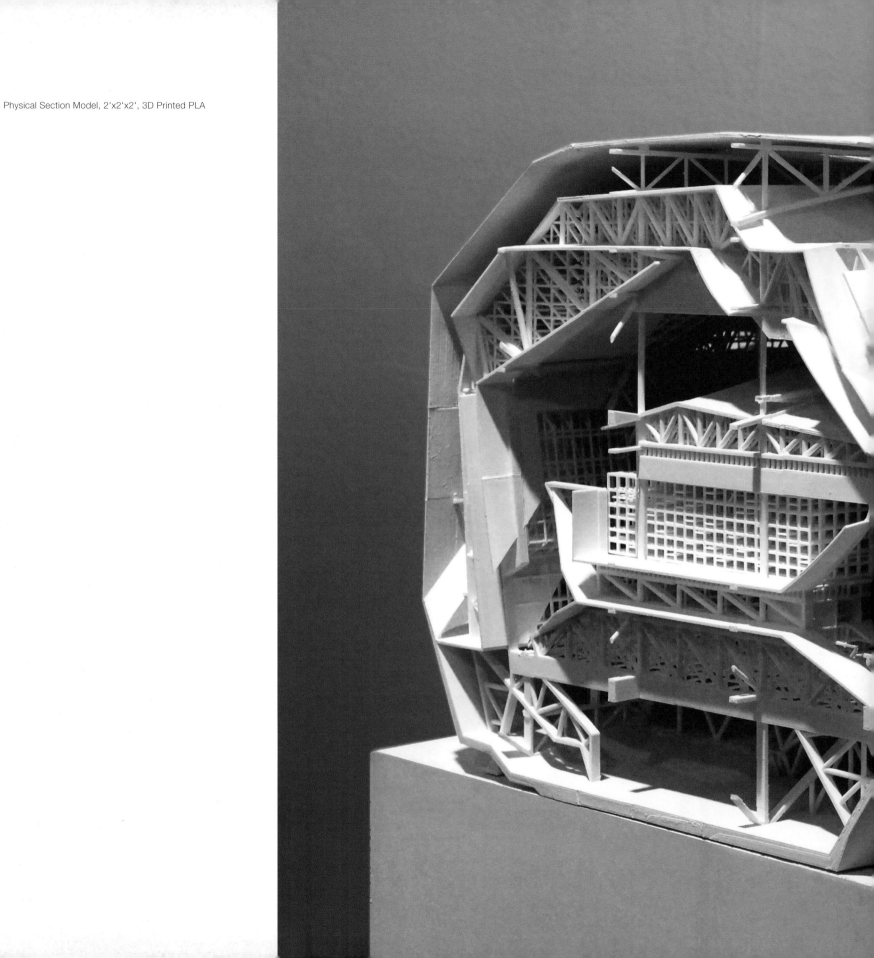

Physical Section Model, 2'x2'x2', 3D Printed PLA

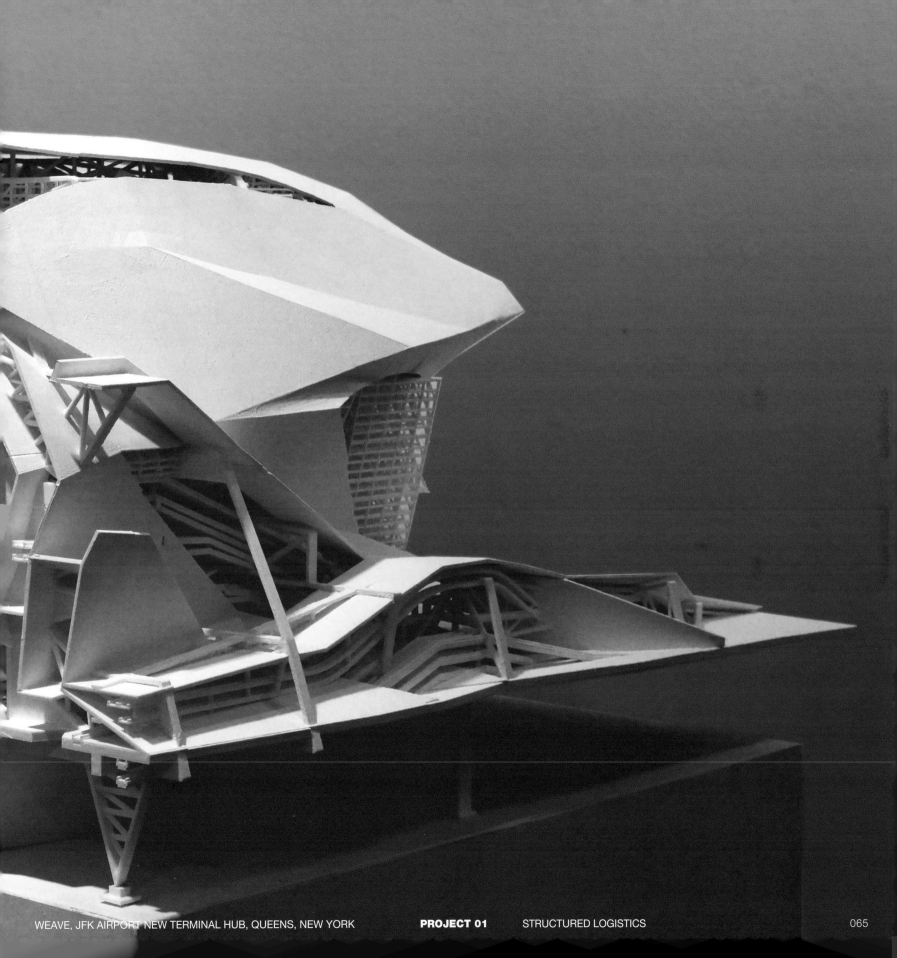

PROJECT 02 **BRAID**

JFK Airport New Terminal Hub, Queens, New York

Xiaoqing Meng, Yuwei Wang, Haozhou Yang

BRAID treats the truss as malleable and inhabitable form, shaping the passenger spaces within a larger solid. Looking at the plan of the project, there are three nodes the project is organized around. The truss is designed as an inhabitable continuous space, spiraling around these nodes and connecting passenger spaces with one another. Looking at the model photograph, the truss is nested within the outer solid which contains logistics and support areas for the main passenger spaces. The juxtaposition between the solid form and the transparent and light weight truss braids the capacities of the structural system being used to produce an aesthetic of fineness and lightness while using the organizational capacity of the logistics system.

Ground Floor Plan

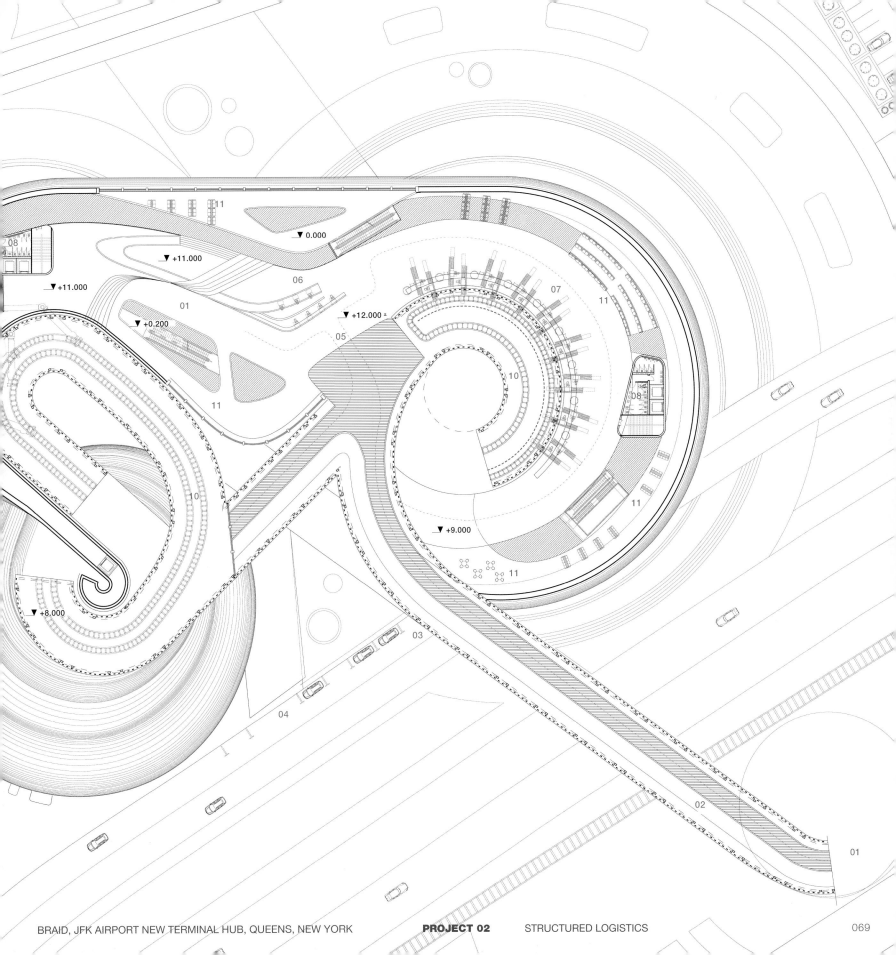

Top Right: Upper Level Floor Plan

Bottom: Long Building Section

01   Baggage Claim
02   Restroom
03   Cargo Sorting Area
04   Cargo Pick-up Area
05   Cargo Transportation System
06   Cargo Storage
07   Pedestrian Bridge
08   Offices
09   Lounge Space
10   Passenger Check Point
11   Atrium

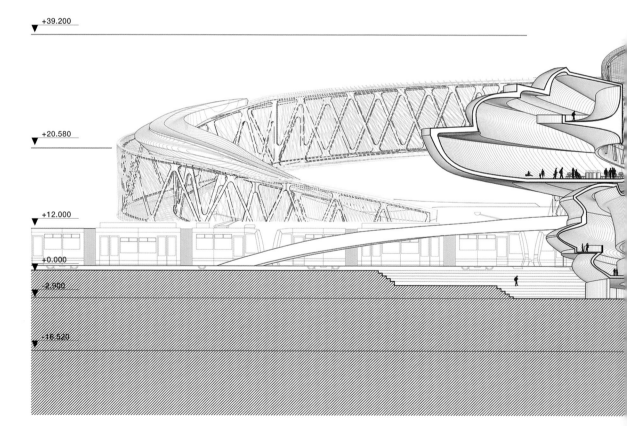

+39.200

+20.580

+12.000

+0.000

-2.900

-16.520

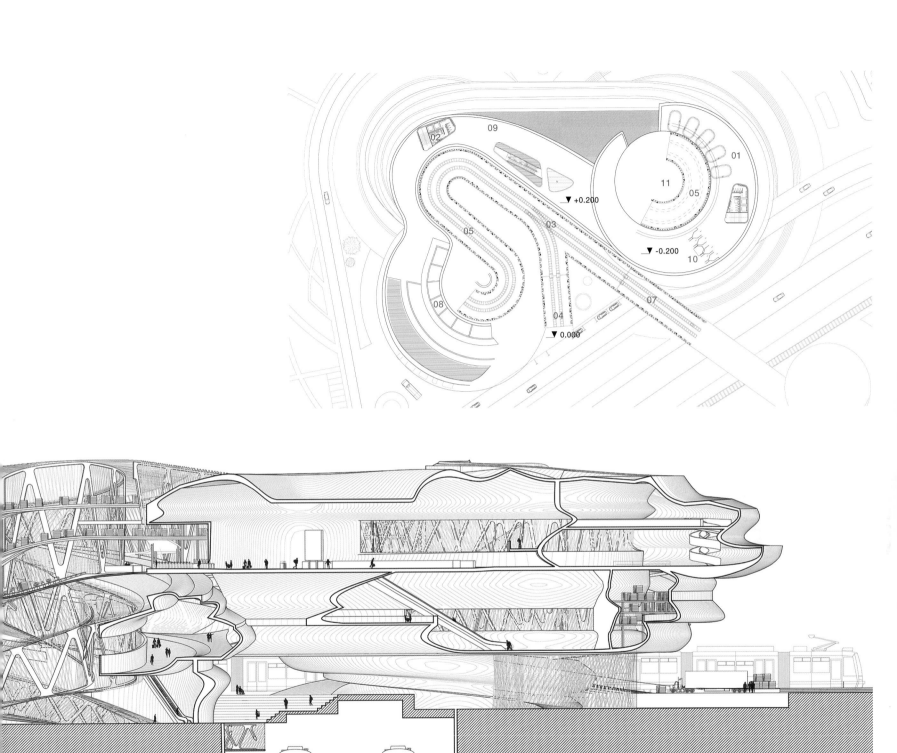

Section Model Rendering

Physical Section Model, 2'x2'x2', 3D Printed PLA

BRAID, JFK AIRPORT NEW TERMINAL HUB, QUEENS, NEW YORK   **PROJECT 02**   STRUCTURED LOGISTICS

PROJECT 03   **INTERSECT**

JFK Airport New Terminal Hub, Queens, New York

Rui Huang, Qi Liu, John Dunn

INTERSECT was conceived as an arrangement of logistics with emphasis on the temporal sorting of different scales of cargo. These different scales of cargo, from containers for large-scale shipments to suitcases, are intersected with each other to develop a language of densities that permeates the organization of the project. The scale of cargo determines different scales of accumulation of material. The temporal nature of these densities being filled or empty changes the perceived porosity of the building from the exterior. The logistics systems developed a series of carved voids that shaped the interior for passengers in plan and section—an interior that exposes the densities and modulates light and shadow while contributing to an animated experience. When the project is perceived from the exterior a clear aesthetic of the airport as a storage container emerges.

Top Right: Upper Level Floor Plan

Bottom: Long Building Section

01 Luggage Distribution System
02 Luggage Drop-off Area
03 Passenger Drop-off Area
04 Air Train
05 Air Train Station
06 Passenger Pick-up
07 Cargo Pick Up and Drop-off
08 Main Hall
09 Cargo Transportation System
10 Cargo Storage
11 Cargo Distribution System
12 Baggage Claim

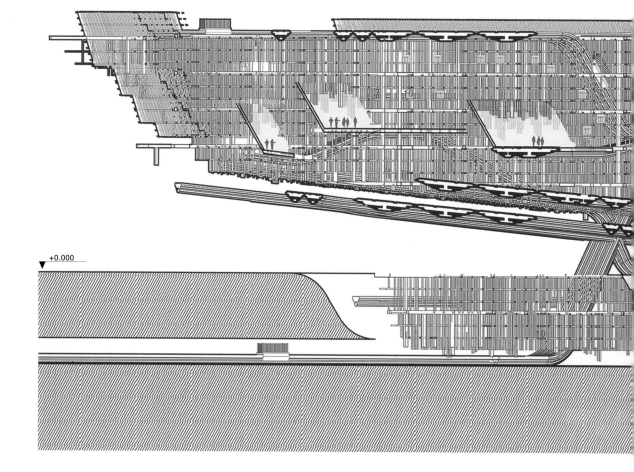

+0.000

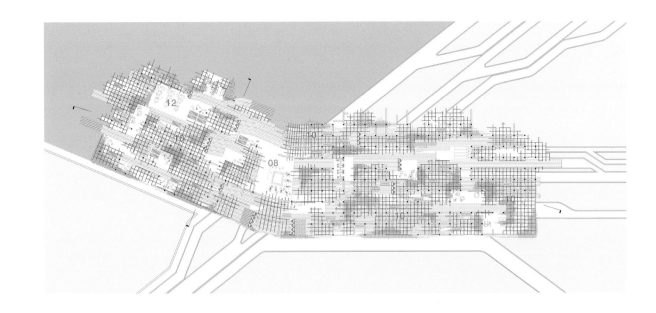

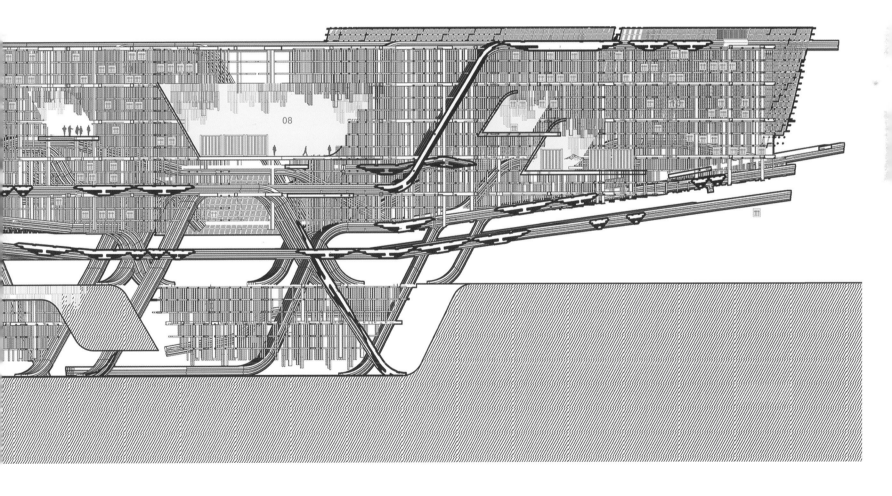

Choisey Axonometric

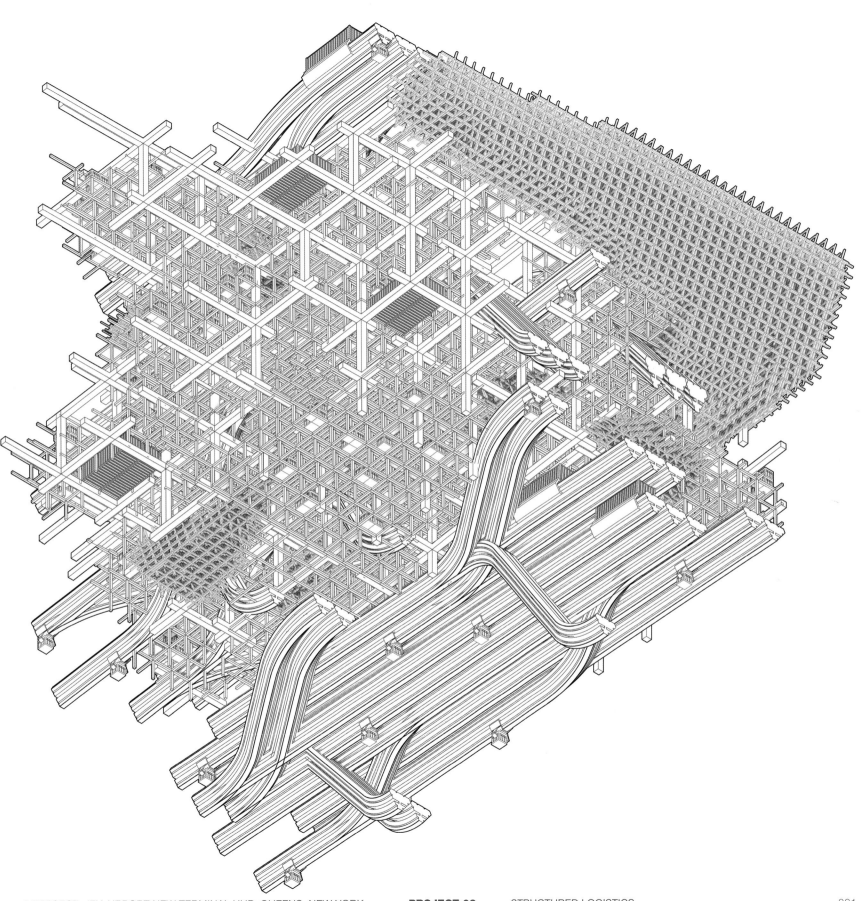

INTERSECT, JFK AIRPORT NEW TERMINAL HUB, QUEENS, NEW YORK   **PROJECT 03**   STRUCTURED LOGISTICS

Section Model Rendering

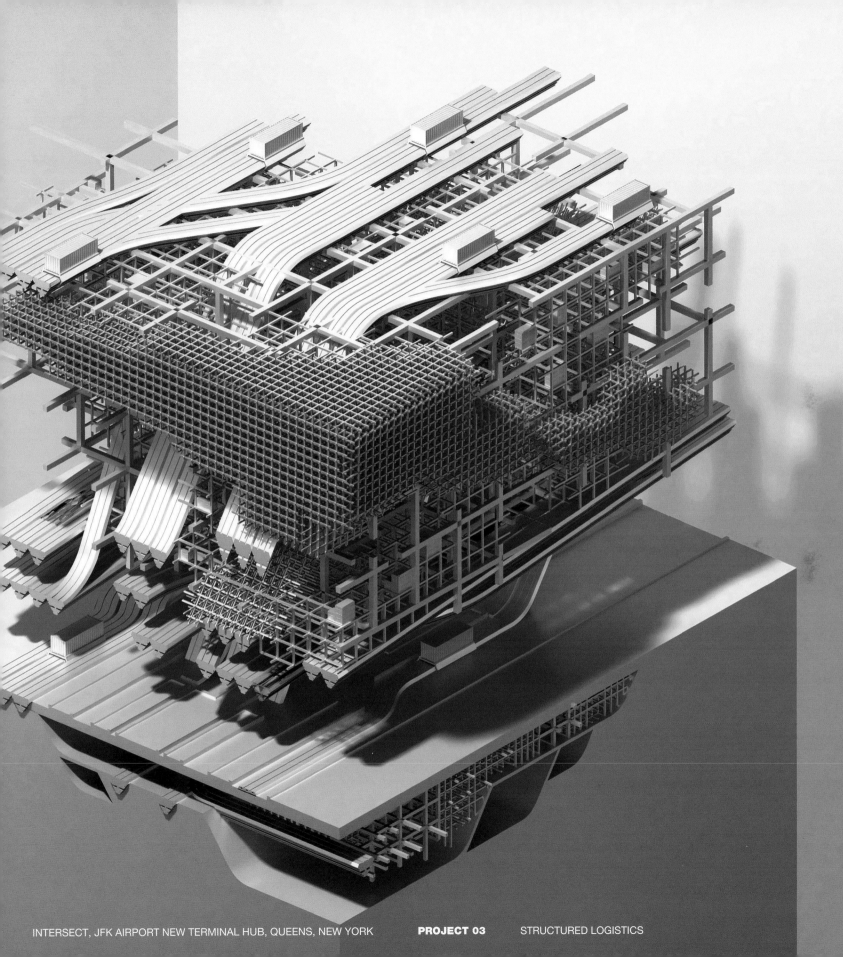

Physical Section Model, 2'x2'x2', 3D Printed PLA

PROJECT 04   **BUNDLE**

JFK Airport New Terminal Hub, Queens, New York

Fangzhou Sun, Wenzhao Xu, Hang Zhang

BUNDLE allows the form and organization of the logistic systems to be expressed in the form of the building. The tension in the skin contributes to the aesthetic of the project while serving as a woven hybrid between structure and logistics. The project has five organizational moments that bundle each node together while providing a tension in the envelope structure that binds the five nodes together. The logistics stacks move arriving cargo and luggage into the highest part of the building where it is sorted based on the length of time it will be in storage. When the luggage or cargo is needed it moves through conduits built into the skin of the project, using gravity to power its descent to the area where needed. The skin of the building is energized with moving packages which disrupt its light and delicate transparency.

Ground Floor Plan

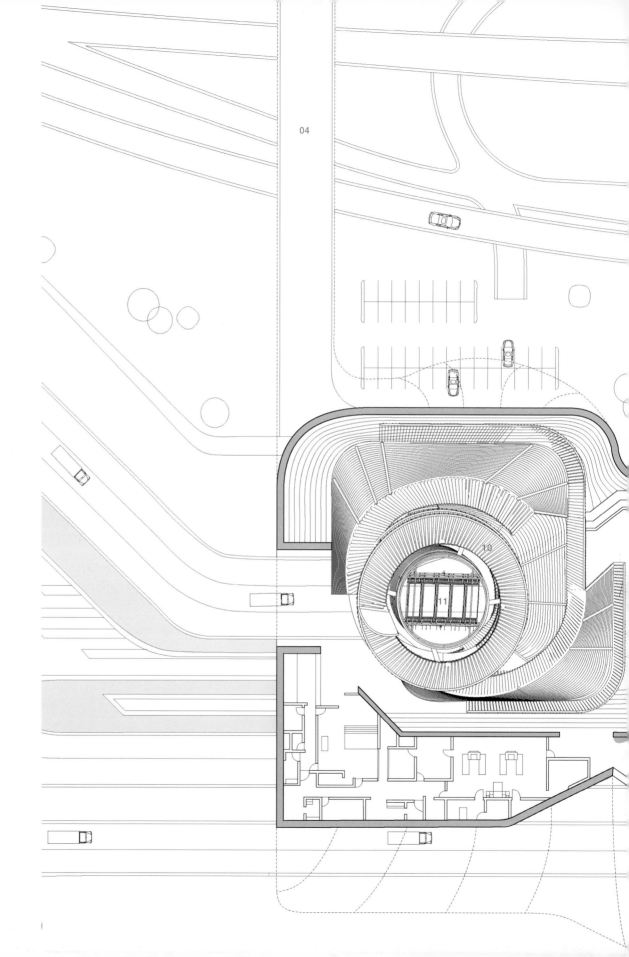

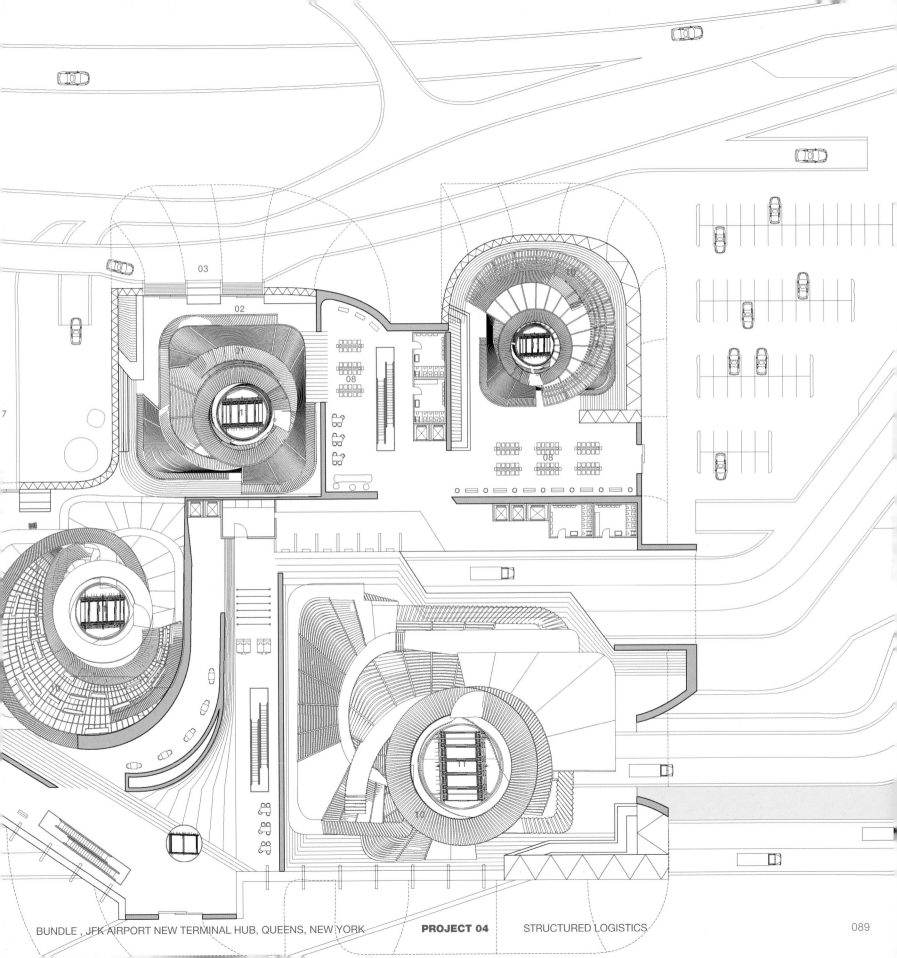

Top Right: Short Building Section

Bottom: Building Elevation

01   Luggage Distribution System
02   Luggage Drop-off Area
03   Passenger Drop-off Area
04   Air Train
05   Air Train Station
06   Passenger Pick-up
07   Cargo Pick-up and Drop-off
08   Passenger Hall
09   Cargo Transportation System
10   Cargo Storage
11   Cargo Distribution System
12   Baggage Claim

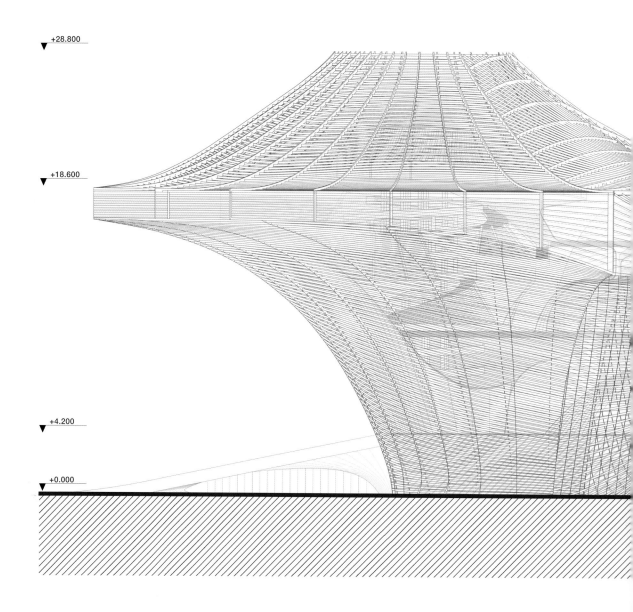

▼ +28.800

▼ +18.600

▼ +4.200

▼ +0.000

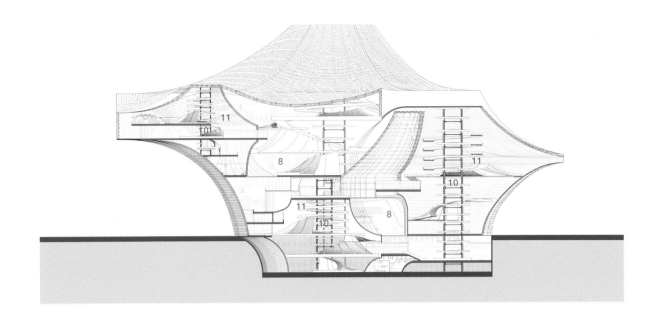

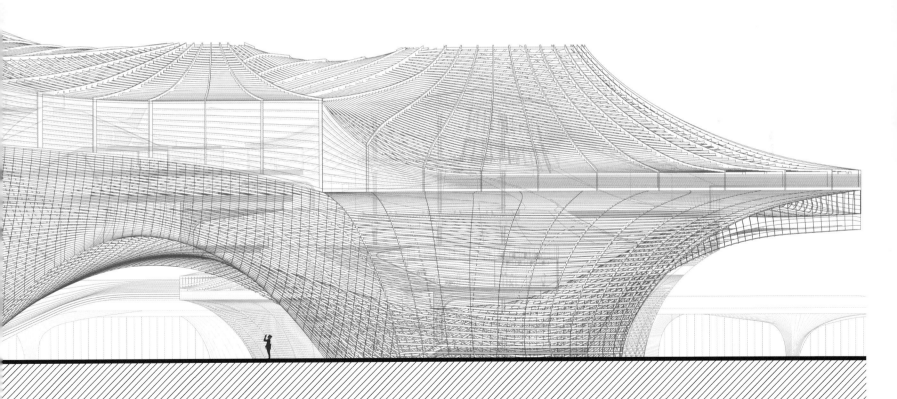

Right: Section Model Rendering

Bottom: Transverse Building Section

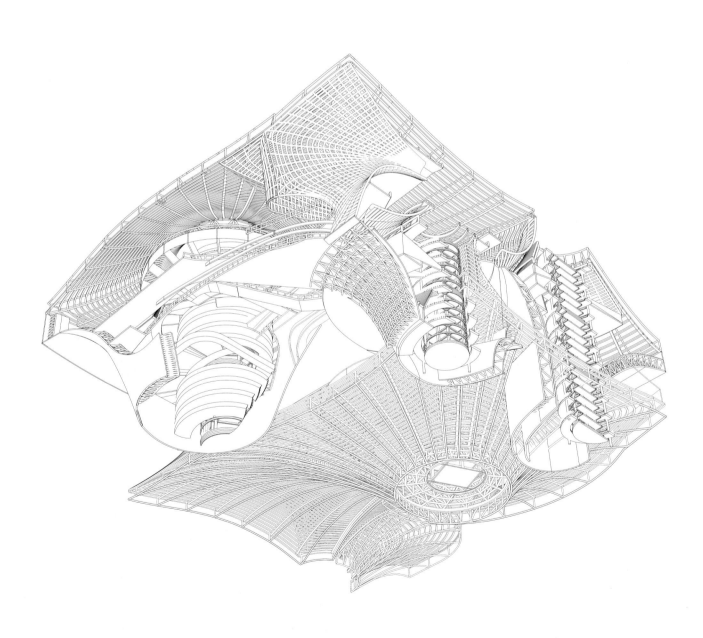

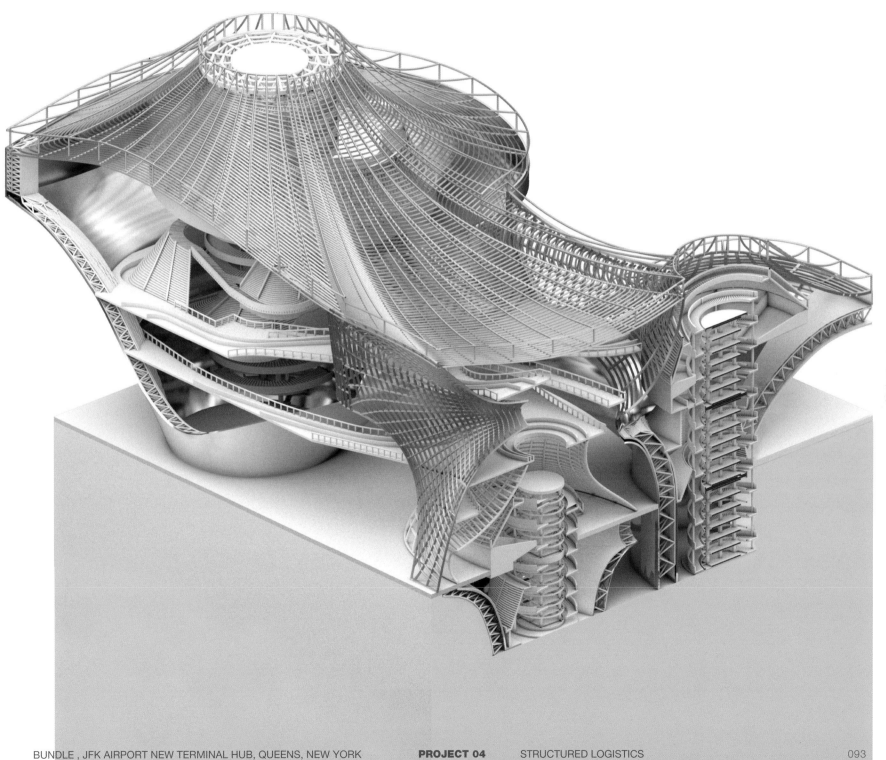

Right: Physical Section Model, 2'x2'x2', 3D Printed PLA

Bottom: Detail View of Physical Section Model

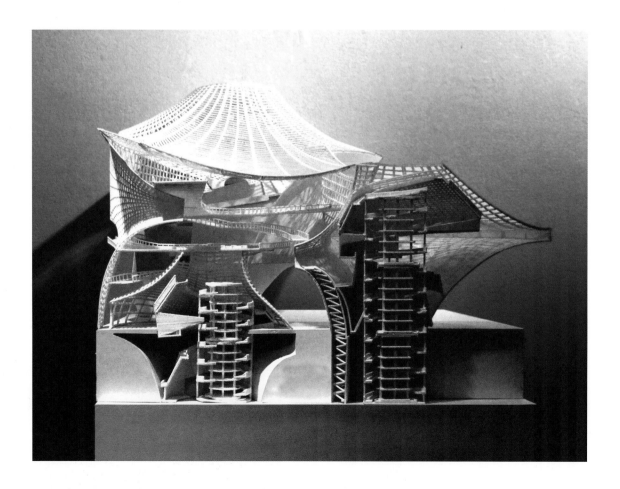

PROJECT 05   **CRADLE**

JFK Airport New Terminal Hub, Queens, New York

Zhenqin Dong, Ruobing Huang,Gengzhe Liu

CRADLE considers the long-span structure as a movable logistics-sorting element within the building, more Ferris wheel than roof structure. Rather than supporting the building, the wheel-shaped structural elements are self-supporting storage containers that allow the cargo and luggage stored within to be cycled through as needed. This innovative storage method allows cargo and luggage stored on a short-term basis to be easily accessible rather than placed deep in a storage stack requiring more sorting and conveyer mechanisms. The storage system is a featured attraction within the building, creating a dynamic passenger experience where the luggage surrounding the public space is constantly in motion. As can be seen within the Choisey axonometric, passengers move between the wheels and even sometimes through the center of them on the way to their destination. In this way, the enclosure of the building is formed by a series of these self-supporting structures cradled in constant motion and communication with one another, transforming the airport into a machine, processing cargo and passengers.

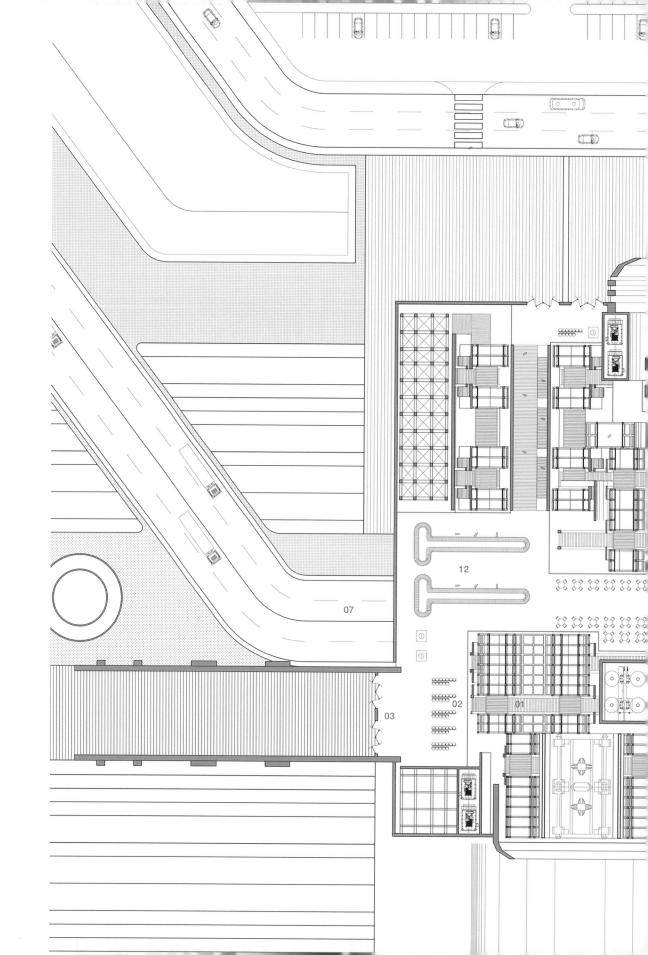

Ground Floor Plan (Arrivals)

01 Luggage Distribution System
02 Luggage Drop-off Area
03 Passenger Drop-off Area
04 Air Train
05 Air Train Station
06 Passenger Pick-up
07 Cargo Pick-up and Drop-off
08 Main Hall
09 Cargo Transportation System
10 Cargo Storage
11 Cargo Distribution System
12 Baggage Claim

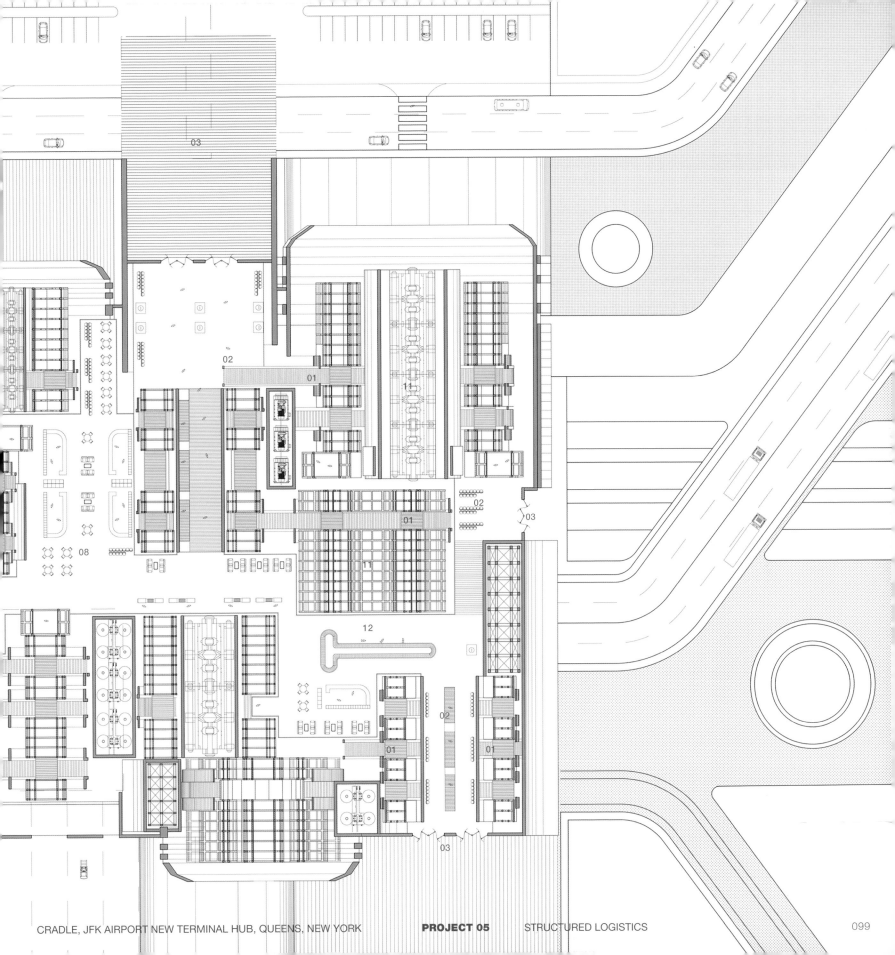

Perspective Section Drawing

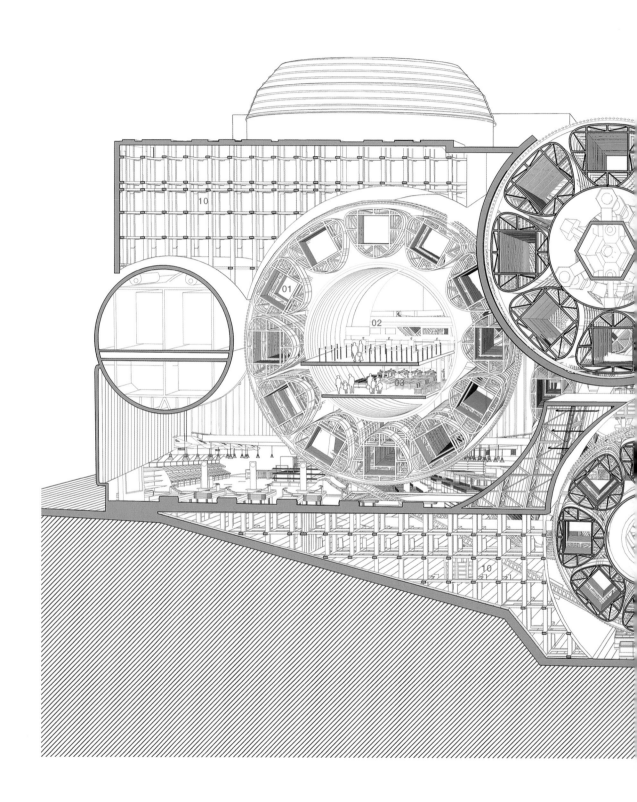

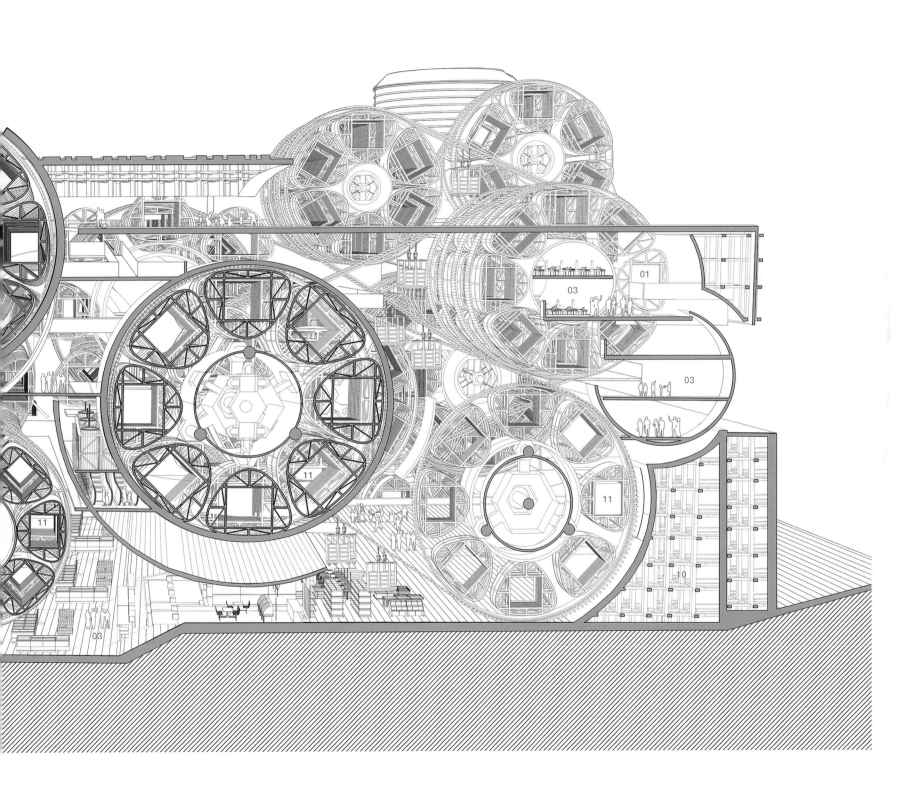

Choisey Axonometric

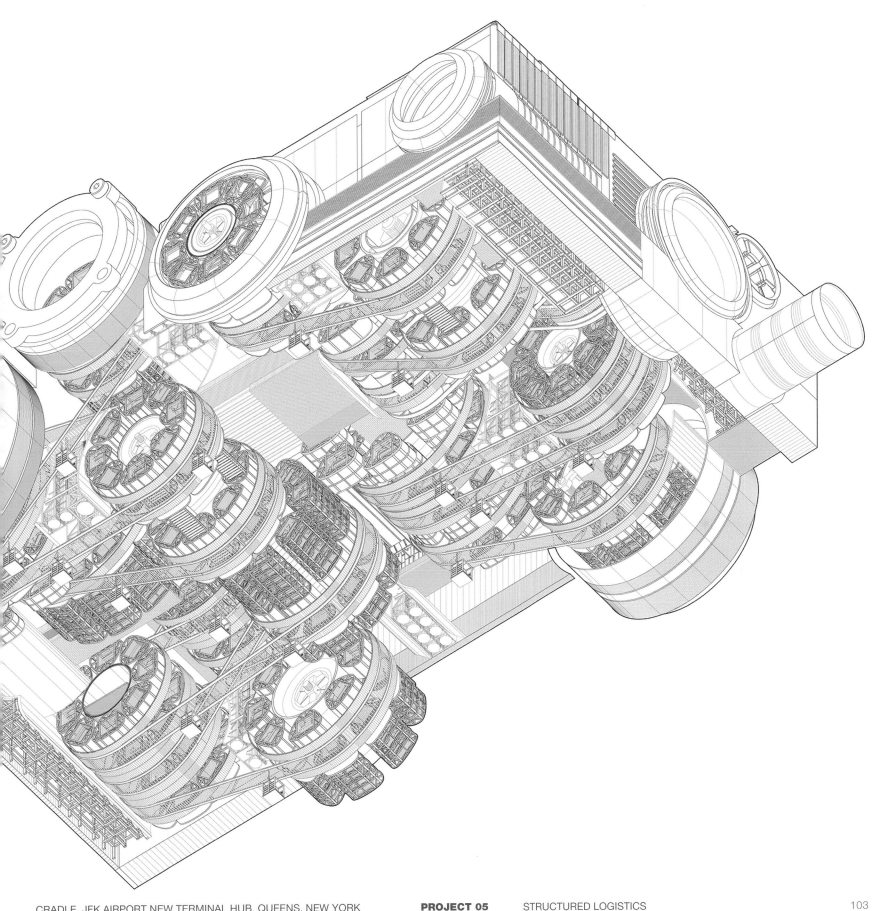

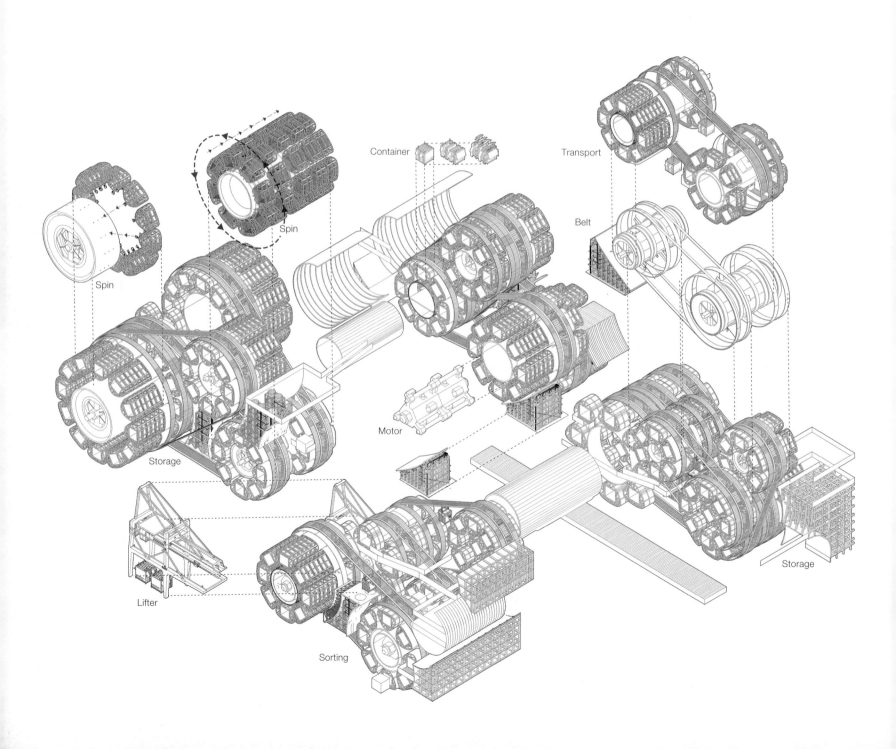

Spin

Spin

Container

Transport

Belt

Storage

Motor

Lifter

Sorting

Storage

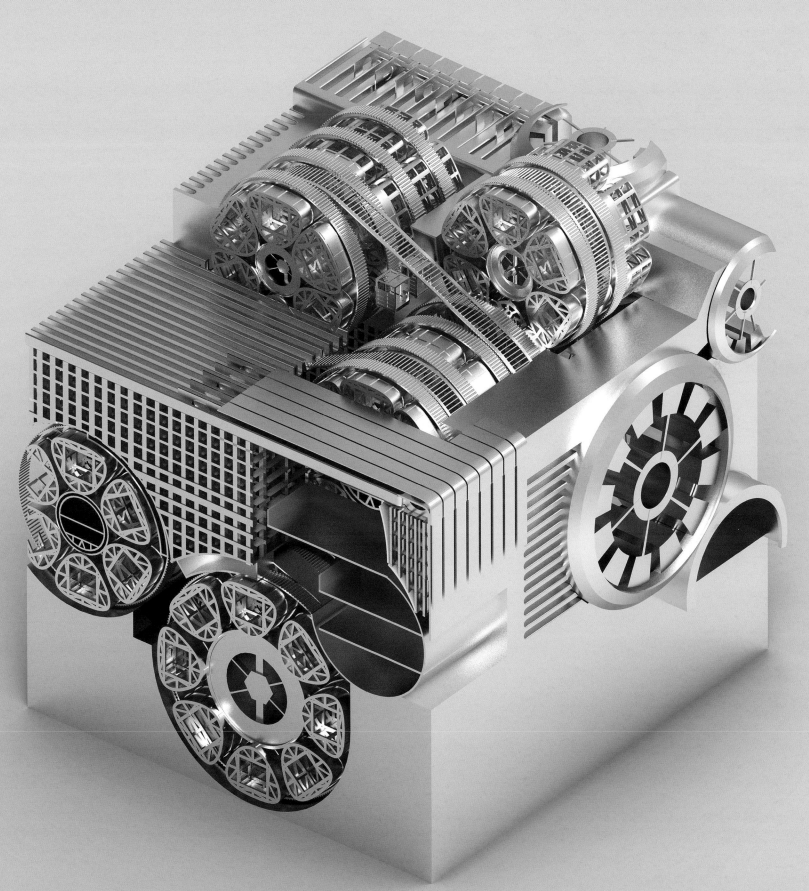

Right: Physical Section Model, 2'x2'x2', 3D Printed PLA

Bottom: Elevation View of Physical Section Model

04 THE EVOLUTION OF AIRPORT STRUCTURE
Preetam Biswas

Airports often reflect the aspirations of a city in projecting an image, a first-impression, to a traveler arriving at its doorsteps. Like the railway stations and shipping ports of the 19th Century, today's airports serve as gateways not only to cities but sometimes to an entire country. Over time, as airport terminals have grown, their designs have typically been a testament to the advancement in technology and progression in modes of air travel. As we move into shaping the airports of tomorrow, the creation of these enormous structures should be both, pioneeringly bold and intentionally responsible. It should be reflective of our commitment to protecting the environment and minimizing the impact to the natural resources of this planet.

UNDERSTANDING THE HISTORY OF AIRPORT TYPOLOGY

Early days of air travel was restricted to the affluent few. While railway stations boasted of grand halls under high majestic roofs, airports were typically smaller buildings occupied by few travelers, making the demand for single level and modest spans more appropriate. They were typically small enough to have an airplane park right next to it. As the demand for air travel increased, so did the need for larger airports. Smaller buildings with walk up access to aircrafts were replaced with terminal buildings with busses that ferried passengers to aircraft parking stalls. However, the additional time and functional requirements of bussing passengers to aircrafts led to the discovery of direct passenger loading bridges, also known as aerobridges. This brought a fundamental change to air travel in terms of speed and volume of passenger handling capabilities. With air travel being more affordable, the demand for larger terminal buildings with multiple levels to segregate different functions became the norm.

However, with larger terminal buildings came the passenger discomfort of large travel distances between the point of entry to the terminal building and the boarding of the aircraft. The concept of Airport terminal building with Multiple Satellite Terminals connected with rapid transit connectors served by a large centralized processing hall started taking shape. With exponential increase in air travel, especially in developing nations such as China and India and with gigantic aircrafts available for commercial air travel, the airport terminal, with millions of square feet of area and large functional spaces interrupted by very few columns, started being built. With the introduction of the super jumbo Airbus A380, with simultaneous loading of passengers at multiple levels of the aircraft, terminal buildings worldwide had to be structurally altered to accommodate such needs. The growth of retail, far more than basic food and beverage services, that can be commercially harnessed have given rise to the concept of airport terminals taking the shape of a "shopping mall" with aircraft gates attached to it. With it has come the need for airports to transform into one-of-a-kind buildings with large heroic roof and structural demands.

PLANNING AIRPORTS AND TERMINAL BUILDINGS

Airports in general and airport terminal buildings, in particular, are dynamic and continuously morphing in their functioning. Advancements in aircraft design and new technologies endlessly impact the functioning of an airport. Changes in laws governing the movement of people and cargo also play an active role in

Bidirectional long-span and independent headhouse roof, Chhatrapati Shivaji International Airport Terminal 2, Mumbai, 2014. Photo by Lucas Blair

the ever-evolving function of airport terminal buildings. When passengers travel through an airport, they go through different zones and depending on the type of travel, i.e. domestic or international, they are subjected to the various processing activities. Each of these have their own specific requirements and their functional demands dictate the structural systems most appropriate for it. However, there is a vast zone of the airport where a passenger never travels through but it is in these zones where clockwork-like precision allows for seamless and timely travel for the passengers. The functional requirements of these areas are sometimes more demanding than the public spaces of an airport terminal.

Like every structure, airport terminal buildings must be designed with appropriate consideration for both its gravity as well as the lateral system. However, given the low-rise nature of the building structure, lateral loads are not predominant controlling factors in the structural engineering of terminal buildings. The various requirements of different functional spaces govern the design of both the base structure and the roof structure of most airport buildings.

Terminal buildings are typically divided into different zones: central processing zone and the gate zone where passenger boarding takes place. Several specific parameters govern the design of the base structural systems in these zones: from column-free areas for ease of baggage carts maneuverability in the baggage claim halls to catering for optimum baggage dolly movements in the baggage make-up and break-up zones. Heavy loading, stringent deflection and vibration criteria of baggage handling and in-line security systems to specific requirement of mechanical, electrical, plumbing, and fire-fighting systems need to be considered while designing the floor framing and supporting vertical structure of the base structure of the terminal buildings. The base structure typically employs distinct structural floor systems in response to functional zones with varying optimal clear-span requirements. The floor-framing systems can be steel or concrete and is typically dictated by balancing many factors including cost, construction methods, future flexibility, etc. At locations that generate heavy passenger congestion such as the baggage claim hall, functional requirements call for a relatively column-free space and this can be achieved by placing columns within the baggage claim

Unidirectional long span truss roofs, Changi International Airport Terminal 3, Singapore, 2008.
Photo by Tim Griffith

Aesthetically expressed roof structure, Pearson International Airport Terminal 1, Toronto, 2004.
Photo by Timothy Husley

belts and having a clear span between belts. The resulting larger structural spans usually require floor-framing systems that span longer distances, such as waffle slab systems for reinforced concrete structures. In the retail areas of the terminal, where maximum flexibility for floor openings and future renovations is desired, the floor systems very often utilize steel framing with composite metal-deck slabs. Besides functional requirements, early in the design process, an evaluation of local construction techniques, available construction materials, and availability of skilled labor should play an important role in the choice of both building materials and structural systems.

INCORPORATING ROOF SYSTEMS AND IDEAS

In response to the functional requirement of the space in the different zones, various column layouts and resulting roof structures are employed. In most airports, the headhouse zone serves as the great hall with high density and very often results in long-span roofs over this zone. In most cases these are projected as the signature element of the entire airport terminal. For headhouse roofs are rectilinear in plan; the requirement for column-free space for central processing can be fulfilled by long spans in one direction with relatively closely-spaced columns in the other direction resulting in unidirectional long-span roofs. For instance, the primary roof of the San Francisco Airport is designed as balanced-cantilevers with spans of over 200 feet and a lightweight spatial truss system. The trusses of Changi International Airport in Singapore have a 300-foot clear span which serves as a back span to the 150-foot cantilever over the roadway. These long-span trusses march along at regular intervals of 45 feet and are supported by columns on both ends, making it an example of a regimental unidirectional long-span roof.

In some cases, the geometry of the central processing zone is a response to the availability of the real estate on an airport site and is not rectilinear in its plan. Such geometries lend themselves to two-way long-span roof systems with strategically positioned columns. In addition, larger spans, maintenance requirements and the desire to have minimal expansion joints in the roof can result in the roof structure to be kept completely independent from the base structures below. This allows the roof structure to move independently in response to loads, particularly expansion and contraction caused by thermal change. The headhouse roof of Chhatrapati Shivaji International Airport in Mumbai, covering 700,000 square feet, is a bidirectional long-span truss grid that spans over seven individual concrete-base structures. Supported by only 30 Composite Mega-Columns, it is designed to move independently from the base structure. Thus, making it one of the largest roofs in the world without an expansion joint.

The geometrical plan of terminal buildings may not always lend themselves to either unidirectional or bidirectional long spans. Additionally, a singular roof structure that encapsulates all functional zones requires a response which is neither one-way nor two-way trusses but more of a spatial truss system that could be broadly categorized as space-frame typology. Beijing International Airport roof is an example of such a roof.

Very often the light weight nature of terminal roofs results in an exposed structural system for the roof. Not only does a logical, structural grid layout and well-conceived long-span elements enhance the overall spatial experience for users, the aesthetics of the structural members and connections also play an important part in the creation of distinct roofs for each airport that sometimes become the signature element of the airport.

STRUCTURING BUILDING ENVELOPE SYSTEMS

Large terminal buildings with high roofs require building envelopes to be structured differently than typical buildings with regular floor to roof stories. The building envelope includes several unique features that create various challenges in the design and detailing of the supporting structure. There are various systems that can be implemented as a structural back-up system to cladding; they could be as simple as an integrated back-up system, inbuilt into mullions or more elaborate back-up trusses to support a unitized cladding system. Another cladding system that is used worldwide is a tension system consisting of cables. A cable wall system, which can offer ultimate flexibility and transparency in terms of design, also has a good response to dynamic loading. For building envelopes of airports, security considerations are probably one of the highest priorities in its design.

MODULATING ROADWAYS AND MULTIMODAL TRANSPORTATION HUBS

Airports, in theory, are a transition point between two modes of transportation and the design of the parking structure or more recently, the design of a multi-modal transportation hub adjoining a terminal that requires an equally well thought system as that of the terminal building itself. Due to the sheer volume of functional spaces, the design of these multi-modal transportation hubs brings several aesthetic

and functional challenges. Designers typically do not want an imposing structure that overshadows the terminal building itself. Geological conditions often limit the depth of excavation and thus working within these constraints, a parking structure must utilize the shallowest floor framing system practically possible. Two-way concrete flat plates with concrete shear walls for lateral support are the most common types, however given time and site constraints during construction, precast and prefabricated structural systems often provide viable alternatives. Compact, automated parking facilities that require the least volume in terms of a building structure are also considered a reasonable alternative. A desire to create compact multi-level parking garages along with multi-modal ground and rail transportation connections below or above ground will trounce any attempt for a heroic structural system that overshadows the main terminal building.

Like the parking garage, the frontage and approach roads are an integral part of a terminal and careful consideration should be given to both their aesthetical and functional characteristics. The structural system consisting of reinforced concrete systems with prestressed and precast long-span beams supported on isolation pads is predominantly the most utilized system worldwide. A cast-in-place reinforced concrete slab interconnects the beams and acts as a diaphragm but given that the roadway slab is exposed to the elements, it is required to be designed to allow for thermal movement due to temperature changes. The roadway structure thus requires expansion joints at regular intervals; however, with functional spaces used by passengers below, water-tightness is a very important consideration in the design. Cast-in-place concrete structures and structural steel beam and girder systems are also used in many parts of the world. Most passengers would experience the roadway structure from above and underneath during departure and arrival respectively, depending on the vertical separation employed by the functional design and hence the design of the system should not be considered ancillary.

PRIORITIZING CONSTRUCTION, ASSEMBLY AND BUILDING MATERIALS

Construction of an entirely new airport along with a terminal building takes years, sometimes decades. An airport terminal site can vary immensely. A brand-new terminal building in a green

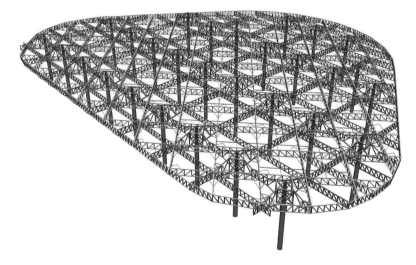

Cable wall system ,Chhatrapati Shivaji International Airport Terminal 2, Mumbai, 2014.
Photo by Robert Polidori

Bidirectional long-span and independent headhouse roof structure, Chhatrapati Shivaji International Airport Terminal 2, Mumbai, 2014.

field airport on one end of the spectrum, and a new terminal building in a phased manner at an existing Airport, on the other end of the spectrum. Sometimes, the new terminal buildings need to be constructed in close proximity of an existing terminal that must remain operational during construction. Thus, the choice of a structural system that can accommodate construction phasing and permit rapid construction are sometimes a function of site more than the actual working of the airport itself. Modular construction utilizing repetitive, self-contained modular designs can be a choice that can greatly facilitate phased construction methods.

There are quite a few airports where modular construction has been used in a way that allows all the function areas of the airport to be housed under one roof. The design for the majority of terminal buildings typically places a high priority on material efficiency and ease of construction. All parts of the buildings that utilize repetitive, modular designs and accommodate construction phasing and permit rapid construction find their way into structural and economic considerations. For a brown field project, ensuring the stability of the individual portions of the terminal buildings throughout the phased construction is an important consideration in selecting the building's structural systems.

Stansted Airport, London, United Kingdom, takes modular construction to a whole new dimension. The modularity was in every system of the airport, the structural system, the mechanical, electrical, and plumbing system, etc. The integration of the systems into modules that could be repeated to make a terminal building of the desired configuration provided significant flexibility.

Built in the 1980s, the Hajj Terminal, Jeddah, Saudia Arabia, employed tensile fabric roofing and supporting mast in a modular fashion never seen in airport construction prior to it. This allowed the airport to be built in phases and expanded when the demand increased. It has proved to be one of the most versatile airports in handling of the annual fluctuation of passenger demand and overall growth of passenger volume over the last three decades.

The choice of building materials plays a fundamental role in the choice of the structural system being employed. Though conventional, reinforced concrete and structural steel have been the material choice for major terminal buildings, the use of non-conventional materials such as glue-lam, timber and CLT are increasingly being explored as materials for various functional zones of a terminal building. Fabric and tensile membrane systems first used in extreme hot weather of Saudi Arabia for the Hajj Terminal and later in the extreme cold weather of Denver, Colorado for the Denver International Airport demonstrated the wide spectrum of the use for yet another non-conventional material for construction of airport terminal roofs.

RESPONSIBLE ENGINEERING
AND PLANNING FOR FUTURE FLEXIBILITY

Light-weight materials that are capable of efficiently spanning large distances are most often the material of choice for roof structures among airport designers. Locally sourced materials which can be used with construction techniques than can be easily implemented in the geographical region where the airport terminal building is being constructed should be one of the basic considerations for a terminal building. Life cycle analysis with materials that have the least carbon demand should be the other fundamental consideration.

We live in the world of finite resources and as responsible engineers we need to be extremely aware it. Utilizing resources beyond the real need of the design, is not just bad economics, it is unethical. If a structural engineer designs an airport beyond the real need of clear-span spaces just to satisfy the ego of the design so that it can be considered as the largest clear-span airport and as a result utilizes 200% more structural materials, it prevents two other airports from being constructed. When an architect asks an engineer the question: "can you do it?" as a responsible engineer, our response ought to be "should we do it?" "Structural Engineers need to be facilitators of dreams not enablers of willful excess," very eloquently noted by Bill Baker, Structural Partner at Skidmore, Owings and Merrill. It is the responsibility of a structural engineer to ensure the needs of a given function is met with the structural design that allows it to function optimally.

Airports are intrinsically connected with the latest technology and therefore the longer it takes for an airport to be constructed after its design the further it is from the latest technology available for various functions of an airport such as security etc. In other words, from the time a design is conceptualized to the time that an airport is open for public use the desire for certain spaces related to the activities of an airport might be completely different or somewhat different from the original intended use of the space. The structural engineering that allows certain flexibility in the layout of spaces and functions within an airport is more timeless then just responding do the present need of design. Open planning and regularized grids can provide great flexibility in repurposing various areas depending on the change in functional requirements. A concept, like stadiums, where portions could be deployed and repurposed depending on functional requirements would start playing a crucial role in the structural planning and design of airports. Movable and Deployable Structures, that can be repositioned and repurposed could become the norm in airport structure to further enhance its ability to morph itself to changing requirements.

CONTINUING THE EVOLUTION
AND SPECULATION ON THE FUTURE OF AIRPORTS

Terminal Buildings that can combine international and domestic operations with utmost flexibility to achieve 24-hour utilization, a new terminal building that can be built in the vicinity of an existing one with minimal disruption to it operations or a terminal building that allows adaptability for newer types of aircrafts are only a few considerations a structural engineer must focus while envisioning a system for an airport of the future. The most crucial questions one must answer is whether the terminal building structure is timeless enough to be useful for next 50 years of air travel and whether it is responsible enough to inspire the next generations of sustainable design.

There are various aspects of future airport design that will play an important part in the engineering of the terminal buildings. These include: data sharing between airlines and airport operations of passenger rosters and cargo, the use of artificial intelligence for airport and personal security, baggage screening, governmental control and catering; and automation technologies for aircraft maintenance, refueling and servicing. Increase in air travel for leisure and corresponding decrease in business travel and passenger preference of point-to-point air travel versus hub

Interior spaces, King Abdulaziz International Airport Hajj Terminal, Jeddah, 1981. Photo by Jay Langlois

and spoke format by major airlines will lead to the movement of passenger and transportation of cargo integrated to a much greater extent than it is currently.

Airports of the future may not have an airside and landside as typically found in current airports where the airside connects to aircrafts and the landside connects to other transportation systems such as cars, buses, trains and land-based transportation. In a not too distant future, one can expect airports to be multi-pronged, serving as a connection between small autonomous aircrafts that take you from your home and a larger aircraft that takes you to your next destination. It could be a hub where hyperloop pods and autonomous ground transportation are integrated with air borne passengers and cargo and brings a new definition to hub-and-spoke system.

The real future airport is one where systems and methods of travel are interconnected, where people and cargo can transition seamlessly from one mode to another, where preconceived notions of differences between operational requirements of different modes of transportation that prevent cross-platform integration are a thing of the past. Airports and its buildings engineered to have the flexibility and adaptability to facilitate the flow of passengers and cargo from origin to destination using various modes of transportation, one or more of which would be air travel, will truly be the airport of tomorrow.

05 LONG-SPAN STRUCTURE:
The Harbinger of Novel Architecture Culture
Caleb White

The long-span structure has always been a product of technology. It is a composition of engineering and material science that allows architecture to do new things. The arch, vault, and dome, revolutionized stone and masonry construction and made taller and larger open spaces in buildings possible with the construction methods of its time. This structural innovation, first used for the infrastructure of the Roman Empire as they built bridges and aqueducts, became an aesthetic feature of their temples, fora, government buildings, and even their homes. As a result, the arch, vault and dome, became a mainstay of Western architecture. Even after the advent of concrete, iron, and steel as structural building methods these masonry innovations remained aesthetic and sometimes structural features of Western architecture up until it was removed from the lexicon by the modernists.

The history of the long-span structure is the repeated story of technological innovation solving logistical and infrastructural problems and in turn being co-opted as a new aesthetic and thus becoming a cultural feature. Obviously, however, not all architecture is a strict translation of technological means. The greatest architectural works enforce their own agendas aided by the available technologies. We can look at some of these works from different periods of history to see how the newest long-span technologies have been incorporated and more importantly, the agenda and means of their incorporation for architectural and design innovation.

It is important for us to understand and acknowledge the ways that new technologies are brought into the field of architecture. This is a continual process which controls the evolution of architecture's capacities and of our aesthetic sensibilities. Furthermore, if we can understand how this has been done in the past it can provide us with an understanding of how to approach innovative technologies and their potential within architecture going forward. There is a three-part categorization of these processes: Recombination, Hybridization, and Synthesis.

Recombination is the method of looking at emerging processes and technologies that work in other industries and modifying them or directly copying them for an architectural purpose. This is a "copy-paste" of a new material or technology. Hybridization, however, implies that there is a translation from the known process to a specific architectural condition that produces something new and different. Translation is the key term here—this implies that there is some modification or innovation of the new technology. Synthesis is a creative process where the underlying factors that make a new technology possible are understood and used to create an altogether new process that is unique and singular for an architectural feature that would have been otherwise impossible.

RECOMBINATION

The Crystal Palace – Joseph Paxton 1851
The advent of iron and eventually steel construction revolutionized the long-span structure during the industrial revolution. As the process of casting iron became cost effective and reliable in the development of factory machinery, the railroad and the steam engine, it also opened the door for use as a viable building

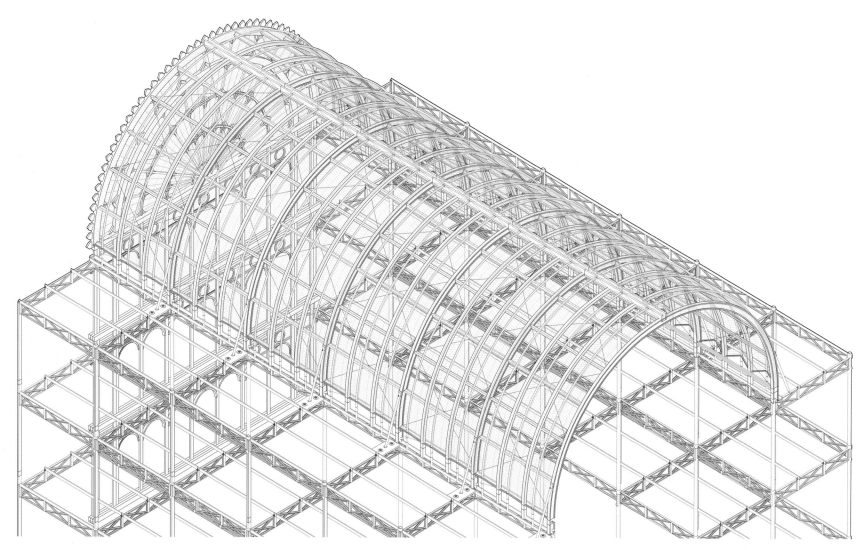

Crystal Palace, Joseph Paxton, London, 1851. Drawing by Quingyang Li, Wenjia Guo, and Yuanyi Zhou

material. Initially, engineers used cast iron to construct bridges and factories. The Iron Bridge in Shropshire, England is a prominent early example of a cast-iron structure, built in 1781 with many similar ones to follow. The technology eventually migrated into architecture via factory design where the slender iron columns saved space and allowed factories and mills to be built taller.

Early rail stations used cast-iron trusses or joists alongside masonry construction. Here we can point to a specific moment where a new technology is brought under the umbrella of architecture—firstly for its advantages as a building material, but also as a new aesthetic feature of an era. The cast-iron trusses were something that had not been seen in architecture before. And for those that were coming to this new architecture to witness rail travel for the first time, they would also have witnessed a new type of architecture—one with new capacities but also with an altogether different aesthetic. Buildings were previously built by craftsmen: skilled laborers who were trained to hew stone and to lay brick. They would be replaced by laborers, a term from the factory, these men would assemble buildings in parts just like mechanics assembling a steam engine.

Joseph Paxton's Crystal Palace took advantage of these new technologies in a holistic way. It was made entirely of cast iron and industrial plate glass—it gave architecture new capacities that it had never had before. Previously architectural design was primarily concerned with surface—buildings had largely focused on masonry systems and therefore were heavy and had great mass. Surface articulation, decoration, and ornament were the architect's tools to modify what was essentially a prescribed building system. Architects dealt with mass and poche. Within the Crystal Palace there was no heavy mass—the elements were thin and light. Covered entirely in plate glass—the building was almost entirely transparent—a quality which buildings had not yet achieved which earned the building its name. With the arrival of new industrial techniques that were initially used for industrial purposes and factory construction, buildings could take on new features and new aesthetics.

Similar to the other products of industry—the steam engine, the locomotive, the steam ship—the Crystal Palace had to be designed in components and assembled as a series of repeated elements. As was mentioned the Crystal Palace was assembled by "laborers" rather than "builders" or "craftsmen." Another innovation of the Crystal Palace beyond just the materials used for construction is also the implications that those materials had for the designer of the building. The structure, a series of cast-iron sections on thin iron columns, was now liberated from the walls of the architecture. The thin structural elements did not have to limit the interior spaces of the building, you could occupy the space in many ways—the interior partitions free of the load bearing structure—a free plan. Joseph Paxton was an architect by trade but began his journey into architecture through horticulture and the building of greenhouses. The innovation of the Crystal Palace is in the recombination of cutting-edge industrial technologies.

Galerie des Machines – Ferdinand Dutert, 1889
Another project that was clearly influenced by the Crystal Palace but also directly borrowed industrial knowledge to produce new architecture capacities was the Galerie des Machines designed by Ferdinand Dutert for the 1878 Exposition in Paris. Dutert borrowed new industrial innovations in bridge building technologies (the three pinned, hinged arch) and more sophisticated metallurgical processes. By recombining these new industrial technologies Dutert built the largest long-span structure of its time. The Galerie des Machines would span 377 feet and have an open space 148 feet high. While the Crystal Palace shocked visitors in London for the new effects and capacities that had not been seen before, the Galerie des Machines would shock visitors with its sheer scale and magnitude. Not to say that there were not also aesthetic qualities to the building—the three pinned hinged trusses were beautifully ornate and their forms were elegant as Dutert designed a series of variations in the geometry of the arches.

HYBRIDIZATION

If the Crystal Palace and the Galerie Des Machines were both examples of recombining industrial innovations into an architectural use then an altogether different method of incorporating new technologies into architecture to produce a novel aesthetic is hybridization. A perfect example of this concept is the exquisite work of Hentri Labrouste. Labrouste, like Paxton, saw the potential of using cast-iron construction in architecture and was also an early adopter. Labrouste, however,

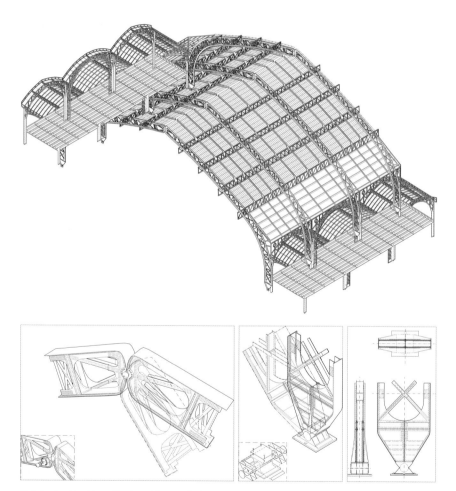

Galerie des Machines, Ferdinand Dutert, Paris, 1889. Drawing by Zhu Sihan, Yang Yifang, and He Liwei

having been trained at the Ecole des Beaux Arts, had a more thorough obsession with the proportion and geometry of classical architecture. His famous reading room in Paris, Bibliothèque Sainte Geneviève (1850), would have been considered radical in its aesthetic at the time, but when seen by the contemporary eye, retains all of the rules and elements of Beaux Arts composition.

The exterior of the library seems traditionally Beaux Arts. It is symmetrical in its composition and adorned with pilasters and arches that give no hint of the innovative interior. Once arriving in the reading room, the user would be astonished by a cascade of cast-iron arches each clad with fine cast-iron decoration. Each pair of arches are supported by a single thin cast-iron column in the middle and resting on masonry pilasters on the outside. It is a hybrid of two building systems and two materials: traditional masonry construction and cast-iron trusses. The project was not simply innovative for its novel materials but was hailed as spectacular for the novel aesthetic that the fine ornate arches produce in relation to the heavy masonry walls.

For his second library built in Paris, Labrouste used the same strategy but brought to the next level. The Bibliothèque National de France (1868) utilized a series of domes rather than vaults. And this time the clear space of the reading room would be much larger as the whole of the reading room would be comprised of a nine-foot-square grid of cast-iron truss-supported domes. The same care and quality were given to the ornate decoration of the dome's components. There was one more added feature, a series of skylights. These were enabled by the deep section of the cast-iron trusses. This section hints at the hybridity of the building. The roof is a fairly traditional shed roof supported by the top chords of the cast iron trusses. Meanwhile, suspended from the bottom chord of the truss is the surface of the domes.

Similar to the Bibliothèque Sainte Geneviève, the whole series of cast-iron trusses are resting on all sides on a Beaux Arts masonry structure. Again, the aesthetic of the space was unique and never before seen. Much of this was attributed to the new materials which enabled the fineness and lightness of the roof structure. In the hands of Labrouste, however, the proportion and geometry of the space was precisely calibrated. These elements were carefully crafted after years of study at the Ecole des Beaux Arts and the

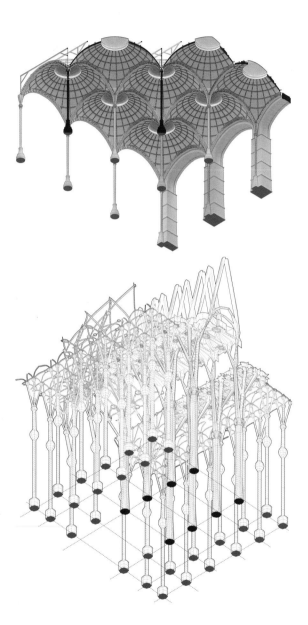

Bibliothèque National de France, Henri Labrouste, Paris, 1868. Drawing by Mengqi xu and Long Ye

Sagrada Familia, Antoni Gaudi, Barcelona. Drawing by Mostafa Akbari, Qiaoxi Liu, and Mariana Righi

years of onsite study in Rome after winning the Prix de Rome. Labrouste transcribed the genetics of generations of classical architecture onto a brand-new building system, enabled by new technologies and producing an altogether new architecture.

SYNTHESIS

Synthesis is a creative process where the underlying factors that make a new technology possible are understood and used to create an altogether new process that is unique and singular for an architectural feature that would have been otherwise impossible. Antonia Gaudi, while designing the Sagrada Familia, famously used a hanging chain model to design and simulate the catenary curve and to model the structure of the cathedral. This unique method was also directly tied to the aesthetic that Gaudi sought to produce in the cathedral. The result is beyond simple recombination of existing structural and material strategies. The hanging chain model represented a geometry for architecture that was beyond existing architectural forms.

It was a synthesis of structural and aesthetic performance. The architect developed a system, a technique to produce the form of the building rather than selecting from an existing repertoire of architectural forms. The structural system that Gaudi developed for Sagrada Familia is one of a kind. While it is typologically similar to a traditional Gothic cathedral its aesthetics do not expressly belong to that category. And while Gaudi is often regarded as an architect of the Art Nouveau period, the three dimensionality and spatiality of his work goes far beyond the ornamental work of his Art Nouveau contemporaries. The work that Gaudi produced at Sagrada Familia is more than a recombination of existing technologies or even a hybridization to produce a new aesthetic. His work was not bound by existing typologies or aesthetics. Synthesis is the creation of something truly new.

It can be argued that architecture is an amalgamation of technological developments or at least a residue of the many technologies that have changed the way we make buildings and what they can do. The question of their origin, or at least their insertion point into architecture, and the method with which they make their way into architecture is of great importance. The various methods of their incorporation, elucidated here, (recombination, hybridization, and synthesis) is an attempt at developing a toolset to understand the coming wave of technologies that have yet to be fully incorporated into architecture. It is not clear what the cast-iron innovation of our day is. Some would argue that the technological innovation of the digital age, by its very immaterial nature, threatens architecture's cultural relevance. It is important that we resist this notion and instead understand these new technological material implications. By doing this we can conceive of architectures new and yet undiscovered capacities.

01   Bridgwater, Derek and Gloag, John. A History of Cast Iron in Architecture. London: Allen and Unwin, 1948.

02   Zanten, David Van. Designing Paris: the Architecture of Duban, Labrouste, Duc, and Vaudoyer. MIT Press, 1987.

06 SPATIAL STRUCTURAL MORPHOLOGY FOR AIRPORTS

Masoud Akbarzadeh

PERFORMATIVE ARCHITECTURAL GEOMETRY

Architectural geometry has two equally-important components: the artistic component, expressing the aesthetic quality, and the performative component, exhibiting the function of the geometry. In contrast to the artistic quality of a specific geometry, which is difficult to be measured, its performative aspects can be assessed by a range of criteria including building physics, environmental impacts, structural endurance, and material and construction techniques. Even though in some projects, the artistic characteristics dominate the performative properties or vice versa, their co-existence is crucial for the successful completion of a project.

Design vs. Analysis
The fact that the performative qualities of an architectural geometry are quantifiable in contrast to its artistic qualities has

been misleading in the design process. It implies that a design must be derived from an idea/approach that can subsequently be analyzed for the performative aspects. This approach indeed disintegrates the design from the performance and considers them as two separate entities, which might cause the following misconception: any property that is related to the aesthetics of the geometry should be called design while the performative qualities should be associated with the analysis which comes after.In this section, I will introduce a design methodology that is based on a performative criterion and will establish design principles that combine design and analysis in the very first stages of the design process. This approach guarantees these performative qualities and results in architectural geometries with inherent artistic elegance.

STRUCTURAL GEOMETRY IN ARCHITECTURAL DESIGN

From all performative aspects, structural performance is one of the key properties without which a project cannot be realized. By structural geometry, I refer to those characteristics that inform the designer on how the forces are distributed in the system and whether the design is physically buildable. The type of structural system of an architectural project can directly affect the techniques of construction and the use of the materials in the entire building. It is a common practice to assess the structural performance of geometry after it is designed, but is it possible to use structural performance as an architectural design method?

Physical Structural Models as a Design Tool
Historically, several architects could successfully combine the artistic properties with the performative qualities of their design. Undoubtedly, Gaudi was one of them who combined structural geometry with Art Nouveau, which made his works timeless. His approach to design was unique; he used physical, structural models such as ropes, sandbags, and hanging chains to find funicular structural geometries as a basis for his designs. Funicular structural forms carry the applied loads in pure tensile forces since the form/geometry of the structure precisely matches the direction of the flow of its internal forces. Robert Hooke first suggested the use of hanging chain models to find funicular forms in the 17th century.[1,2] More importantly, he showed that by flipping the geometry of a hanging chain, one could find a form of an arch

A side view of the boarding gate and the interweaving structural geometry of the terminal. Project by Tian Ouyang and Jasmine Gao

in pure compression: the principle that Gaudi used extensively in materializing his designs. Aligning the geometry of a structure with the direction of its internal flow of forces maximizes the structural performance and minimizes the use of construction materials.

Physical form-finding methods have been used extensively by master builders such as Antoni Gaudi, Heinz Isler, Frei Otto, and many others throughout the history of architecture and structural design.[3][4] Although these methods are quite powerful and intuitive in conveying the concept of efficient structural forms, building such models is quite cumbersome as any design iteration requires a new model. Moreover, the process of translation from smaller scales to the larger scales using physical models is quite difficult.[5][6]

Numerical Form-Finding Methods
Advances in computer science and engineering have allowed the development of techniques to simulate the physical behavior of materials to find the optimal geometry of the structure under the given loading conditions. Physics simulation engines,[7] particle-spring systems,[8][9] force density methods,[10][11] and dynamic relaxation[12] are among them. These methods are the primary substitutes for the tedious physical form-finding techniques.[13] In all these techniques, the final geometry is the result of various computational processes, and therefore, the contribution of the designer is minimal. There is not an explicit relationship between the structural geometry and the state of equilibrium that makes it difficult for a designer to recognize the effective parameters in the design process. Besides, their underlying mathematical concepts are not trivial, and the mechanism to control the geometry of the structure is not clear for the designer. As a result, they do not provide a desirable level of control in the design process.

GEOMETRY-BASED FORM-FINDING METHODS

Many eminent engineers and designers such as Guastavino,[14] Maillart,[15] Eiffel, Koechlin,[16] Nervi, and Dieste relied on geometric methods of structural design, known as graphical statics (GS), to design their architectural structures. graphical statics (GS) methods represent a group of powerful and intuitive geometric techniques for form finding and analysis that originated in the pre-digital era and continue to be used and developed even today.[17][18] [19][20][21][22][23] In this method, the equilibrium of forces in the structure

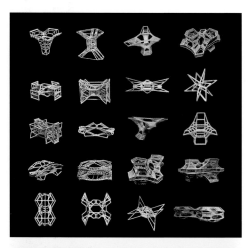

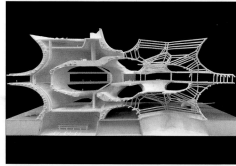

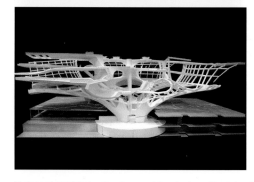

Variety of spatial structural geometries designed by using 3D graphic statics and controlling the force polyhedrons.

Structural model of a terminal where the internal space is designed as a multi-story spaces to receive drones on the top and conventional airplanes on the side.
Project by Zhou Xieyang and Duan Xiaoyu

Example of a terminal design using 3D graphic statics in form of a multi-layered funnel structure.
Project by Huang Ye and Liu Yuchen

is explicitly represented by a geometric diagram composed of closed polygons.

Each closed polygon represents the equilibrium of forces in a node of a structure. The closeness of the polygon shows that the force vectors are in equilibrium in a node, and the length of each edge of the polygon represents the magnitude of the force meeting at the same node in the physical structure. As a result, the number of polygons in the geometry of the force is equal to the number of nodes of the structural form that is in equilibrium. Therefore, in graphic statics, we have two geometric diagrams: one represents the geometry of the structure and is called the form diagram; and the other represents the geometry of the internal and external forces of the structure which is called the force diagram. These two diagrams are geometrically dependent: in a two-dimensional space, each edge of the form diagram is parallel (or perpendicular depending on the convention) to one and only one edge of the other diagram. Hence, the change in one diagram affects the geometry of the other, and a designer can explicitly control the magnitude of the forces in a structural system simply by modifying the geometry of the force diagram. That is the main reason that many eminent engineers constantly used graphic statics in the design of their masterpieces.

Designing the Geometry of Force
If a closed polygon in the force diagram represents a node in equilibrium in a physical world, then a designer can start by designing these force polygons and explore a variety of structural solutions in equilibrium through a series of explicit geometric drawings. This geometric representation of forces makes this method quite intuitive and powerful compared to any other structural form-finding technique. Moreover, the closeness of the polygons of the force diagram guarantees the existence of a structural form in equilibrium compared to other design techniques where the equilibrium of the system needs to be analyzed.

Design in the Dual Space
Note that in this design approach, in contrast to any other design method, a designer does not directly design the structural form; in fact, the designer creates the geometry of the force from which they subsequently extract the geometry of the structure by procedural/computational techniques. Therefore, the main

challenge is to understand the properties of the force polygons and realize how the manipulation or modifications of force can change the geometry of the structural form. Before expanding on this new design methodology, the topological relationship between these two diagrams should be explained. A fascinating example of topology is related to the "The Konigsberg bridge problem" proposed by Euler in 1736.[24]

The problem inquires as to whether it is possible to start from a location and pass only once over all the bridges of the city of Konigsberg and return to the starting point. The connectivity of multiple parts of the city to each other, using a graph regardless of the number of bridges. This graph represents the topological relationship between multiple parts of the city with no geometric information. The graph also divides the space into sub-spaces. The connectivity of these sub-spaces results in another graph, which is the topological dual of the first graph. Based on this duality, the number of edges of both graphs is equal; the number of sub-spaces in one graph corresponds to the number of nodes in the other graph and vice versa.

In the method of graphical statics, the form and force diagrams are the topological dual of each other (i.e., in a two-dimensional space, the number of polygons in the force diagram equals the number of nodes in the form diagram, and the number of edges of both diagrams is equal). The geometric dependencies of these two diagrams, together with their topological relations, results in reciprocal properties between the two that can be exploited in a new design methodology explained in this article.

Designing the Geometry of the Force

The force diagram of compression- or tension-only structural forms consists of closed, convex polygons. For a given set of applied loads and support locations, a designer can aggregate or subdivide the force polygons to construct a group of closed convex polygonal cells as a force diagram. Each force diagram can then represent a topologically different structural form for the same boundary conditions.[25 26] As a result, the designer has control over both the geometry of the structural form and the magnitude of internal and external loads, a property that none of the other form-finding techniques provide for the designers.

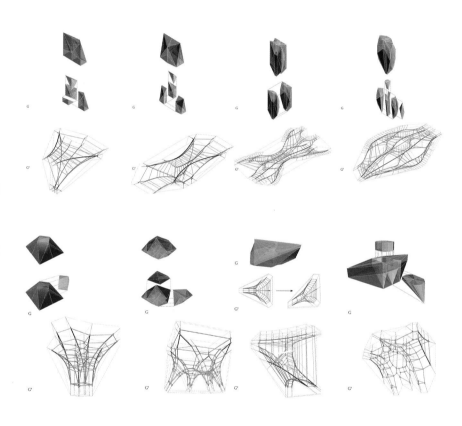

The process of designing the geometry of the force diagram (G) and multiple stages of exploration to control the geometry of the structure (G⁺) with specific curved boundaries and sectional varieties.
Project by Zehua Qi and Qi Liu

Various geometric studies to design single versus multi column, and opening versus funnel geometry that can be used for the design of two interweaving structural systems for the terminal project.
Project by Tian Ouyang and Jasmine Gao

Graphical methods beyond 2D Despite its evident strength and advantages, traditional graphical statics were based on 2D diagrams, and therefore, a designer could only design 2D abstraction of three-dimensional structures. Moreover, the lack of computational and representational tools in the 19th century limited the use and progress of graphical statics. It encouraged many researchers to shift to numerical methods at the end of the 19th century. Since the 19th century, several methods have been developed to extend graphical statics to three dimensions, including the cremona method based on reciprocal (non-planar) polygonal diagrams[27][28][29] and the works of Föppl based on projective geometry.[30] The advances of computational and representational tools gave a rebirth to a new extension of these methods in the field of architecture and structural design. Some recent developments include the Thrust Network Analysis for finding compression only funicular shells[31][32][33][34][35] and the methods based on Combinatorial Equilibrium Modeling.[36][37] These methods were not entirely successful in fully extending the methods to a variety of 3D problems.

3D GRAPHIC STATICS
USING RECIPROCAL POLYHEDRAL DIAGRAMS

In 2016, I was among the very first people who developed an extension of graphical statics in three dimensions based on a 150-year-old publication by Rankine[38] in Philosophical Magazine.[39][40][41][42] (Rankine's principle was limited to a short paragraph without any proof or illustration, and the highly ambiguous language of the proposition, together with technological limitations at that time, made it very-well hidden among other historic scientific publications.) In this method, which is called 3D Graphical Statics using Reciprocal Polyhedral Diagrams, the equilibrium of the forces in a single node is represented by a closed polyhedron or a polyhedral cell with planar faces. Each face of the force polyhedron is perpendicular to an edge in the form diagram. And, the magnitude of the force in the corresponding edge is equal to the area of the face in the force polyhedron.[43][44][45][46][47][48][49]

Topological Relationships

Similar to the 2D methods of graphical statics, in 3D, there are geometrical and topological relationships between the form and force diagram. Each closed cell in the force diagram represents the equilibrium of a single node in the form diagram. Hence, the number of cells in the force equals the number of vertices in the form. Moreover, each edge in the form is perpendicular to a face in the force diagram and vice versa. Therefore, the number of faces in the force diagram is equal to the number of edges in the structural form.[50] This topological information can be used in design; for instance, a designer can design an aggregation or subdivision of force cells and explore a variety of non-conventional spatial structural geometries. As a result, the method provides a new horizon in the design and construction of spatial architectural geometries that only their 2D examples were previously explored.

Computational Design Tool for Design
The process of design using force polyhedrons will not be very efficient without a computational tool. Therefore, at the Polyhedral Structures Laboratory (PSL), we have developed a software plugin called PolyFrame for this purpose.[51] The tool receives the geometry of the force diagram as a group of faces and finds all the convex cells and establishes the force diagram from which a designer can extract the geometry of the structural form and manipulate it further.

Stereotomy of the Force Diagram
Understanding the topological relations of the form and the force diagram is necessary to sculpt the structural form in three-dimensional space. In this regard, the conventional architectural geometries should be redefined according to their corresponding dual diagram. For instance, a spatial curve in the structural form is a result of an aggregation of polyhedral cells that converge to a point or line in 3D space. Using this method, a synclastic or an anticlastic surface in structural form can be designed by designing their dual diagrams, as shown in Fig.upper left. The intersection of these surfaces establishes a spatial volume for which all the conventional rules of stereotomy apply[52][53] (Fig.upper left). Indeed, this is a nonconventional design approach that requires creativity and artistic vision to design highly-articulated structural forms.

Definition of the Design Problem
The technological advances in the transportation industries such as drone taxis and Hyperloop will change our perception of commuting, transitional space, and the so-called terminals.

The terminals will be the interstitial spaces that occur at the intersection of multiple transportation modes. Therefore it is an interesting architectural question to be used for this exercise. Designing such architectural spaces requires utilizing specific structural language. The designs presented in the following examples are the results of a semester-long Design Research Studio in 2018 and 2019 at the Weitzman School of Design, University of Pennsylvania.

The studios concentrated on the development of non-conventional architectural structures that can respond to the needs of such spaces and programs more concise than the conventional solutions. The design exercise had two main objectives: (1) exploring formal structural typologies suitable for common airplanes as well as the future modes of transportation; and (2) studying the programmatic aspects of such architectural structures, including the spatial and sectional quality of spaces for architectural programs within the terminal.

In the images above, I present multiple exercises that utilize the use of this new design approach in developing non-conventional architectural structures for an airport terminal. The Terminal E of the Philadelphia International Airport was considered as a potential site for the project, and the students were asked to design for a new generation of terminals considering the new modes of transportation to and within the terminal to fulfill the mentioned objectives. Each project uses a particular design approach; aggregating/subdividing the force polyhedrons meticulously and deliberately in the dual space.

CONCLUSION

Unlike any other structural design technique, the performance of complex structural concepts can be described by geometric diagrams. Therefore, a designer has two design domains: the form domain which is the same as the common design domains and the force domain that always guarantees the equilibrium of the resulting form and many surprising structural forms can result from working in this domain. This property makes graphical statics a unique and intuitive approach for architects and designers. Since the magnitude of forces in 3D graphical statics (3DGS) are represented by the area of the polyhedral faces, the optimization

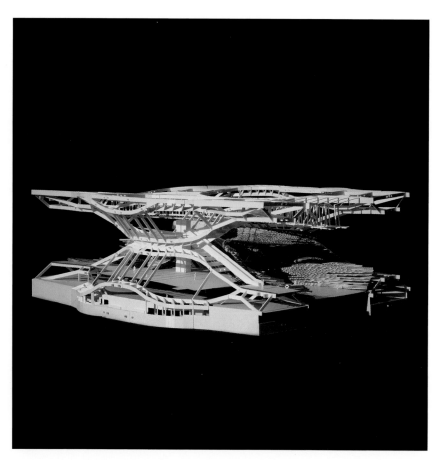

Physical scale model of the terminal structure. Project by June Zhu, Linnan Yu, and Yiwei Gao

criteria become entirely understandable and will open a new field of research in architecture, material science, structural engineering, and computer science.

Fabricating design concepts usually involves lots of post processing and construction rationalization. Using 3DGS in deriving structural geometry can significantly facilitate the fabrication process of the concepts; the inherent planarity constraints between the form and force diagrams dictates the resulting concepts to include planar facets which makes their construction much easier.

Therefore, this method can combine structural form-finding and fabrication logic in one design attempt. The reciprocal relationships between the form and force diagrams can be used in an interactive environment to help students understand structural concepts more intuitive than ever. Since the change in each diagram results in a change in the other; for instance, changing the magnitude of the applied forces will change the form and its internal forces. This property can teach students what parameters control their design and how they can deliberately modify those parameters to achieve certain design criteria. None of the existing structural design methods have the mentioned properties.

01   Poleni, G. Memorie Istoriche della gran cupola del tempio vaticano. No. 33. Padova: Nella Stamperia del Seminario, 1748.

02   Hooke, R. A description of helioscopes, and some other instruments. London: John Martyn, 1675.

03   Ibid.

04   Otto, F. and Rasch, B. Finding Form: Towards an Architecture of the Minimal. Edition Axel Menges, 1996.

05   Collins, G.R. "Antonio Gaudi: Structure and form," Perspecta 8: The Yale Architectural Journal, pp. 63–90, 1963.

06   Addis, B. "History of using models to inform the design and construction of structures," in Proceedings of IASS Symposium 2004, Shell and Spatial Structures: from Models to Realization, (Montpelier, France), 2004.

07   Piker, D. "Kangaroo physics," 2013.

08   Kilian A. and Ochsendorf, J. "Particle-spring systems for structural form finding," in Journal of the International Association for Shell and Spatial Structures, vol. 46, no. 2. pp. 77–85, 2005.

09   Kilian, A. "Cadenary tool v.1 [computer software]." http://www.designexplorer.net/projectpages/cadenary.html, 2004. (Accessed March 1, 2009.)

10   Linkwitz, K. and Schek, H.J. "Einige Bemerkung von vorsgepannten Seilnetzkonstruktionen," Ingenieur-Archiv, vol. 40, pp. 145–158, 1971.

11   Schek, H.J. "The force density method for form finding and computation of general networks," Computer Methods in Applied Mechanics and Engineering, vol. 3, no. 1, pp. 115–134, 1974.

12   Barnes, M.R. "Form finding and analysis of tension structures by dynamic relaxation," International Journal of Space Structures, vol. 14, no. 2, pp. 89–104, 1999.

13   Adriaenssens, S., Block, P., Veenendaal, D., and Williams, C. (eds.). Shell Structures for Architecture: Form finding and optimization. London: Taylor & Francis – Routledge, 2014.

14   Freeman M. and Ochsendorf J. Guastavino Vaulting: The Art of Structural Tile. Princeton Architectural Press, 2013.

15   Billington, D.P. The Art of Structural Design: A Swiss Legacy. New Haven, USA: Yale University Press, 2003.

16   Fivet, C., Ochsendorf, J., and Zastavni, D. "What maurice koechlin's scientific contribution tells about his life" (1859–1946). Proceedings of the 5th International Congress on Construction History, vol. 2, pp. 71–78, 2015.

17   Maxwell, J.C. "On reciprocal figures and diagrams of forces," Philosophical Magazine and Journal Series, vol. 4, no. 27, pp. 250–261, 1864.

18   Culmann, K. Die Graphische Statik. Zürich: Verlag Meyer & Zeller, 1864.

19   Cremona, L. Graphical Statics: Two Treatises on the Graphical Calculus and Reciprocal Figures in Graphical Statics. Oxford: Clarendon Press, 1890.

20   Wolfe, W.S. Graphical Analysis: A Text Book on Graphic Statics. McGraw-Hill Book Company, Inc., 1921.

21   Block, P. "Thrust Network Analysis: Exploring Three-dimensional Equilibrium." PhD thesis, MIT, Cambridge, MA, USA, 2009.

22   Fivet C. and Zastavni, D. "Constraint-based graphic statics: New paradigms of computer-aided structural equilibrium design," Journal of the International Association of Shell and Spatial Structures, vol. 54, no. 4, pp. 271–280, 2013.

23   Akbarzadeh, M., Block, P., and Van Mele, T. "Compression-only form finding through finite subdivision of the external force polygon," in Proceedings of the IASS-SLTE Symposium 2014 (O.J.B. and R. Tarczewski, eds.), (Brasilia, Brazil), 2014.

24   Euler, L. "Solutio problematis ad geometriam situs pertinentis," Comment. Acad. Sci. U. Petrop., vol. 8, pp. 128–40, 1736.

25   Akbarzadeh, M., Block, P., and Van Mele, T. "Compression-only form finding through finite subdivision of the external force polygon," in Proceedings of the IASS-SLTE Symposium 2014 (O.J.B. and R. Tarczewski, eds.), (Brasilia, Brazil), 2014.

26   Akbarzadeh, M. "3D-Graphic Statics Using Polyhedral Reciprocal Diagrams." PhD thesis, ETH Zürich, Zürich, Switzerland, 2016.

27   Maxwell, J.C. "On reciprocal figures and diagrams of forces," Philosophical Magazine and Journal Series, vol. 4, no. 27, pp. 250–261, 1864.

28   Maxwell, J.C. "On reciprocal figures, frames and diagrams of forces," in Transactions of the Royal Society of Edinburgh, vol. 26, no. 1, pp. 1–40, 1870.

29   Cremona, L. Graphical Statics: Two Treatises on the Graphical Calculus and Reciprocal Figures in Graphical Statics. Oxford: Clarendon Press, 1890.

30   Föppl, A. Das Fachwerk im Raume. Leipzig: Verlag von B.G. Teubner, 1892.

31   Block, P. "Thrust Network Analysis: Exploring Three-dimensional Equilibrium." PhD thesis, MIT, Cambridge, MA, USA, 2009.

32   Höbinger, M., Pottmann H., Vouga, E., and Wallner, J. "Design of self-supporting surfaces," ACM Trans. Graph., vol. 31, pp. 87:1–87:11, July 2012.

33   Guo, B., Liu, y., Pan, h., Snyder, J., and Wang, W. "Computing self-supporting surfaces by regular triangulation," ACM Trans. Graph., vol. 32, pp. 92:1–92:10, July 2013.

34   Alliez, P., Desbrun, M., De Goes, F., and Owhadi, H. "On the equilibrium of simplicial masonry structures," ACM Trans. Graph., vol. 32, pp. 93:1–93:10, July 2013.

35   Block, P., Panozzo, D., and Sorkine-Hornung, O. "Designing unreinforced masonry models," ACM Transactions on Graphics – SIGGRAPH 2013, vol. 32, pp. 91:1–91:12, July 2013.

36   D'Acunto, P., Fivet, C., Jasienski, J.P., and Ohlbrock, P.O. "Vector-Based 3D graphic statics (Part III): Designing with Combinatorial Equilibrium Modeling," in Proceedings of the IASS Annual Symposium 2016 on "Spatial Structures in the 21st Century" (Kawaguchi, K., Ohsaki, M., and Takeuchi, T., eds.), IASS, 2016.

37   Kotnik, T. and Schrems, M.J. "Statically motivated form-finding based on extended graphical statics (egs)," from Open Systems: Proceedings of the 18th International Conference on Computer-Aided Architectural Design Research in Asia (CAADRIA 2013) (Stous, R., Janssen, P., Roudavski, S., and Tuner, B. eds.), 2013.

38   Rankine, M. "Principle of the equilibrium of polyhedral frames," Philosophical Magazine, vol. 27, no. 180, p. 92, 1864.

39   Akbarzadeh, M., Block, P., and Van Mele, T. "Equilibrium of spatial networks using 3d reciprocal diagrams," in Proceedings of the International Association for Shell and Spatial Structures (IASS) Symposium 2013 (Obrebski, J. and Tarczewski, R. eds.), (Wroclaw, Poland), September 2013.

40   Akbarzadeh, M. "3D-Graphic Statics Using Polyhedral Reciprocal Diagrams." PhD thesis, ETH Zürich, Zürich, Switzerland, 2016.

41   Beghini, A., Beghini, L.L., Baker, W.F., Carrion, J., and Schultz, J.A. "Rankine's theorem for the design of cable structures," Structural and Multidisciplinary Optimization, 2013.

42   McRobie, A. "Maxwell and Rankine reciprocal diagrams via Minkowski sums for 2D and 3D trusses under load," International Journal of Space Structures, vol. 31, pp. 115–134, 2016.

43   Stokes, G.G. Mathematical and Physical Papers. Cambridge: Cambridge University Press, 1905.

44   Akbarzadeh, M., Block, P., and Van Mele, T. "On the equilibrium of funicular polyhedral frames and convex polyhedral force diagrams," Computer-Aided Design, vol. 63, pp. 118–128, 2015.

45   Akbarzadeh, M., Block, P., and Van Mele, T. "Spatial compression-only form finding through subdivision of external force polyhedron," in Proceedings of the International Association for Shell and Spatial Structures (IASS) Symposium, (Amsterdam), August 2015.

46   Akbarzadeh, M., Block, P., and Van Mele, T., "3D Graphic Statics: Geometric construction of global equilibrium," in Proceedings of the International Association for Shell and Spatial Structures (IASS) Symposium, (Amsterdam), August 2015.

47   Akbarzadeh, M. "3D-Graphic Statics Using Polyhedral Reciprocal Diagrams." PhD thesis, ETH Zürich, Zürich, Switzerland, 2016.

48   McRobie, A. "Maxwell and Rankine reciprocal diagrams via Minkowski sums for 2D and 3D trusses under load," International Journal of Space Structures, vol. 31, pp. 115–134, 2016.

49   Block, P., Lee, J., and Van Mele, T. "Form-finding explorations through geometric manipulations of force polyhedrons," in Proceedings of the International Association for Shell and Spatial Structures (IASS) Symposium 2016, (Tokyo, Japan), September 2016.

50   Akbarzadeh, M., Block, P., and Van Mele, T. "On the equilibrium of funicular polyhedral frames and convex polyhedral force diagrams," Computer-Aided Design, vol. 63, pp. 118–128, 2015.

51   Akbarzadeh M. and Nejur, A. "PolyFrame: Structural form finding tool using 3D graphic statics." https://www.food4rhino.com/app/polyframe, 2017–2019.

52   Warren, S. Stereotomy: Problems in Stone Cutting. In Four Classes. I. Plane-sided Structures. II. Structures Containing Developable Surfaces. III. Structures Containing Warped Surfaces. IV. Structures Containing Double-curved Surfaces. For Students in Engineering and Architecture. J. Wiley and sons, 1875.

53   Warren J. and Weimer, H. Subdivision Methods for Geometric Design: A Constructive Approach. Morgan Kaufmann, 2001.

PROJECT DESCRIPTIONS   ATMOSPHERE

Airports consist of habitual experiences that travelers are expected to negotiate as they travel. Check in, security, and immigration are routine if travelling abroad. The nature of these experiences is not differentiated through the architecture but is coded with systems such as the weighing scale or metal detectors that necessitate experiences. These projects question the norms of mundane experience through their design of the interior and exterior. Logistics are introduced as intensified experiences that are revealed at moments that punctuate and excite. The materiality of the airport is not related to the internal organization of the airport but strives to go beyond the machinic quality of airports to forge a fabrication logic within the assembly of building. The exteriors use refined material pieces that are accumulated and assembled to design the envelope. The buildings yield an atmosphere that contributes to the overall airport.

PROJECT 06   **ACCUMULATED SURFACE**
JFK Airport New Terminal Hub, Queens, New York
Xiaoqing Guo, Hanning Liu, Yingxin Zhang

ACCUMULATED SURFACE uses a series of folded and layered surfaces to produce a rippling aesthetic on the exterior of the building. From the section, however, it becomes clear that these folded surfaces are connected to clusters of shelving systems on the interior of the building. There interiors are also shaped by surfaces. Between these surfaces appear hints of the storage components of the logistics systems that punctuate passenger experience with atmospheric effects. The calibration of these atmospheres seeks to alter the experiential mundane that occurs within the typical airport.

Top Right: Ground Floor Plan

Bottom: Long Building Section

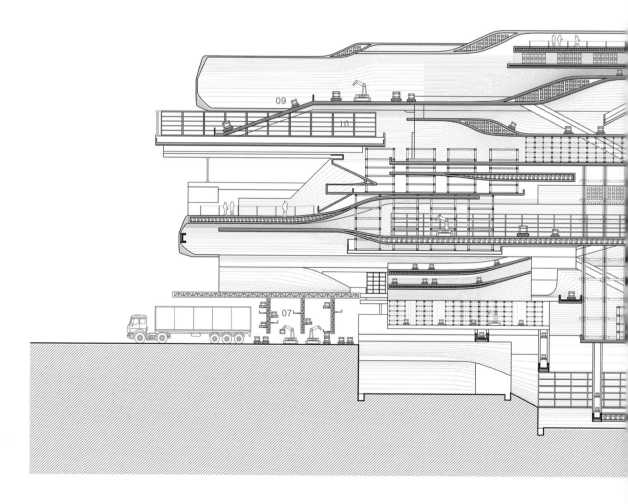

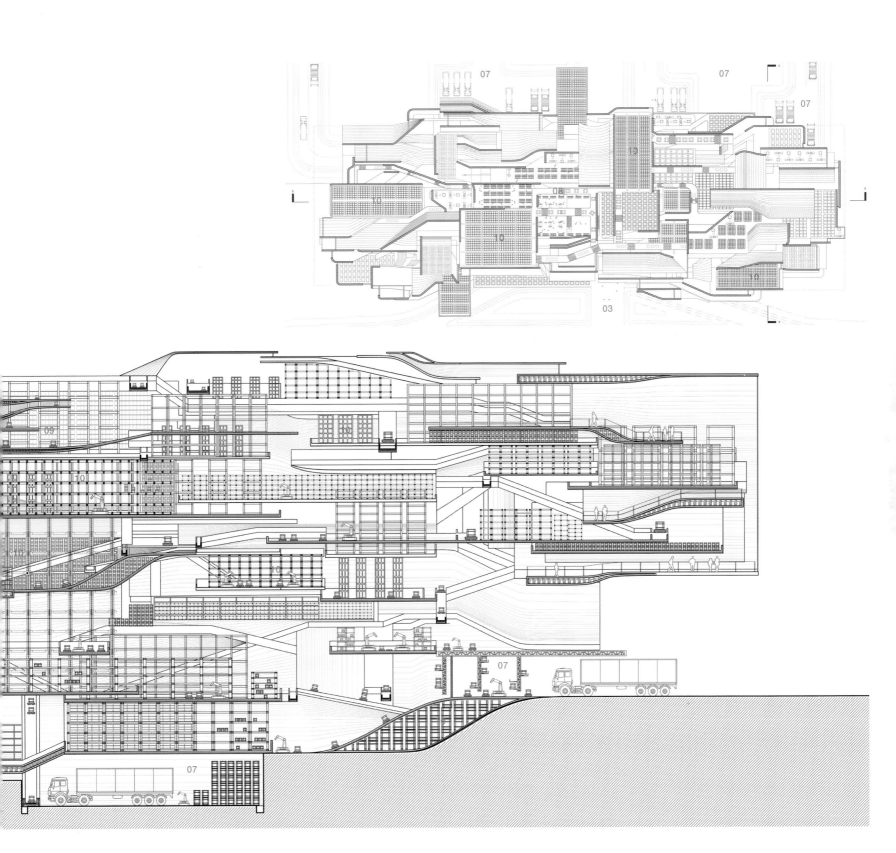

ACCUMULATED SURFACE, JFK AIRPORT NEW TERMINAL HUB, QUEENS, NEW YORK **PROJECT 06** ATMOSPHERE

Section Perspective Drawing

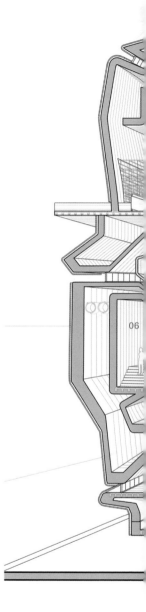

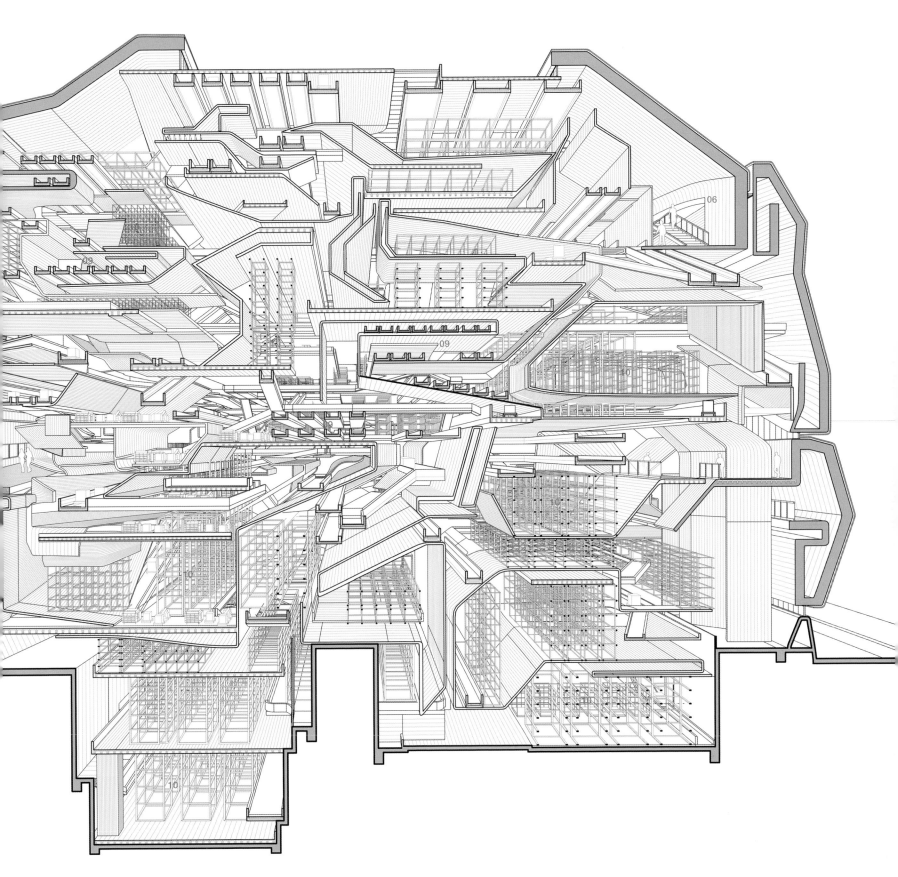

ACCUMULATED SURFACE, JFK AIRPORT NEW TERMINAL HUB, QUEENS, NEW YORK **PROJECT 06**   ATMOSPHERE

Physical Section Model, 2'x2'x2', 3D Printed PLA

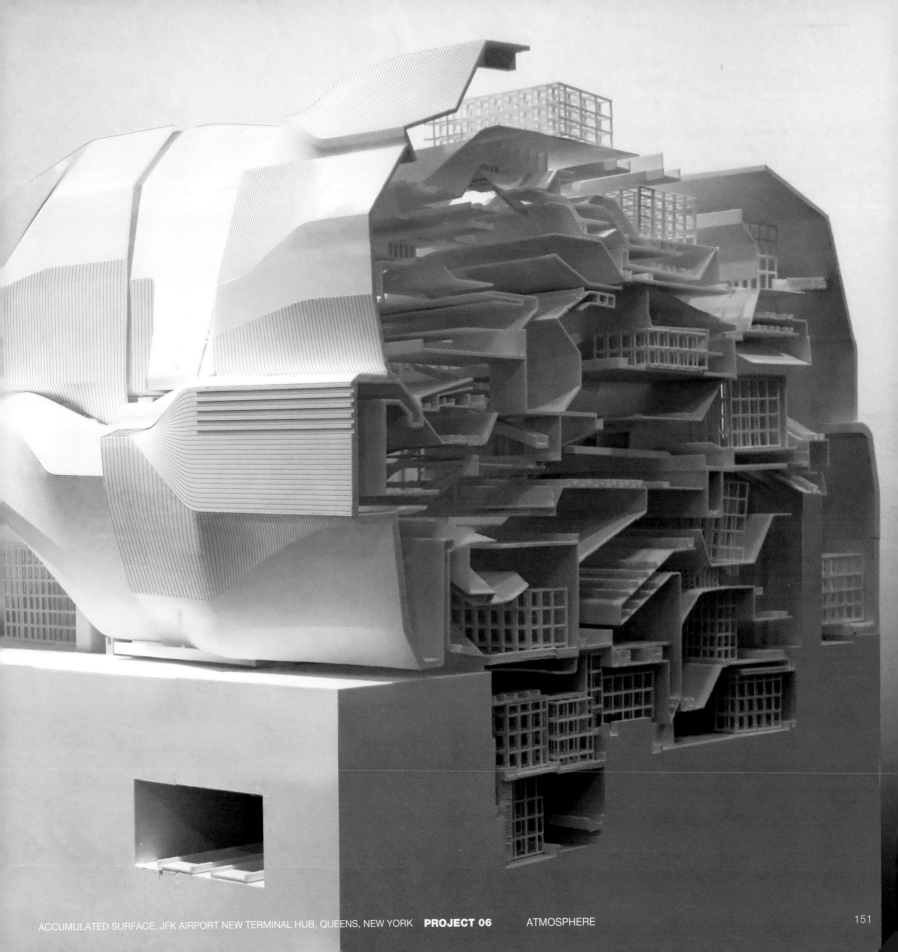

Physical Section Model, 2'x2'x2', 3D Printed PLA

PROJECT 07   **STRIATION**
JFK Airport New Terminal Hub, Queens, New York
Pu Pang, Hasan Uretmen, Qishi Zhang

STRIATION produces a flatness to an otherwise curved building. The material is inlaid further developing a smooth but materially differentiated envelope. This proposal allows the bends in the logistics systems to caress the experiences through the terminal while concealing the systems within the airport. The smoothness and curvature of the interior reinforces the desire to create flatness in the project. The smoothness of these surfaces is highlighted with light that is brought through the roof and façade. As the interior becomes the exterior it gains finer articulation developing an atmosphere that is separate from the rest of JFK.

Right: Ground Floor Plan

Bottom: Short Building Section

01 VIP Lobby
02 Waiting Area
03 VIP Lounge
04 Lobby
05 Luggage Transportation System
06 Offices
07 Cargo Sorting System
08 Luggage Check-in Area
09 Rest Area
10 Restrooms
11 Mechanical Room
12 Baggage Claim
13 Cargo Storage

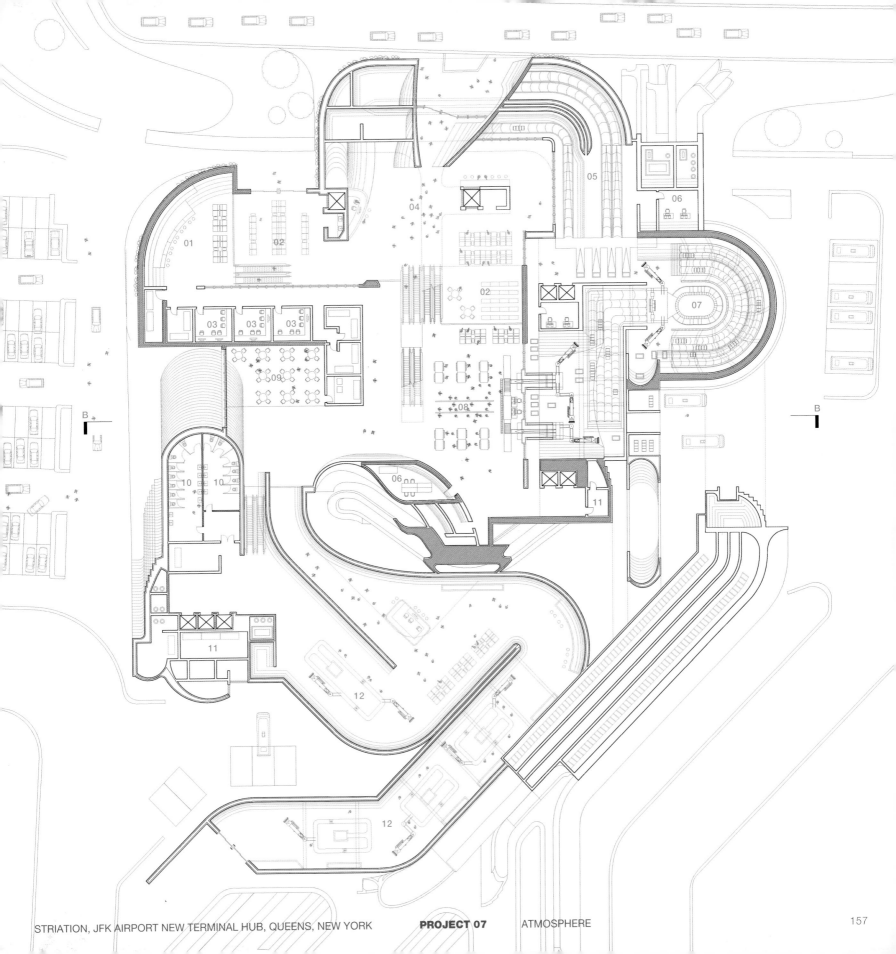

Long Building Section

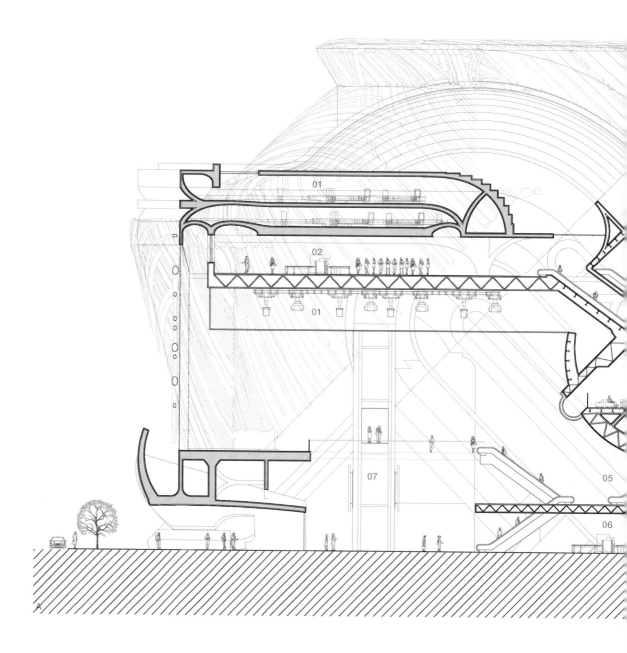

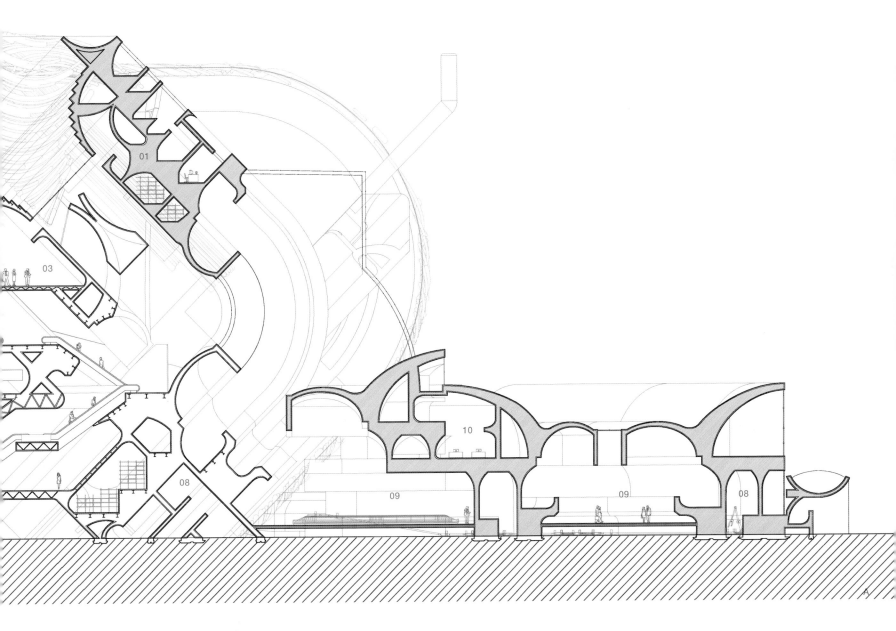

Right: Section Model Rendering

Bottom: Elevation Drawing

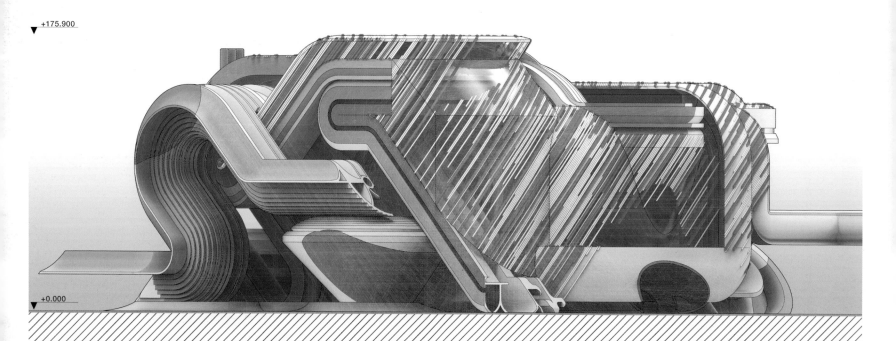

+175.900

+0.000

PROJECT 08

FROTH

JFK Airport New Terminal Hub, Queens, New York

Zihao Fang, Chaeyoung Kim, Ruochen Wang

FROTH uses new materials to create a lightness and depth on the façade of the building. The glass, reinforced-concrete panels accumulate to develop a watertight surface that is constructed in layers of smaller pieces producing a delicacy and fineness. The assembly of these parts contributes to the exuding of atmospheric effects that alter the way people perceive typical envelopes of building—particularly in airports. The interior in contrast is majestic and contains large surfaces that allows for circulation around the arrival hall that is the center of human experience. The logistics are carefully inserted as poche except for one instance where the majestic surfaces are penetrated revealing a moving walkway for boxes for all to see.

Ground Floor Plan

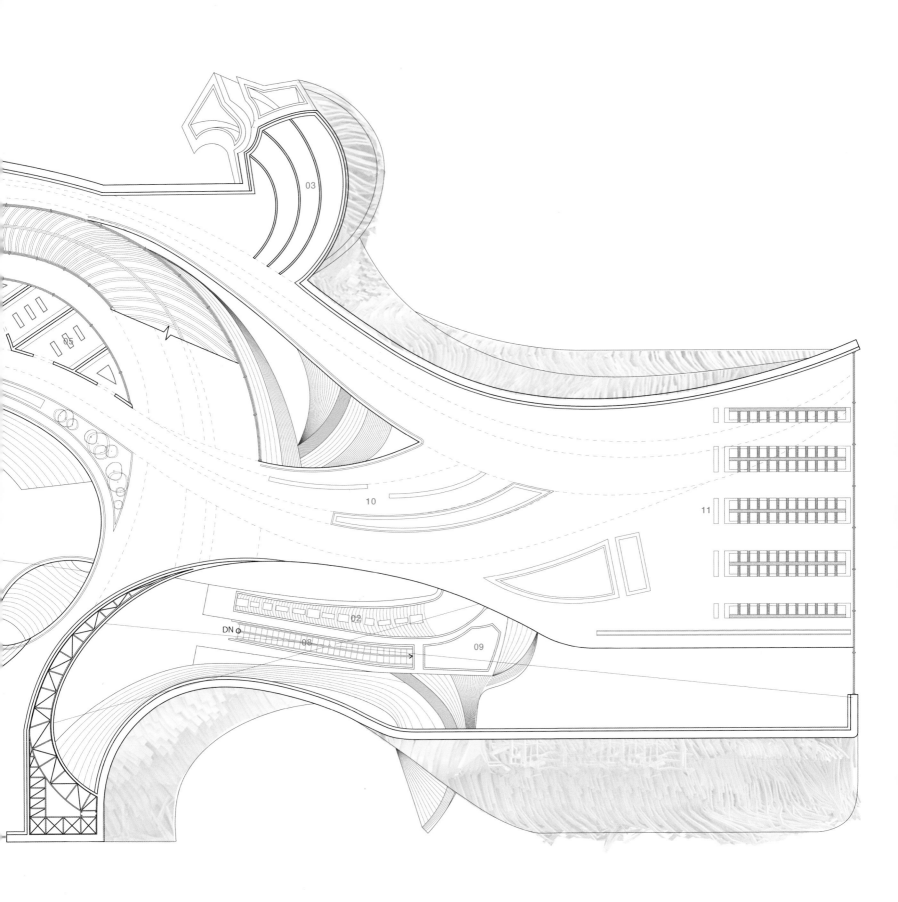

03

05

10

11

DN

02

08

09

Short Building Section

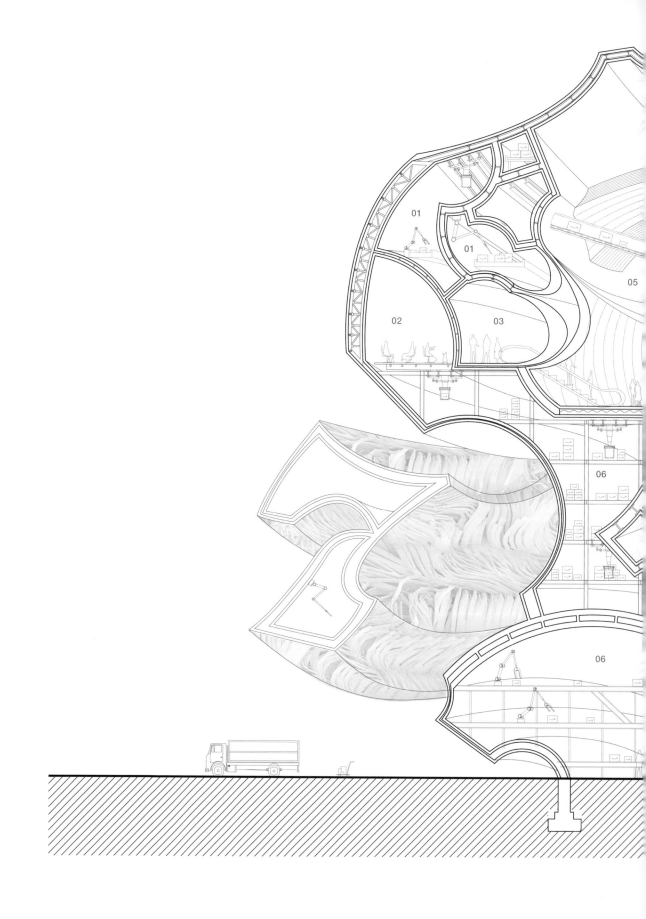

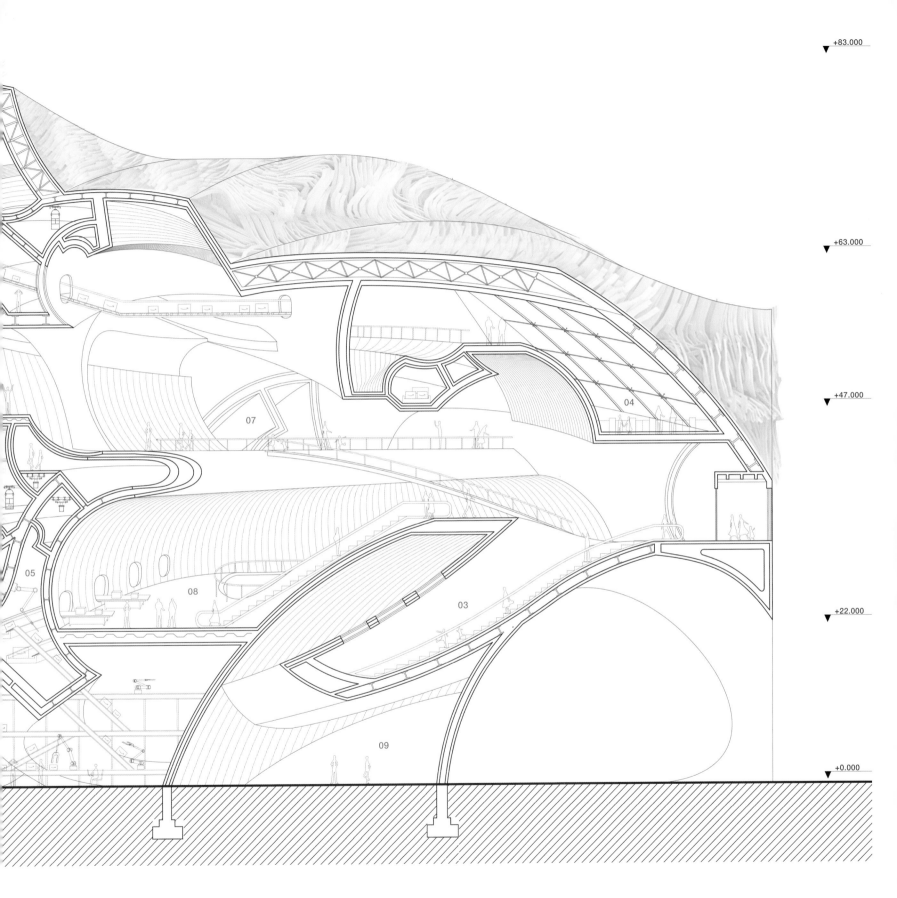

FROTH, JFK AIRPORT NEW TERMINAL HUB, QUEENS, NEW YORK   **PROJECT 08**   ATMOSPHERE

Right: Section Model Rendering

Left: Exploded Axonometric

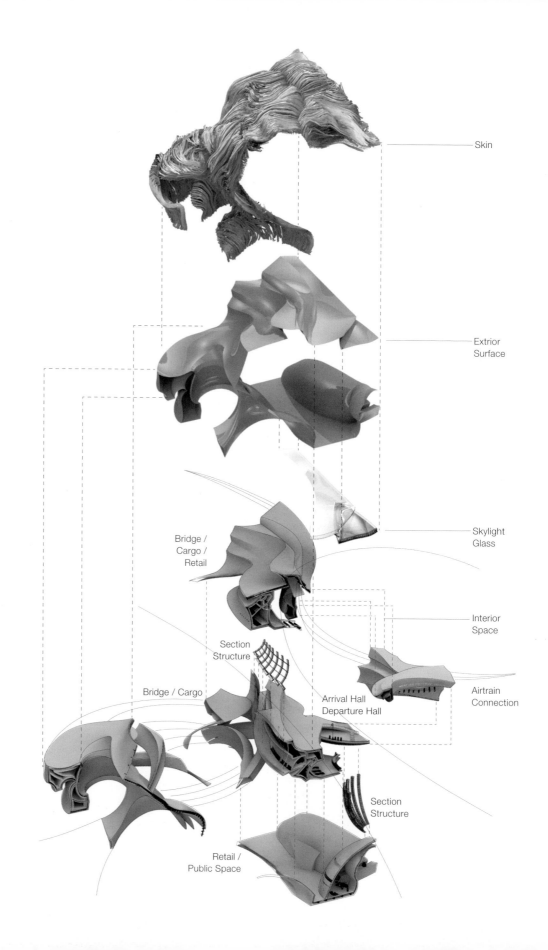

Skin

Extrior Surface

Skylight Glass

Bridge / Cargo / Retail

Interior Space

Section Structure

Arrival Hall Departure Hall

Airtrain Connection

Bridge / Cargo

Retail / Public Space

Section Structure

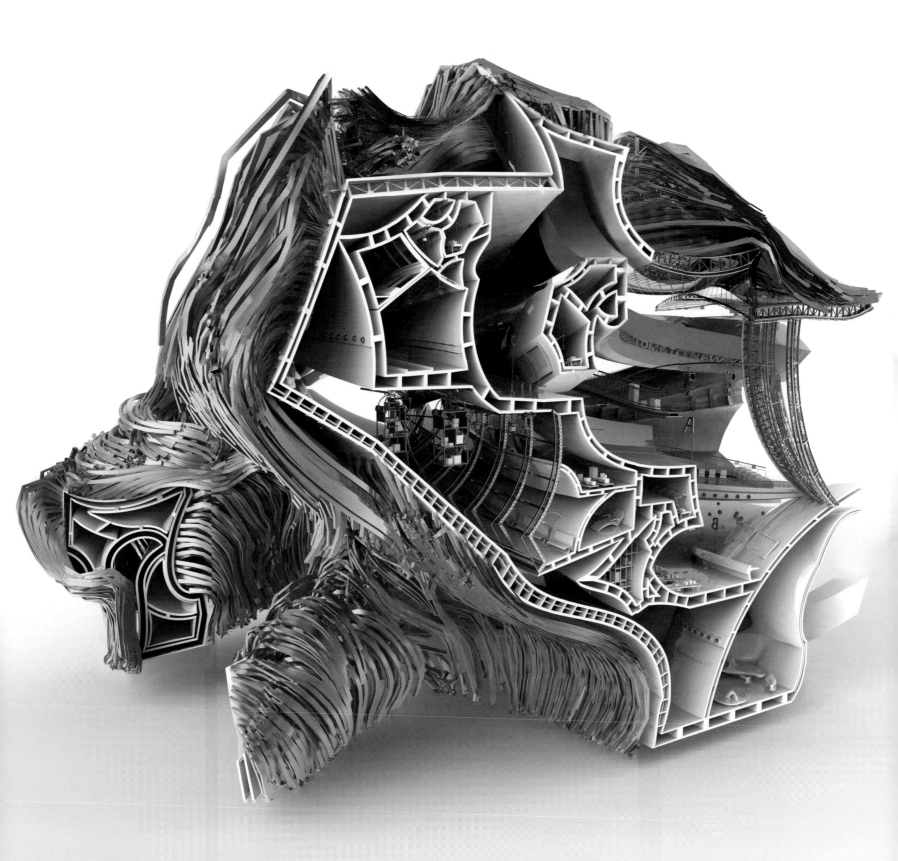

FROTH, JFK AIRPORT NEW TERMINAL HUB, QUEENS, NEW YORK   **PROJECT 08**   ATMOSPHERE

PROJECT 09   **QUILT**

JFK Airport New Terminal Hub, Queens, New York

Dongyun Kim, Qianni Shi, Zhaoyuan Gou

QUILT utilizes different methods of stacking and storing cargo to produce quilted patterns and textures as in nature. The aesthetic is sublime from the exterior. The quilted fields of logistics take on differing three-dimensional rotations that contribute to the variation and density of the storage containers. As one enters the building, which is a carved area through the entire building, the quality of space continually shifts due to the ephemeral quality of the environment acting on the envelope.

Section Perspective Drawing

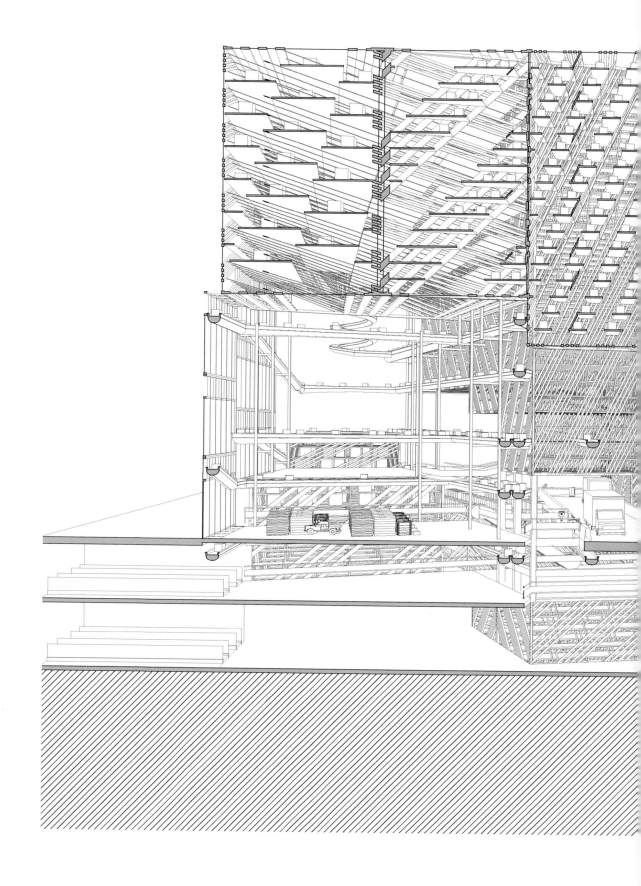

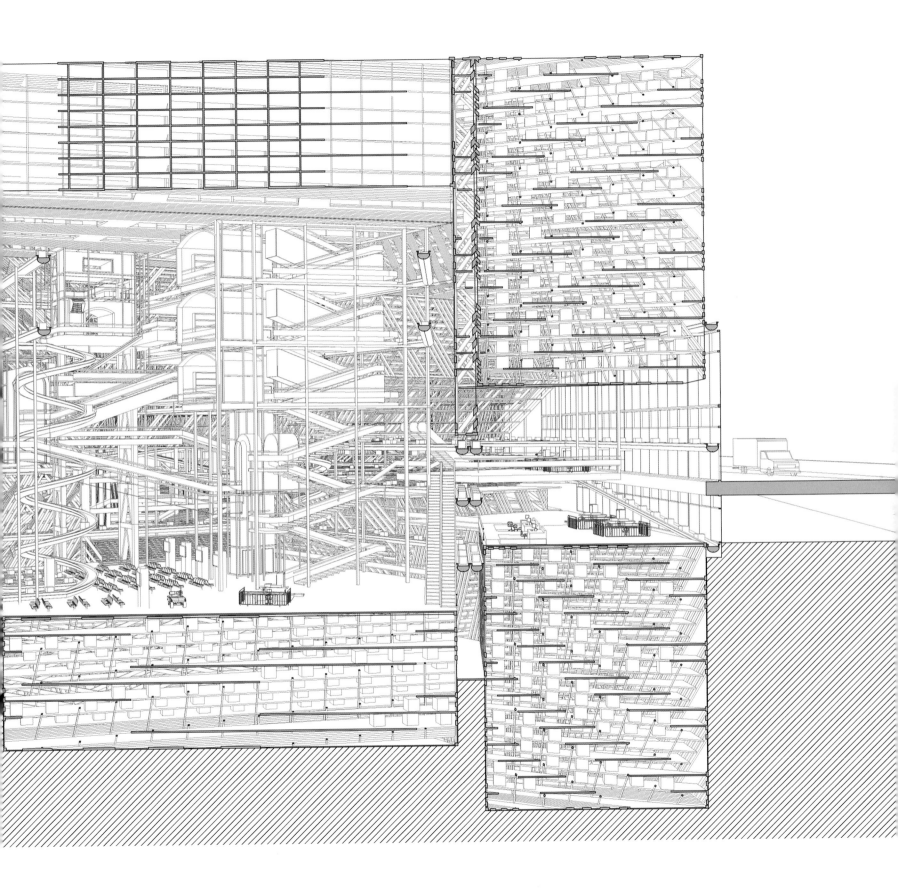

QUILT, JFK AIRPORT NEW TERMINAL HUB, QUEENS, NEW YORK   **PROJECT 09**   ATMOSPHERE

Top Right: Ground Floor Plan

Bottom: Section Perspective Drawing

01 Truck Path
02 Truck Dock
03 Cargo Control Room
04 Cargo Transportation System
05 Passenger Drop-off
06 Entrance
07 Departure Check-in
08 Passenger Waiting Area
09 Luggage Control Room
10 Cargo Storage

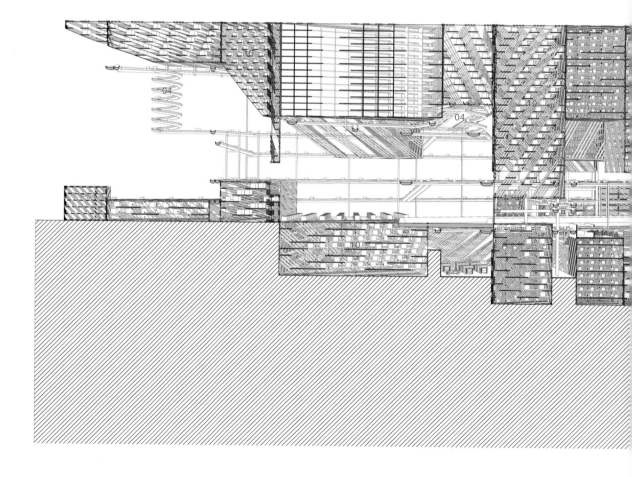

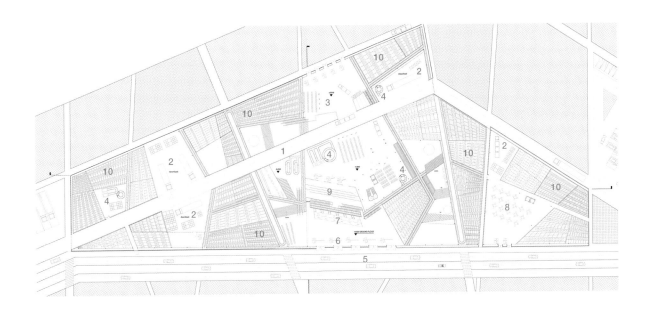

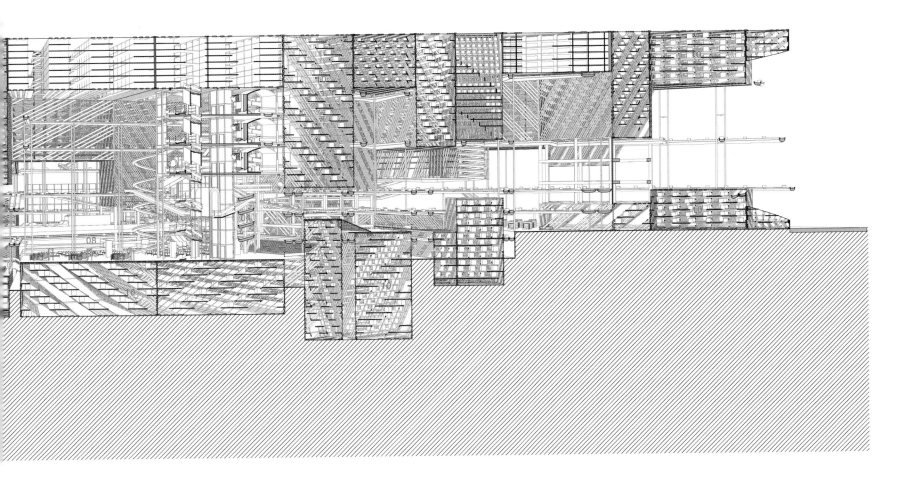

QUILT, JFK AIRPORT NEW TERMINAL HUB, QUEENS, NEW YORK **PROJECT 09** ATMOSPHERE

175

Right: Section Model Rendering

Left: Exploded Axonometric

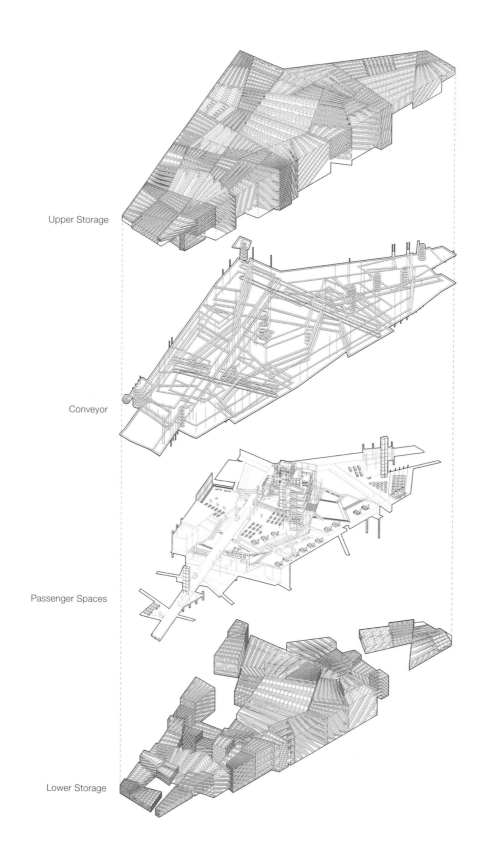

Upper Storage

Conveyor

Passenger Spaces

Lower Storage

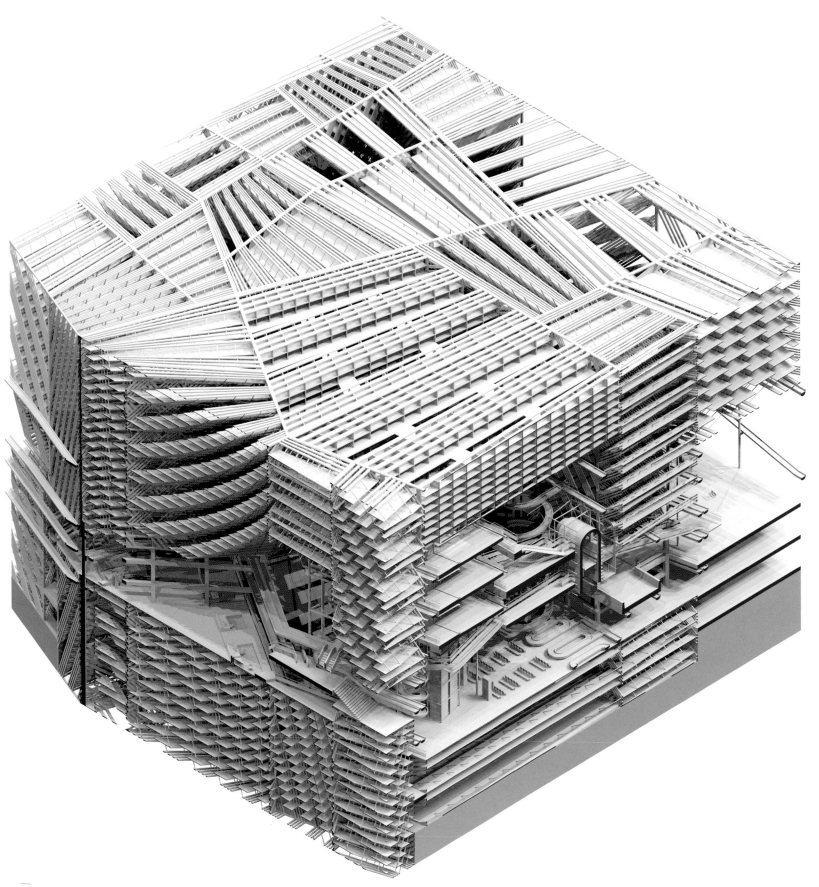

QUILT, JFK AIRPORT NEW TERMINAL HUB, QUEENS, NEW YORK   **PROJECT 09**   ATMOSPHERE   177

Right: Physical Section Model, 2'x2'x2', 3D Printed PLA

Bottom: Detail View of Physical Section Model

Physical Section Model, 2'x2'x2', 3D Printed PLA

QUILT, JFK AIRPORT NEW TERMINAL HUB, QUEENS, NEW YORK   **PROJECT 09**   ATMOSPHERE

07 BEIJING DAXING INTERNATIONAL AIRPORT:
A Planetary Building Block
Cristiano Ceccato

CREATING A META-ECUMENOPOLIS

In the first Star Wars saga prequel, The Phantom Menace, George Lucas introduced the core planet, Coruscant. Besides being the seat of all galactic power, this planet had the remarkable feature of being covered in one giant, planetary city. Star Wars lore has it that Coruscant's urbanization took a thousand centuries, so perhaps remains comfortably in the imagination of futurist filmmakers. Such a contiguous planetary urban condition does not yet exist on Earth and probably never will; but the notion of an "ecumenopolis," a contiguous urban region, was first considered by the Greek architect and city planner C.A. Doxiadis (1913–1975), denoting a continuous inter-city reticulum of construction that spans beyond the nexus of a single urban core.

An increasing number of such regional ecumenopoli have been emerging on Earth, and are continuing to expand in number, size, and population: The Pearl River Delta (PRD) is perhaps the prime example today; the clustering of Abu Dhabi, Dubai, and Sharjah in the United Arab Emirates; Tokyo-Yokohama; the Southern California clustering between Los Angeles and San Diego; the Ruhr region in Germany; and so on. These urban regions tend to be densely innervated through railway and automotive transport networks, and the promise of urban air mobility (local drone-based accessibility for people, such as Uber Elevate and similar services) will further intensify urban and regional connectivity.

Concurrently to the growth of larger urban agglomerations, the emergence of fast, safe, and relatively inexpensive global air travel through jet aviation over the past fifty years has fuelled a voracious demand for near-instant human communication which has been accelerated by, but not replaced with, the Internet. Advances in aircraft efficiency and safety, global air traffic control protocols and tracking technology, and the fundamental adherence to stringent international standards set by universal bodies such as ICAO and IATA, mean that aviation has become the world's primary mode of transportation, allowing anyone to reach the furthest corners of Earth within a day or little more.

It could be inferred, therefore, that the networking of mega-cities and regional urban agglomerations through aviation can be considered a global "Meta-Ecumenopolis": while not being the single contiguous urban space of Coruscant, the interconnectivity of the world's major urban areas has created cities which nowadays share a common set of business, cultural, and scientific offerings which allow them to be effective actors on a global urban stage, each with their own part to play.

THE RISE OF THE MEGA-TERMINAL

If the jet aircraft is the vehicle that has enabled such a global network, then the complementing infrastructure that has made this possible is, of course, the emergence of the International Airport, with its embedding into the railway (including high-speed inter-regional rail) and roadway fabric (and, in the case of facilities such as the Hong Kong, seaways and ferries). More specifically, we are speaking of passenger terminals, and in particular, the emergence of the mega-terminal as both a regional and national gateway.

Beijing Daxing International Airport, Zaha Hadid Architects, Beijing, 2019. Photo by Hufton+Crow

Before we can begin discussing and comparing terminals, it is important to understand how they are sized. Most typically, passenger terminal capacity is measured in (a) passengers throughput per hour, especially at peak hours, and (b) yearly capacity as "millions of passengers per annum," abbreviated as MPPA or MAP (millions of annual passengers). As a rule of thumb, roughly 10,000 square meters or 100,000 square feet of floor area are required per one MPPA capacity.

A second factor in an airport layout is the walking distance. The IATA ADRM (Airport Design Reference Manual, effectively the "Neufert of Airports") specifies walking distances between the perimeter of the terminal's central processing and retail areas to be typically within 550 meters; this can be tweaked through the use of devices such as travellators or an Automated People Mover (APM), though the latter are costly to install and maintain. All this needs to be reconciled with prescribed performance requirements such as Minimum Connections Times (MCTs) required by airlines that must be guaranteed by the airport operator in its design. There are further rules in sizing a terminal, such contact stand frontage (façade linear length for aircraft docking) and other factors but are not relevant to the subject of this article.

A further aspect of airport planning is terminal morphology, as a means of achieving the required performance criteria within boundaries of cost, geographic constraints, and geotechnical limitations; and a possible longer-term expansion plan requiring phased investment and flexibility. Some terminals have one or more piers branching out from the core processing area; others have remote satellites which are accessed by an APM; and so forth. The configuration options for a terminal are virtually unlimited which is what makes them such a fascinating typology in architecture today.

Determining the size and configuration that a passenger terminal should have is therefore not easy. In very general terms, a small passenger terminal will serve anywhere from 3-10 MPPA; a medium-sized passenger terminal will serve 15-20 MPPA, and a large one up to 30 MPPA maximum. Anything above that is to be considered a mega terminal and brings passenger facilities of this size into a class of their own.

London Heathrow is currently operating well over its planned design capacity of 69 MPPA, at almost 90 MPPA distributed across five terminals, with British Airways' Terminal 5 being the largest. It is one of six airports in the greater London region, providing a combined processing capacity of nearly 150 MPPA in an urban catchment area of fourteen million people. In the early 2010s, the then-Mayor of London, Boris Johnson, campaigned for a new London airport which would have a projected capacity of up to some 200 MPPA, centralizing passenger capacity into one single integrated facility.

The question, therefore, is how many such large hub airports are required to service a particular population; what local connectivity must they have in order to succeed, and what will be politically required to make such projects a reality —and by that we don't just mean the terminal itself, but the necessary land-based infrastructure that enables fast and easy access to the airport; without this, the airport will be starved of throughput and will ultimately fail (in broad terms, see Montreal Mirabel Airport).

MEGA-HUBS VS. THE PROMISE OF ULTRA-LONG HAUL

An additional factor within this discussion is the fact that airports today are not only serving so called O&T (Originating and Terminating) passengers who arrive or depart; but in some cases cater more to transfer passengers who use the airport as a hub-and-spoke connector between destinations which may not have a direct connection. Airlines capitalize on this significantly, building brand loyalty through status and perks.

Airline alliances such as Star Alliance or OneWorld, and code-sharing operations between airlines, often mean that the transfer traffic can be as large as, or as in the case of Dubai or Atlanta, larger than, the O&T traffic. Capturing this traffic has become the subject of ferocious competition, particularly in the Middle East, where Dubai, Abu Dhabi, Doha and the recently opened Istanbul Grand Airport all effectively compete for the same traffic—all with ever-larger, ever grander mega-terminal facilities. In fact, if the anticipated Dubai World Central (Al-Maktoum) airport is realized, it will have a staggering combined terminal boasting over 200 MPPA capacity.

The perceived risk, of course, lies in two factors: first, when is a terminal too large? When does the scale of a building not only dwarf the passenger but risk jeopardizing the all-vital connection capability? The second one is the rise of ultra-long haul flight operations. Nonstop flights such as Doha–Auckland, Singapore–New York or the recent London–Perth mean that distant points can be connected without the need for transfer. The latter example was long considered the holy grail, connecting Britain and Australia non-stop, now achieved with the Boeing 787-9 Dreamliner; the forthcoming 777X aircraft will have ultimate range to connect London and Sydney. While the challenges of hosting passengers on twenty-hour nonstop flights is for others to determine, a rebalancing between mega-hubs and direct routes is an inevitability.

BEIJING DAXING: A NEW GATEWAY TO CHINA

A recent example, which the subject of this article, is the new Beijing Daxing International Airport (BDIA; ICAO Code: ZBAD; IATA Code: PKX). This facility is a new greenfield airport located to the south of Beijing in the rural Daxing district, straddling the border with neighboring Hebei Province. Together with the Three Gorges Dam on the Yangtze River and the entire national Hight Speed Rail network (roughly 16,000 kilometers or 10,000 miles in length at the time of writing), the Beijing Daxing International Airport (BDIA) is one of three National Capital Projects in China today. Although other similarly large airports are concurrently being built or expanded in China (Shanghai Pudong; Guangzhou Baiyun; the new Chengdu Tianfu airport; and of course, the Hong Kong International Airport's own Third Runway Concourse expansion), it is Beijing's uniquely central position at the fulcrum of China's geopolitical system that has led to BDIA being classified as a National Capital Project and therefore fundamental in determining investment and decision-making at the highest national level of the Chinese Government itself.

Unlike Shanghai or the PRD's primarily industrial- and trade-driven growth, Beijing's expansion in domestic and international air travel has been equally mandated by its political and cultural pre-eminence. BDIA is therefore symbolically and politically, as well functionally, a new gateway to China: BDIA sits on the southern end of the ancient ceremonial entrance axis into Beijing. It is, quite literally, the first gateway into Beijing and thus into the very heart of China itself.

As an emblem of Chinese culture and technological progress, BDIA's new passenger terminal is highly functional and necessarily visually iconic, while achieving outstanding operational efficiency through several technical and functional innovations on par with the highest standards of contemporary international airport design. The terminal itself, as a civic project, is conceived as a new addition to China's long, and considered, tradition of public architecture—in particular, as one of the crowning national achievements of the Xi Jinping Administration, which has sought to develop a new generation of public buildings that combine the best international planning and design standards with distinctly "Chinese" design characteristics.

More than just an airport, BDIA is first and foremost a Multimodal Transfer Hub. This means that all forms of ground transportation are tightly interwoven with the airport functionality from the outset within a single, integrated structure, with the goal of bringing rail, metro, bus, car and taxi facilities as close as possible to the aircraft themselves. Whereas most airports have a separate, typically adjacent or off-site Ground Transportation Centre (GTC), which is often added to historical airport structures, BDIA integrates a large mainline rail and metro station right underneath the passenger terminal building itself. In fact, by combining direct access to the national high-speed rail network with regional rail, airport express and the Beijing metro, as well as coaching services and car access, BDIA can be considered agnostic of the preferred form of travel chosen: while most passengers will be transitioning to and from aircraft, a sizeable amount of regional commuters as well as airport employees will make use of the GTC as an interchange station in its own right.

Following an international design competition, BDIA's terminal was designed from 2014 onwards by the Joint Design Team (JDT) under the leadership of the Beijing New Airport Headquarters (BNAH), bringing together ADP Ingeniérie (ADPI) and Zaha Hadid Architects to collaborate on the optimized design, subsequently working with BIAD (Beijing Institute of Architecture and Design) and CACC (China Airport Construction Company) to deliver the project.

The selection of ADPI's competition entry as the winning scheme provided the JDT with a basic functional framework for the development of the final design project; ZHA's architectural scheme was applied as the basis for the creation of an architectural masterpiece that would redefine the aviation terminal typology and fulfil the Chinese Government's ambition for a new national gateway. Together, under the leadership of BNAH, the collaboration of ADPI and ZHA yielded a new functional layout that is harmoniously integrated with, and expressed by, a fluid and dynamic architectural language that provides BDIA with an unmistakable identity and spatial character.

Within the JDT, ZHA functioned as the Terminal Design Architect, providing a unified architectural language across the terminal, from the exterior form of the building to the seamless architecture of the interior, and the distributed pod planning arrangement for the retail design. ADPI acted as the terminal planning architect for the project, leading the development of the terminal's functional schema and technical specifications.

Following the completion of the JDT unified design scheme, the project was delivered by local design institutes BIAD and CACC, responsible for the detailed design and delivery of the terminal building's architecture; and the technical design and implementation of the terminal's aviation functionality as well as the apron, runways and air traffic systems. The close partnership between BIAD and ZHA, in particular on the interiors of the terminal, benefitted from ongoing collaboration between the two firms across multiple architectural projects across China, to ensure the delivery of the new terminal to exceptional standards.

ICONIC DESIGN AS A NATIONAL FORM OF EXPRESSION

Echoing principles within traditional Chinese architecture that organize interconnected spaces around a central courtyard, the terminal's design guides all passengers seamlessly through the relevant departure, arrival or transfer zones towards the grand courtyard at its center—a multi-layered meeting space at the very heart of the terminal which celebrates the excitement of air travel with a distinct language of form and space that give the building a unique identity.

Flowing forms within the terminal's vaulted roof reach to the ground to support the structure and bring natural light within, directing all passengers towards the core of the building. Natural daylight plays a central role in leading passengers from the center of the terminal down each pier, providing an intuitive form of wayfinding through the building.

The use of column-free long-span structures, with distances spanning as much as one hundred meters, gives the central terminal spaces a powerful sense of uncluttered grandeur, while providing a high level of flexibility for any future reconfiguration of the internal spaces. The compact radial form of the terminal allows

Beijing Daxing International Airport, Zaha Hadid Architects, Beijing, 2019.
Photo by Hufton+Crow

a maximum number of aircrafts to be parked directly at the terminal with minimum distances from the heart of the building itself, providing exceptional convenience for passengers and flexibility in operations. Every aircraft pier radiates directly from the terminal's main central court where all passenger services and amenities are located, enabling passengers to walk comparatively short distances without the need of an Automated People Mover (APM) within the main terminal. As a result, the terminal's compact design minimizes distances between check-in and gate, as well as connections between gates for transferring passengers.

INNOVATION THROUGH PEOPLE-CENTERED DESIGN

Innovation is achieved in many ways, not only in size and speed of execution, or through the universal deployment of security and processing technologies, but within the building's spatial arrangement itself. Specifically, the terminal's design directly responds to the evolving demographics of China and the emergence of a new entrepreneurial merchant class—tech-savvy, high-frequency, national commuters who will rapidly travel between Beijing and other Chinese cities on a regular basis.

Research has found that China now boasts the highest per-capita adoption of so-called smart phones; and that Chinese app platforms such as WeChat now manage nearly all aspects of everyday life—including financial transactions and banking. It is in considering this evolution of the Chinese traveller, as well as the manifest need to maintain maximum domestic passenger throughput in Beijing, that the BDIA passenger terminal has achieved true functional innovation.

Firstly, the BDIA terminal shrinks the building's footprint by vertically stacking international and domestic facilities in the core processing zone: for example, international and domestic reclaims are stacked on top of one another, not side by side. This configuration further shortens walking distances and accelerates passenger throughput. Secondly, it introduces the concept of an additional separate departure level for such high-frequency domestic travellers.

Basic conventions of airport design generally mandate two levels of processing which are generally well understood by the travelling public: a departures concourse on the upper level; and an arrivals concourse typically on the ground level. BDIA extends this paradigm by adding an intermediate third functional level which is positioned between the departures and arrivals level. This additional floor is a new dedicated self-processing level that enhances throughput for high-frequency domestic travellers. This fully automated floor hosts self-check-in, automated baggage drops with self-tagging systems, and facial-recognition security facilities for domestic passengers, all of which is distinct from the conventional full-service check-in on the traditional departure level above.

COMMERCIAL REVENUE AND THE PROBLEM OF TRANSIENCE

Designing airports—specifically, airport passenger terminals—presents a particular conundrum. As architects, we see buildings as permanent fixtures in the city, as destinations in themselves with a particular function or purpose. I go to the stadium to see sport; I go to the museum to look at art; I go to the library to borrow books. In an airport, you go there to pass through—to not actually dwell there at all. Yet the creation of an attractive shopping location—the terminal as a commercial revenue source—has become fundamental to the financial viability of the terminal and the overall success of the airport as a whole.

A passenger terminal today must typically generate as much as 50% of the airport's revenue—from retail, concessions, parking, advertising and other forms passenger-related commerce. Airport operators are recognizing that while travellers may want to shop for the odd convenience en-route, most travellers are enjoying the moment of discovery in a location that is all about the transience, the impermanence, the continuous movement. The terminal becomes a showcase on the world as much as it is on the specifics of its locale; it becomes a temporal window of desires that may otherwise be beyond reach—it becomes a global showcase, a window-shopping experience that stimulates brand awareness and loyalty, and the long-term value that this brings, beyond the immediate revenue of limited on-the-spur purchases.

In the case of the Beijing Daxing International Airport, the client team was aware of the lack of commercial performance achieved by its previous flagship terminal, the Terminal 3 at Beijing Capital Airport due to a combination of insufficient retail density, a lack of concession diversity and a deficient focus on traveller demographics. For BDIA, the conscious effort was made to compact the airside retails areas, while offering a more diverse range of concessionary options on the landside, which is generally directed as much at those collecting or dropping off passengers as it is to the travellers themselves.

In 2015 the ZHA team won a separate competition to plan retail strategy and design the commercial units for BDIA. This allowed the team to maintain a continuous design approach within the terminal, from the expanse of the roof envelope on down to the human scale of retail pods and shop frontages. More importantly, it provided the client with an optimized strategy for retail densification and diversification that was in tune with a carefully assessed travelling demographic: passengers today are much more savvy in terms of their shopping preferences and desire to explore, rather be spoon-fed, a range of commercial offerings. In the case of BDIA, this was captured by considering the retail pods as "pebbles in a Chinese stream," with the passengers flowing past them like water, in a landscape of densely packed volumes. This arrangement, backed by considerable research into the commercial shopping trends of the Chinese travelling public, create an effective commercial solution without the alienation of forced-fed shopping.

AN AIRPORT OF SUPERLATIVES

Beijing Daxing International Airport is a project of superlatives, whether in terms of time, scale, and collaboration effort; as well as the political will required to make it a reality. BDIA is being delivered in three phases: Phase 1—which commenced operations in late September 2019—provides the 700,000 m² Terminal 1 building and an 80,000 m² ground transportation center (GTC) as well as airport hotel, administration facilities and car parking for some 4000 vehicles, with four runways and an initial capacity of 45 MPPA. Phase 2 will expand terminal's capacity with a new satellite Concourse to 72 MPPA at 1,100,000 m² and five runways by 2025; Phase 3 will further grow to 1,500,000 m² with a new terminal in the south, seven runways and a currently planned capacity 100 MPPA by 2040.

From the time of selection of a combined design team of ZHA and ADPI in the summer of 2014, later joined by Chinese LDIs BIAD and CACC, total design time was less than three years. Using a 24-hour cycle collaboration between Europe and China, the integrated project team developed the new terminal design in record time, producing a fully coordinated set of digital documents containing all the information required to enable BIAD to execute the project.

BDIA Terminal 1's star-shaped layout is compact and efficient: the terminal has almost eighty contact stands in a single building, but its compact radial form keeps it a "walkable" terminal requiring no APM assistance beyond travellators to achieve required performance levels. Together with its ample sources of natural daylight, this terminal is highly sustainable as a low-energy building bathed in sunlight, achieving China's coveted three-Star environmental rating.

A HERCULEAN CONSTRUCTION EFFORT

The expanse of BDIA's passenger terminal is vast: within the central processing area, Heathrow's Terminal 5A could fit inside almost three times; the star-shaped layout of the piers measures over 1450 meters tip to tip, stretching from Green Park past Piccadilly Circus to Covent Garden in London. Its cumulative area of almost 800,000 m² is the size of over 110 football pitches and has a footprint that straddles an area the size of Mayfair in London. Together with its southern satellite concourse, BDIA Terminal 1 can process a total of 72 million passengers per year, which equates to more processing capacity within a single terminal building than the entire 69 million planned design capacity of all five Heathrow terminals combined.

Ground was broken on 26th December 2014, and construction was completed on the 30th of June 2019, exactly four years and six months later, with services commencing on the 26th of September. In this time, a herculean construction effort was undertaken with few parallels today. Within the central processing area alone, 10,000 piles were driven to support the main terminal and the underlying 14-track railway station. This required three million m³ of earthworks, and 600,000 m³ of concrete were poured, totaling over 1.6 million m³ for the entire terminal project including piers, all achieved by as many as 40,000 workers at peak of construction working 24 hours a day manning over 80 tower cranes.

Success on the execution of BDIA was achieved through four primary factors:
1. The first factor, already described above, was the political will in China to produce a piece of national infrastructure at previously unimaginable time and scale, only made possible through the combined efforts of the Central Government and its funding arm, the National Development and Reform Commission (NDRC); the Civil Aviation Administration of China (CAAC); the Beijing Airport Holdings (BAH); the airlines themselves; and finally the reliability of the Beijing New Airport Headquarters (BNAH) as the primary delivery partner orchestrating a project of this magnitude.

2. The second factor was the highly successful design collaboration between ZHA and ADPI, and the immediate camaraderie of shared design goals that established itself on the Joint Design Team under the leadership of BNAH. Without this understanding of shared common goals, it is unlikely that a unified design of the functional efficiency and aesthetic quality of the Beijing Daxing terminal would have been achieved. In fact, the collegial integration achieved across both teams was such that the boundaries of

ZHA's primary remit of architectural design and ADPI's focus on functional planning quickly blurred: the team effectively merged into one combined studio.

3. The third factor is the continued collaboration between ZHA and BIAD. Beijing Daxing is the fourth collaboration between the two firms, ranging from the Galaxy and Lize SOHO developments in Beijing to the Infinitus project in Guangdong Province. The maturity of this collaboration, and BIAD's experienced understanding of ZHA's architectural language and interior design materiality meant that the original design intent could be translated faithfully from an international best-practices airport design to a China-specific airport project without losing the spatial, material and geometrical qualities of the building as originally conceived.

4. The fourth factor was ZHA's intimate experience of the Chinese construction industry; an understanding of its maturity; and the evolving capability and quality of Mainland Chinese Contractors. Previous successful experiences with China State Construction and Beijing Urban Construction Group provided confidence that not only would a high-quality and faithful execution of the project be achievable, but that a shared understanding of the primary technological solutions for the project be understood—in particular, the long-span spaceframe roof system.

SPATIAL FLEXIBILITY THROUGH LONG-SPAN STRUCTURES

The space-frame structure of the long-span roof is fundamental to the project in two ways: first, it provides the open interiors spaces that harmoniously encapsulate the terminal's flowing design. The second, and perhaps more important reason is that the long-span system allowed for an essentially column-free roof support: A limited number of peripheral touch-down points and only six central main columns mean that all other internal elements of the project essentially become a collection of small buildings under one giant envelope. This is fundamental to the terminal's flexibility and therefore its long-term viability over the course of a 50- to 70-year lifespan; the interior elements can be modified, reconfigured, and relocated in response to changing passenger processes, retail trends and other unforeseeable changes over time, without fundamentally altering the building's character or basic design characteristics.

The actual roof shape was achieved through computationally-assisted structural form finding, resulting in a shell-action performance spanning up to 120 meters, enough to park two Airbus A380s neck-in-neck. It relied on significant research into the maturity of Chinese space-frame fabrication capabilities, developed on past projects such as Terminal 3 at Beijing Capital Airport. Without this understanding, such a design could not have been responsibly proposed to the client.

The space-frame span elements are constructed onsite by skilled steel workers using two primary elements: hollow steel spheres up to as much as one meter in diameter, and round hollow section steel tubes connecting them. Weld-points are surveyed from the 3D-model coordinates onto each sphere, these are then connected through arc-welding of the tubes, held in precise positions through a series of steel shunts that are also derived from model information.

The design and construction of this space frame system was conducted in record time: detailed design was completed in just three months, with fabrication taking only four months. For the central terminal area, 400 onsite welders and 2000 joiners assembled 60,000 individual elements into 77 preassembled units over 180,000 m² while still achieving 100% weld-testing.

Once assembled, the space frame spans are synchronously lifted by strand-jack systems atop the main fabricated steel mega-columns, immediately achieving shell-action performance across tripod load point configurations. Above the space-frame, the roof is primarily enclosed with a conventional build-up consisting of a secondary steel support, a lightweight perforated metal deck with insulation and covered with a flexible, variable-geometry aluminum standing-seam system. Decorative colored rain-screen panels are placed atop the envelope to achieve the continuous, flowing exterior form.

Building closure was completed in late December 2018, with internal fit-out completion on the 30th of June 2019. Following six months of concurrent ORAT (Operational Readiness And Transfer), Beijing Daxing International Airport was officially opened by President Xi Jinping on the 24th of September 2019, with service commencing the following day.

Beijing Daxing International Airport, Zaha Hadid Architects, Beijing, 2019. Photo by Hufton+Crow

EPILOGUE: CONSIDERING THE FUTURE OF AVIATION

Beijing Daxing International Airport is undoubtedly a milestone in aviation and aviation architecture. Its role as a new national gateway is enshrined by the Chinese Government's emphasis on the symbolism of the project as an icon of national achievement as much as its vital role in expanding the country's transport capacity. As a true multimodal transport hub, it will rapidly play a central role within the Chinese transport system, and as a new building block in the global network of Meta-Ecumenopoli it will become a recognized as a major node in international air connectivity.

After the opening of projects such as BDIA and Istanbul's new airport, what remains to be seen is the global balance that will emerge between global O&T travel, familiar hub-and-spoke operations and new, long-range, smaller-scale direct routes. Projects such as Dubai's Al-Maktoum are significantly delayed and in danger of outright cancellation. The premier vehicle for high-capacity hub operations, the Airbus A380, has been cancelled in favor of a growing offering of medium-sized, long- and ultra-long-range airliners such as the A350 or Boeing's Dreamliner and 777X. Whether the demise of the world's largest passenger aircraft will be reflected in the eclipsing of mega-terminal design in favor of smaller, more flexible structures remains to be seen. What is clear is that aviation, and aviation architecture, will remain one of the fastest evolving and dynamic fields of urban and infrastructural development for many years to come.

08 DISSIMULATION,
SUBLIMINATION, AND IMMERSION:
The Impossible Architectures
of the Logistics Revolution
Christopher Hight

As with the adage that no one wants to see how the sausage
is made, pleasures of consumption often require willful acts
of forgetting. That is, certain intensive material processes
of production, often messy, often offensive to aesthetic and
ethical sensibilities, are be sublimated in the final object for it to
induce the desired sensation for its subject. In this way, Marx's
description of capitalism as an effervescent process in which of "all
that is solid melts into the air" finds its apotheosis in the logistic
revolution. Beginning in the late-20th century the knowledges and
technologies of the logistics have catalyzed exponentially more
efficient but complicated economies of commodity production
and consumption. Packets of information and material move
faster and farther, seeking ever more connectivity and maximal
flow, with apparently increasing ease and immediacy. Of course,
this ambient metaphorical cloud of commodities is hosted by

structures of immense and innovative material production. Datacenters, multi-modal cargo terminals, containerized shipping yards, and product distribution hubs, are central to the culture of advanced capitalism and are among our largest, technically sophisticated and most expensive buildings of our age. Yet by the inherent logic of the economy they bear, their intensive material construction must be suppressed the appearance of inevitability, instantaneity and ineffability.

A useful analogy can be made to the transportation revolution of the 19th century and early-20th century (one in which the speed of movement first exceeded that of the horse or sail). Then as now, a paradigmatic transformation in speed and connectivity required vast physical infrastructures punctuated by new types of buildings. From Le Corbusier's adoption of the ocean liner and automobile to train terminals and market halls with vast iron and glass sheds, such conduits and terminals became beacons for early modern architecture. With Gustav Effile's Gallerie Des Machines and Paxton's Crystal Palace employs, such infrastructurally derived tectonic sheds were transposed as expressive and symbolic types, hosting massed urban crowds in the celebratory displays of cultural and technological achievement.

In contrast, today's logistical enclosures necessarily resist representation and have been seen as peripheral to the architectural discipline. To maintain the ideology of total flow and massive connectivity, these enormous structures need to be as invisible and as slight as possible. Unlike the vast volume of 19th-century industrial shed, the logistical shed is optimally packed almost solid, stuffed with canyons of shelves and servers, filled with pipes and ducts, chutes and ladders. Literally they are almost solid. This solidity cannot be expressed for monumentality for that would belie the premise of instantaneity and frictionless flow. Their envelopes contain immense interiors that increasingly are not designed for human occupation let alone perception. Instead robots and conveyer belts churn in an endless night. Constellations of blinking status indicators are occasionally punctuated by momentary flashes of illumination for fleeting human access or repair. Phenomenally, they are lacunas within the built environment, black holes around which global economies whirl, the poche of junk space.

Paris Charles de Gaulle Airport Terminal 1, Paul Andreu, Paris, 1974. Photo by Paul Maurer[1]

Nor can today's logistical sheds be decorated. Or rather, they render the strategy of the decorated shed as hyper-duck. They necessarily resist meaningful representation to the extent possible. They are often located in distant hinterlands not only for real-estate value and proximity to vital transportation, electrical and information infrastructures and water for cooling, but to reinforce the idea that anywhere can be everywhere and nowhere. The roof, typically by far the largest surface of the shed envelope, returns the satellites' gaze with a blank membrane, inverting the blacked-out text within an unclassified document, as white mark of redaction amid the dark green canopy or grey city scape. Ideally, they would appear on google maps as a smug or blur like top-secret military installations. Practically, they appear more like Area 51, the desert locale where the alien space craft and remains are kept, a mappable but infamously elusive site of rumor and conspiracy beyond reason. If proximity to more dense populations is logistically necessary, "nature" is often used as camouflage (landscape buffers, green roofs, forested screens) or contextual provides a curtain-wall cloak of invisibility within regional specificity.

If neither redaction nor camouflage are feasible for practical or marketing reasons, more sophisticated dissimulations may be required, and disciplinary talents of architectural subterfuge may become of service. One approach might be called the "screen saver" and can be extrapolated from Jeffery Kipnis's description of Herzog de Muron's work as supplanting decorative ornamentation with the "cunning of cosmetics." Perhaps Hezog & Demuron's Basel signal tower will become the Bramate tempietto of our age. Situated in the middle of the rail yards, twisting copper ribbons wrap around an existing prosaic-brick building filled with signaling equipment and offices. Kipnis notes that rather than ornament raw structure or form, their architecture is applied in the way cosmetics are upon skin, alternatively accentuating and applied as a surface upon a substrate rather than a structure, one which can slip in relation to the form within, one which is not concerned with the articulation of tectonic assemblage or formal plasticity so much but employs pigmentation and shadow to create effects that vary with the angle of light and mood. The copper ribbons shimmer in the sun, patina in the rain, and become semi-diaphanous at night, providing a shadowed outline of the body they enshroud. Toyo Ito's Tower of the Winds offers a different and older flavor. Ito shrouded a ventilation chimney required by subterranean infrastructure with a tube of perforated aluminum. Like the Basel signal tower's ribbons, this screen offered a relatively sedate appearance of shimmering opacity by day. A metal lattice between the concrete chimney and diaphanous aluminum contains a technologically precocious array of lights (as much a fixture for the lighting and wiring harness as traditional architectural structure). At night, the tower responds to contextual cues of noise and breeze through a panoply of various effects in which the diaphanous sheen of the aluminum shroud is rendered as variously translucent, transparent, reflective. In both examples, copper ribbons or perforated aluminum belie cues of scale and relative opacity during the day, creating an inscrutably mute object by day and an ineffable performance at night. Lighting and surface effects are the matter and means of architecture, not a supplement to it. Rather than signify as façades, such envelopes are like the invisibility armor worn by the "Predator" in the eponymous films, cloaking the body with an iridescent shimmer. They do not valorize the infrastructure they shroud with significance or give the function within symbolic form. The architecture does not seek to communicate so much as dazzle, confound and entrance, supplanting semiotics with effect.

A complementary approach lays in sublimation, for which SANAA's development of aspirational minimalism for cultural institutions served as a beta market test. Their architecture has key commonalities with Jonathon Ive's designs for Apple. Most importantly, they seek to intensify the desire of the object by removing indices of its assembly (both as a process of construction and as an assemblage of manifold heterogenous components). Curved glass that demands caress is held in with impossibly thin bezels (what used to be called roofs or mullions). As with Apple's "unibody construction" that not only carved out space for its electronic componentry out of solid billets of aluminum but is designed systematically promotes the appearance of the final product as itself solid, that case is the computer hardware, and almost as if it was found rather than made. In both, incredible feats of construction and complicated details are employed to minimize the appearance of seams, material disjunction or mechanical connection. The high-tech rococo of mechanical connection or the critical regional expression of tectonic specificity has been supplanted by an architecture that

Apple Park, Foster and Partners, Cupertino, 2018. Photo by Shinya Suzuki[2]

Grace Farms, SANAA, New Canaan, 2015. Photo by Leon Yi-Liang Ko tries to approach product design: snap friction fit, glued, and as seamless as possible. More recently things seem to have come full circle—literally—as architecture of logistical dissimulation emerges from its programmatic and typological wombs. Apple's new corporate headquarters building integrates all three of the above dissimilative techniques. Obscured from public/external by landscape buffers: check. Use of envelope to create cosmetic slippage and shimmering effects: check. Minimalist fetishization of tectonics to transform architecture into a product design for techno-erotic consumption: check. Perhaps it is entirely fitting the Jonathon Ive was portrayed as a co-equal author with Foster Associates in popular press coverage. The conventional concerns of the architectural discipline are subsumed much the way that Apples hardware engineering becomes enveloped by unibody aluminum and gorilla glass.

These are objects without interior or at least one which is blatantly inaccessible and inscrutable, non user-servable, non-upgradable, unalterable. Like the alien monolith of 2001: A Space Odyssey that inexplicably manifests itself and that exists beyond our grasp, contentless yet enthralling. That is to say, the object's material conditions of assemblage are sublimated in favor of fetishization, conflating, commodification, and objectification with objectivity and desire.

The projects presented in this publication point to another approach, one of immersion. Situating the projects at Kennedy Airport provides a pragmatic and disciplinary premise. Saarinen's JFK terminal is perhaps the most overtly symbolic architecture for a program often laden with such metaphors within the history of modernism. Its virtuosity and specificity also participated in its rapid obsolesce, and thus the antithesis of the shed is the dominate logistical type (it is perhaps not incidental that Saarinen's terminal at Dulles, which maintains the shed type, has been more resilient). Tafuri's critique of modernist urbanism as oxymoronically attempting to control the dynamics process capital into a static formal plan that would be obsolete the moment it was complete is relevant here.

A more important antecedent is Terminal One at Paris Charles De Gaulle, designed by Paul Andreu between 1966 and 1974. A multi-story torus with elevator tubes crisscrossing within its center

Washington Dulles International Airport, Eero Saarinen, Dulles, 1962. Photo by Balthazar Korab[3]

to make different connective flows, the terminal attempted to make the networks of movement into a monument. As an object, it is a pure diagram of logistical operations and the sorting of bodies and objects while incorporating all the transport infrastructures, from the approaching roads, spiral ramp and rooftop parking garages to satellite gates and airplanes, to a master plan based on its multiplication. The use of transparent elevator tubes connecting to the glazed envelope of the internal space contrasts to the heave, opaque, and mute exterior. Indeed, Terminal One transposes Foucault's understanding of the panoptic prison type into the airport logistical map. For Foucault, the panoption offered an example of how an architecture can also be "a figure of political technology." Terminal One involuted the panoptic diagram. Instead of a central tower from which authorities can observe prisoners in isolated cells arrayed along the interior perimeter, the travelers circulates around a transparent interior central void and are gazed upon from a continual perimeter that also contains various layers of control, immigration, security, customs, and so on. Rather than the pantopic diagram of disciplinary power, Terminal One can be understood as a diagram of what Deleuze called the Society of Control, which operates upon individual bodies in a diffused but omnipresent manner. Like Foucault's presentation of Panopticon, Terminal One offers not simply a symbolic form so much as an "infrastructure of subjectification" that refers both to a specific program and as a more generalizable diagram of the disciplinary system of power it distills.

The hybrid of cargo and passenger terminal requires one understand the architecture as an infrastructure of subjectification, one that tracks the development of biopower via transport logistics. Through this program and siting, therefore, the studio is positioned as an extension of longstanding and inherent disciplinary concerns. These programs are not, therefore, necessarily marginal to the discipline but integral to the construction of its discourses. Moreover, the architectural agenda rejects dissimulation or sublimation in favor of material maximalization. While the projects have remarkable differences in terms of specific formal approach, none operate according to an aesthetic of the seamless and smooth. Rather, there appears to be an ethical commitment to an accelerated-architectural agenda of material articulation and formal intricacy. The studio's decision to include human transport and program along with freight is important and offers a challenge from architecture to the logisticians for the premise of opening the interiors of the logistics envelope to "public" runs counter to its normal ideology. Interestingly, many of the projects employ the shelves that would hold commodities as a lattice like structure, and the storage space as a new sort of poche and thickening of space. On the exterior the projects do the opposite of hide; they intensely foreground themselves as objects but also as constructed propositions. The formal specificity always depends on its elaborate constructed condition. This is true in terms of the architecture represented but just as importantly in the nature of the representations of the architecture both in terms of the careful and innovated ways the drawings are constructed as anything but neutral presentations and in the commitment to large scale models. While many projects are relatively opaque to the interior, the envelopes are often convoluted, laminated, or partially diffused; geometries rarely terminate within a space so such to extend beyond as a vector, another space beyond. Often the spatial effect is to not pass an extensive threshold to the outside or inside so much as becoming enfolded. Interiority and exteriority is always relative to adjacent spaces and provisional; one is always both on the exterior of one space and in a deep interiority. This labyrinthine spatial enfolding has no center nor exit in a certain sense. While one is never outside the logistical systems of global capital, its spaces are not uniform or universal but variegated and contingent. Rather than the 19th-century agoraphobia, these architectures tend towards an almost haptic envelopment of its subjects. Rather than vast empty sheds with crowds, or even an inverted panopticon, these architectures encompass and immerse subjects within a manifold that has finite exterior size but which tends to almost infinite surface area within.

By extension, this raises the important and difficult question of the agency of design in regards to bio power and their figuration, between operation and representation.

01   Maurer, P., Photographer, 1974. Paris Charles de Gaulle Airport Terminal 1 [Photograph]. © ADP/Paul Andreu - Artists Rights Society (ARS), New York / ADAGP, Paris 2020.

02   Suzuki, S., Photographer, 2018. Apple Park [Photograph]. Retrieved from Flickr, https://www.flickr.com/photos/shinyasuzuki/39663468794/in/album-72157692905899024/. CC BY-ND 2.0 / Desaturated from original, https://creativecommons.org/licenses/by-nd/2.0/.

03   Korab, B., Photographer, between 1958 and 2000. Dulles International Airport, Chantilly, Virginia, 1958-63 (Expanded by Skidmore, Owings & Merrill, 1998-2000). Interior [Photograph]. Retrieved from the Library of Congress, https://www.loc.gov/item/2018673570/.

09 TERMINAL FULFILLMENT
Nate Hume

I don't know what the hell this 'logistics' is that Marshall is always talking about, but I want some of it."

– Admiral E. J. King

Over the past few decades, this sentiment has moved from the realm of military deployment to pervade countless fields as the relationship between the movement of people, goods, supplies, and information has accelerated. Automation, artificial intelligence, and computational organization have fueled this expansion in intensity and speed of exchange at every level from the organization of complex fleets of vehicles to the stocking of toothpaste on a grocery shelf or the use of conference room three at noon. Logistics no longer remains a concern of merely transporting things from origin to destination, but it is rather the domain of controlling and capitalizing on the entire web of interrelated variables including the steps before the origin point and the intersecting industries on the other end. Logistics has long ago spilled over from the sphere of the military and shipping industries to become a central component at driving the operations of rapidly growing companies such as WeWork, Amazon, Katera, and Starbucks. In most of these cases, logistics has been key for moving large amounts of goods and supplies in the quickest and most cost efficient means possible while also optimizing scheduling and space allocation for the physical offices, warehouses, and points of customer contact. One major pressure on architecture from these companies has been the drive to pack space more efficiently and eliminate any areas of unused real estate. WeWork for example has used their collected data on the office place to drop the square footage for each user by 80%.[1] To create the systems organizing and operating these spaces, new agents have populated these sits including sensors, robots, and logistics software for monitoring and managing the flows of activity.

For architecture, this offers a host of possibilities and challenges as spaces become densely packed and in many cases the space for human occupants becomes secondary as it is compressed by size constraints and the growing back-of-house spaces for machines. One global industry, which is being dramatically altered through logistics, is the airline industry, although the architecture of the terminal and handling facilities still perpetuate a century-old genre of space. New pressures on the location, organization, and allocation of space will force the terminals of the next decade to break with these ongoing tendencies. The terminals and their spatial experiences are ripe for a massive retooling which can capitalize on these technological developments rather than default to an ever more efficient shed producing one of the most generic spatial experiences offered by any building type. The terminal acts as a case study for two of the major spatial reconfigurations developed out of the rise of logistics as an organizing device.

Firstly, space will become much more densely packed in the pursuit of ever more efficiency, especially in urban areas with higher real-estate costs. This drive for density opposes the vast spaces of types such as the twentieth-century airport terminal with its vast expanses of horizontal space and soaring cavernous halls. The static endless spaces become packed and coiled to form dense layered and stacked spaces. The empty space flowing overhead is given over to the ever-expanding volume of cargo and the necessary robotics for its management. This inversion

One-point Perspective. Project by Adriana Davis, Yu Mao, and Wenhao Xu

is bringing about the second shift in the expansion of servant space, or poche, of unseen mechanical spaces to a volume competing with the human served space. The back of house takes over and essentially becomes the architecture. Human users in these offices, warehouses, and hubs share space equally with the nonhuman agents sorting and passing through. New spatial conditions arise as the hierarchy of users reverses and new relationships with technology in these spaces unfolds. The next generation terminals now opening already look to largely intertwine humans and robots. This shared space brings an awareness of the complex logistics wiring contemporary life and act as a physical manifestation of this interface producing entirely new spatial experiences.

Over the lifetime of the airport terminal as a building type, it has continually reorganized in reaction to monetizing a captive audience, increased security concerns, the continual race for new conveniences, and several overhauls in technology for sorting people, planes, and cargo. However, through all of these changes and insertions, the spaces and experiences of these buildings have changed rather insignificantly. They have expanded immensely in size, but in most cases, this has been done through redundancy as they still break down into a series of lofty vacuous entrance halls repeated and joined across the site. As the terminals expand they all generally share a similar spatial sequence of a series of endless corridors occupied by people shuffling to gates surrounded by small retail stores and often dismal food vendors. At times the shed roof becomes more ornate with shaped skylights or the structure of the long-span expressed as ornament, but fundamentally the spaces are generic and lack any surprise besides the weary travelers racing through these interminable tunnels. This continual stretching counters the need for the ever denser zones of space organized by contemporary logistics, especially as the division of space shifts to accommodate a rising volume of real estate given over to processing space for cargo handling.

Almost all airlines earn a significant percentage of their profit through non-passenger cargo as most commercial passenger planes have given over a sizable portion of their hold to capitalize on the booming business of shipping goods. The International Air Transport Association reported that in 2018 the goods carried by

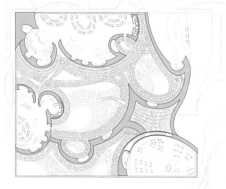

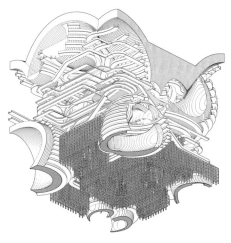

Ground Floor Plan.

Second Floor Plan.

Choisey Axonometric. Project by Yihao Zhang, Heyan Xu, and Jingwei Sun

commercial airlines would exceed $6.2 trillion representing more than 34% of global trade by value.[2] Examples cited include auto parts, pharmaceuticals, livestock, flowers, mail, and food. The margins for air cargo versus passengers implies the proportions may shift in coming decades to people hitching a ride on cargo planes rather than the other way around.

A large, lofty shed filled with goods being processed for shipping defines one of the largest growing building types across the United States—the fulfillment center. Instead of empty interior spaces filled with humans skirting through, these are densely packed structures with conveyor belts, hoppers, sorters, kivas, and picking towers for dealing with the rapid movement of an endlessly diverse array of goods. These spaces are rich with a dynamism that far outstrips the airport. Here the machine and cargo rule the space with humans beings embedded at key moments for monitoring or interacting with the process. The terminal stands to learn quite a bit from the contemporary fulfillment center. Already, logistic techniques and software are being adopted from these centers for other businesses including the airline industry which has adapted them to influence flight scheduling and gate sorting. Besides the efficiency of moving people and their cargo from city to city, the airport could benefit from the spatial richness of these lively machinic spaces. The rich variation of moving things quickly through complex arrays of conveyor belts points to a new spatial landscape for the airport.

The ancient people movers and golf carts of the 1970s laid out in endless corridors would be supplanted by new technologies for quickly connecting people to their destinations. The movements of the fulfillment center are ones of diagonals, arcs, vertical stacks, and hanging which move the terminal from horizontal arrangements to ones that stack, crossover, and intricately weave. As cargo overtakes human passengers, processing space will envelop more real estate and perhaps control the focus of the airport. Instead of cargo disappearing into the enlarged mouse-hole in the wall it will fill the once airy halls. The back-of-house becomes the airport with the passenger now embedded throughout its new Piranesian spaces formed from the interweaving movements of people and cargo. The incessant corridors now coiled and bundled to create animated vistas and oblique views cutting across eliminating the static hall.

Besides the incorporation of logistics systems to organize scheduling, the airport has brought in many other technologies and strategies such as fulfillment centers including diverters, sorters, pick-and-put to light systems, and automated storage and retrieval systems to update their traditional system of carousels. To manage these machines, a new level of robotics and automation have begun to enter terminals around the world. Tokyo Airport deploys friendly-looking robots to help with airport security, transportation, logistics, and translations. Like the Kiva robots of Amazon, these robots roam the airport with their jobs and no human controller. They manage the flow of people as well as act as the airlines main point of contact with the passengers during their time in the terminal. These robots largely frame the experience of the passenger as they move through the space which is now equally shared between cargo, humans, robotics, and sorting equipment.

The spatial impact of this is a shift from a clear front of house experience and initial check in at a barrier manned by human attendants to an expedited path customized by these robots to move the customer through the space. This allows real-time adjustments to be made to where passengers are not only boarding planes but guided to wait, shop, and eat. It also reduces some of the barriers or redundant features of airport space such as the relentless check in counters. These automated services also reduce the time necessary to move from entering the airport to boarding the plane by eliminating paper documents and less efficient line- and human-attendant services. Like a fulfillment center where goods can enter any dock and be stored at random in any picking tower because of the ability for the Kiva system to track, locate, and move, this allows for a more fragmented and continually reshaping space. If fixed counters and gate desks are removed this allows for expanded spatial flexibility throughout the daily cycle of the airport. The space opened up through these shifts does not need to remain as open dead zones but can contract or more likely be given over to the space of cargo and shipping, handling and processing. The back-of-house becomes equal and more than likely quite a bit thicker than the needed space for passengers producing new spatial configurations and shifting empty long-span space to active zones inhabited by nonhuman agents.

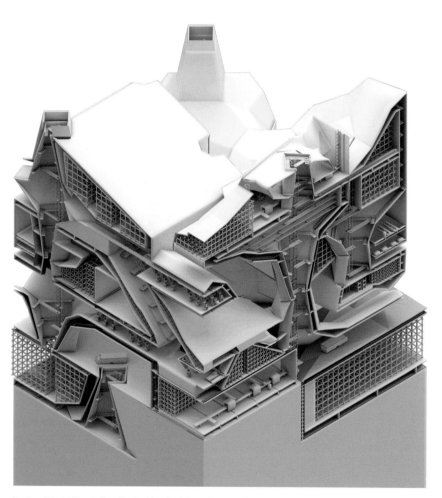

Section Model Rendering. Project by Jiaqi Suo, Sanxing Zhao, and Lizao Chen

Airports are not only moving closer to the organization of a fulfillment center, but in many cases they are sharing land and physically merging together to reduce transport times and capitalize on the growing E-commerce industry. Early fulfillment centers reused inexpensive, remote warehouses close to major highways while the more recent centers are being constructed in proximity to airports and urban centers. The first generation centers were massive sheds sometimes over one million square feet in size. The newer ones are reduced in size in order to get closer to customers and faster modes of shipping. Rather than fewer remote oversize hubs, these new smaller centers form a massive and diffused system near urban centers. Amazon has several airport projects in the works in Washington and Kentucky with many more urban airports currently courting distribution centers from a number of large companies. The potential economic impact of these centers provides huge incentive to the cities as well as an economic prop to the airports to diversify beyond human passengers as their only source of income. The airport and global movement of consumer goods have become entwined and this will continue as parcel shipping has been rising 28% a year.[3]

Similar to the fulfillment centers shift from lonely structure to dispersed-urban network, the airport of future decades may radically alter its locations and footprint. Some projections see VTOL (Vertical Take Off and Landing), which the FAA has begun officially testing in 2016, as being one major component of that change. These planes are capable of leaving from more congested areas and eliminate the need for extended runways. This would allow for a more distributed network of points of shipping and passenger hubs bringing air travel closer to its largest base in growing urban centers. Amazon has begun building smaller picking centers in cities which allow for same day delivery and limit shelf time by using quick delivery through couriers, local carriers, and even drones. The airport likewise may be less of a place to be stuck for hours than an experience which begins from home and is coordinated through logistics networks to bring you and your cargo rapidly and seamlessly to your final destination. Real time traffic updates will maintain a smooth overall flow by not only updating the gate time but also the time needed to leave home and negotiate traffic at any given moment. These will no longer be unknown variables, especially delays and cancellations only alerted after arriving at the terminal. The logistics used by the cargo industry to handle up-to-date tracking, traffic, and weather information to coordinate the shipping of 74 billion packages annually serves as a template.[4]

The airport will become less of a timeless, placeless zone of uncertainty and more of an efficient hub and experience it's always promised. With that the spatial experience would change from one of expansive spaces for waiting to one of optimized sorting and processing with key moments for reprise, leisure, or retail. Use of mobile technology and automation can free the terminal from set parameters of space boundaries, allowing space to be reconfigured at different times of the day or year based on the needs of the airlines rather than fixed assignments. The airport complex will become fragmented into separate vertical terminals dispersed throughout the city opening up new possibilities for configuration, experience, and real-estate arrangements. The immense static spaces of the first two generations of terminal design will be replaced by dense machines offering dynamic architectural experiences building from the sophistication of logistics moving billions of people and parcels through the air annually. These shifts will offer new potentials for the role and use of poche and circulation with all aspects of the building being inhabited in new nontraditional ways and by a myriad of user types many of which are non-human.

01   "Why WeWork Thinks its Worth $20 Billion" by Jessi Hempel in Wired. September 6, 2018.

02   IATA Annual Report 2018.

03   Pitney Bowles Parcel Shipping Index August 2018.

04   Ibid.

10 DEEP AESTHETICS:
A Cultural Design Process
Ali Rahim

Beyond the austerities of technique, aesthetics entails refinement, precision, and opulence. Aesthetics mediates and enables complexity. Rigorous technique is required to mold precise surfaces that incorporate the distinct formal features required by architecture. Technique also enables these features to be assembled in meticulous ways, yet the results are potentially chaotic. Negotiating and restraining the turbidity of complex architectural compositions is an operation that requires an aesthetic sensibility that can only emerge from the act of designing a project. Aesthetics probes desire and unleashes visual intelligence pertinent to design at all scales. Architectural compositions require an aesthetic approach as rigorous and sophisticated as the current techniques used to generate form, an approach that will elevate architectural discourse. The design works presented in this book raise aesthetic issues by displaying a simultaneous maturation of technique and material practice. Beyond refined technical mastery, these projects move towards an integration of aesthetic desire. Moreover, they demonstrate that the seemingly disjunctive multiple necessities, functions, and extents of the future airport can be resolved with compelling results through an aesthetic approach—that aesthetics can be a powerful generative design tool as much as (and more than) it is an end result.

FROM DIGITAL TECHNIQUE TO AESTHETICS

The development of new techniques is essential for innovation in design. However, technical mastery, whether in design, building construction, or both, does not necessarily yield great architecture. Cultural and technological innovations are continually establishing new circumstances and platforms from which to initiate design. Design research embraces an iterative process of conceiving and making simultaneously, where technology can play both pragmatic and generative roles. Design research practices use design knowledge grounded in making to guide technological and cultural innovations and stay ahead of new developments. Reinvention can transpire through existing techniques, such as artificial intelligence and open-source software programs that are mined or retooled for their potential. Plug-ins and custom programming can change the capacity of existing software to develop new techniques for architectural design and manufacturing. Such techniques will continue to be developed and alter the way architectural practices operate in the near and long term. They form a basis from which design research influences the form, space, and material conditions of architecture.

Design research practices can develop new techniques by investigating technologies emerging on the horizon of other fields. Technologies with the most potential contain feedback, are inter-relational, and destabilize their current contexts. Techniques borrowed from other spheres can assist architectural practices in becoming more synthetic—seamlessly integrating the design, testing, and manufacturing of material formations. For example, in the automobile industry, virtual crash testing (VCT) directly engages the material condition of the chassis of the automobile by calculating forces in a collision while predicting the deformation of the vehicle. The material impact is visualized in real time. VCT allows for technique to aid in the production of form in a way that can deepen the architect's role in the design of structures and material selection.

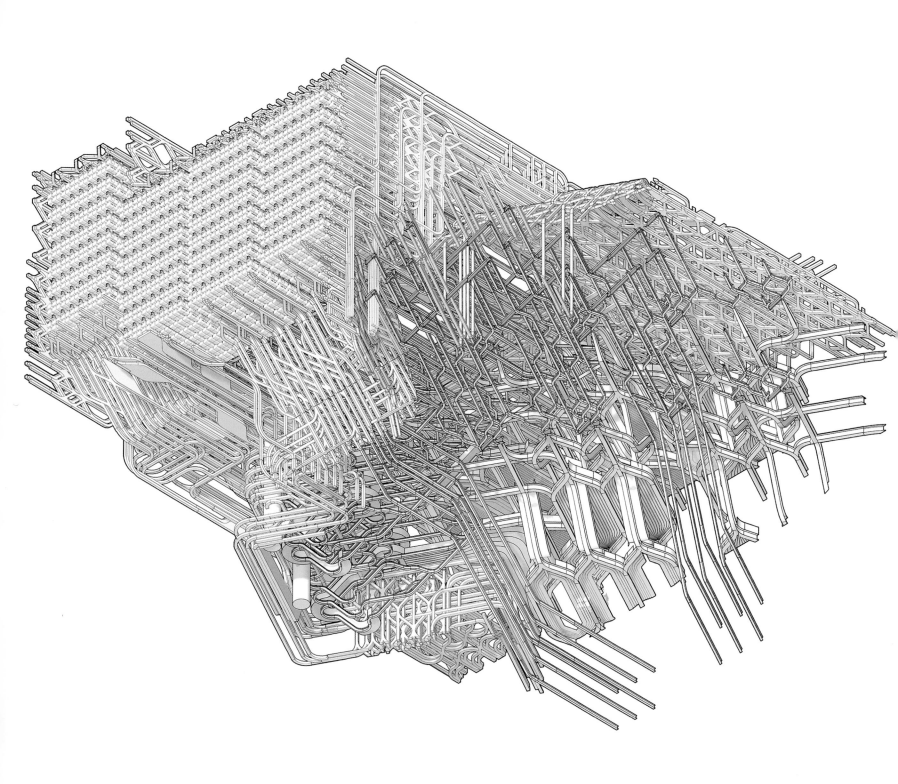

Choisey Axonometric. Project by Agata Jakubowska and Shi Zhang

Technology opens up new frameworks for considering synergies between technology and aesthetics. Architects who have been able to add such a layer of aesthetic sophistication to their designs share several characteristics that are key to the current design discourse. Their projects use techniques that inform new generations of techniques while bypassing methods completely dependent on the rigorous application of scientific standards. Their focus is notably on qualities of space as opposed to efficiencies. Design ability enables these architects to also incorporate the myriad conditions for architectural creation including, but not limited to, constraints associated with zoning, building codes, organization, space, program, circulation, fabrication, assembly, and cost.

The Master of Science in Design in Advanced Architectural Design program at the University of Pennsylvania Weitzman School of Design is very interested in aesthetics that have arisen from the use of digital techniques. These include folds, nests, weaves, braids, and branches to name a few. There is an emphasis on achieving nuance and aesthetic sensibility within the formal development of projects. A necessary starting point is the mastery of digital techniques for the design and fabrication of buildings and assembly systems. A reliance on prescribed scripting procedures rarely yields architecture that can take on the robust nature of the discipline. Manipulation of code through discreet modeling software and the mediation of digital technique is essential to formulating aesthetics. Working through the process of mastering techniques is a necessary, internally driven underpinning to developing a sensibility to the formal features achieved through the course of design.

The projects represented here exhibit a logic of thought that eschews the concept of mapping or revealing specific technical processes as strategies to generate a project's form. Instead, mastery of the techniques used allows each designer to assume a more sophisticated relationship with the creation of form. Aesthetic sensibilities emerge from negotiating the complexities of each project in the design process, as means of finding resolution to multiple, often conflicting needs and desires.

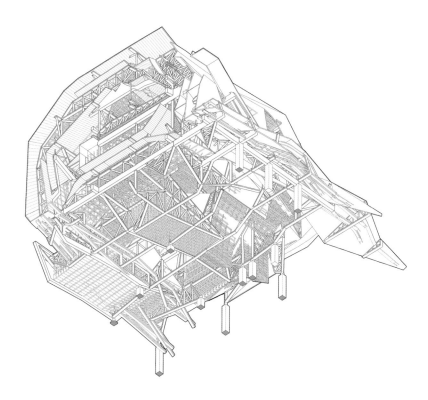

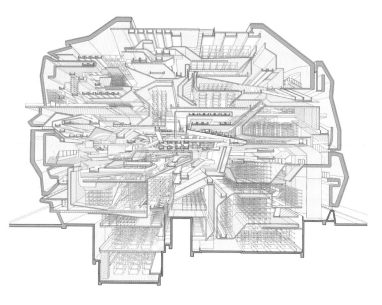

Weave Choisey Axonometric. Project by Han Zhang, Andi Zhang, and Yanang Ding

Accumulated Surface One-point Perspective. Project by Xiaoqing Guo, Hanning Liu, and Yingxin Zhang

DIGITAL TOOLS, ELEGANT FORMS—THE PURSUIT OF AESTHETICS

Frei Otto used one parameter to generate all his landmark research on tensile structures: gravity's relationship to the coefficient of material elasticity. Driven by an interest in the minimal use of materials, his research employed analog-computing methods to yield singularly constituted results—for example a catatonic curve or a derived surface that repeated itself to produce larger formal organizations. These analog methods, however, did not have the capacity to produce two competing relational criteria as a means of generating form.

As highlighted throughout this book, the airport specifically and architecture more broadly have multiple complexities that are difficult to condense into a single formal criterion. A more interrelational set of criteria is needed in order to develop architecture that has the complexities of an airport. As more factors such as pedestrian, vehicular, and cargo circulation as well as storage are incorporated, the ability for a greater number of formal features to emerge becomes possible. For instance, Bundle by Fangzhou Sun, Wenzhao Xu, and Hang Zhang uses a series of composite nodes that combine structural, logistic, and programmatic performance and provide an overall formal organization to the project. The presence of several criteria allows for a genealogy of interrelated features and forms to be constituted in the work; however, these arise only with specific intentions or goals for the project. When multiple criteria are employed, an aesthetic approach can unify discreet systems in a formal resolution while providing a visual language that subsumes technique. As such, the processes of design is not decipherable in the final form.

The act of design, then, is ultimately framed not by a singular aesthetic outlook, but rather grounded by and derived from the multiple constraints and ambitions of a given project as negotiated by the architect. Aesthetics neither prepends nor appends the design and construction logic but is the very the basis for navigating a project. To develop such aesthetic work, layered levels of design intelligence are required which incorporate organizational and spatial aspects.

Spatial configuration and organization act as criteria relative to the form of a project. Organizationally, the traditional concept of program is redefined through visible relationships between space and use that fluctuate between logistics systems and spatial ambience, blurring the relationship between human and mechanistic spaces.

By this logic, the blurring of traditionally separated human and mechanistic spaces may yield relationships that emerge through the ongoing interactions between the two. The projects highlighted in the Structured Logistics section of this book all develop aesthetics by intertwining traditionally separate programmatic and technical systems in airports, reimagining passenger experience in the process. Weave by Han Zhang, Andi Zhang, and Yanang Ding uses the truss to organize the building programmatically. The truss expands and contracts across the project to operate plurally as structure, storage space for cargo, and inhabitable space for people. Further, in certain areas there is an intermingling of cargo logistics and human occupation. A new aesthetic logic emerges from these formal and programmatic fluctuations and juxtapositions, which, in turn, informs, permeates, and distinguishes the project both from its differentiated counterparts as well as the predominant modern airport typology.

Spatially, the interior reveals its organization through the gradual transformation of relationships it forms to the moving human body. In addition, this internal organization is adapted to site constraints and the greater environment that it operates within. Aesthetics is achieved when rather than allowing external constraints to alter and compromise the internal organization, the internal organization is manipulated and transformed to adapt to external constraints. This requires a highly developed design and aesthetic sensibility; reliance on technique alone yields average buildings. Projects in the Atmosphere and Form sections all show ways in which external constraints can be deployed across a project as the very fabric of architecture. For instance, in Quilt, designed by Dongyun Kim, Qianni Shi and Zhaoyuan Gou, cargo is interpreted in terms of storage time frames and sizes of packages, which are articulated and mechanized in complex sorting and organization arrangements hidden within a highly legible exterior box. There is also a separation between the top and bottom of the building, which creates an space and allows for views from the passenger

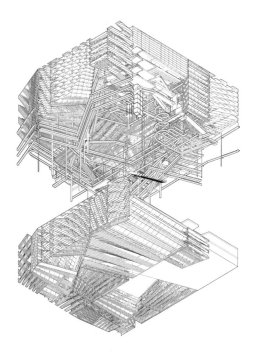

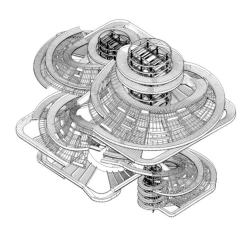

Quilt Choisey Axonometric. Project by Dongyun Kim, Qianni Shi, and Zhaoyuan Gou

Bundle Choisey Axonometric. Project by Fangzhou Sun, Wenzhao Xu, and Hang Zhang

drop off to the airplane runway. Aesthetically, this project along with others featured here, notably Froth, Striation, and Contort, moves beyond the singular iconicity of form latent in airport design towards a manifold and nuanced, perhaps "post-industrial," typology.

During the process of learning and mastering technique, a fineness of manner and expression develops through the cultivation of refinement, exactness, and precision with respect to form, space, and bodily movement. The projects that result are highly customized. Once technique is controlled and coordinated in a repertoire, formal features allow for gracefulness and movement to express the precision and mastery achieved with specific techniques. Through gracefulness, the external appearance of the form allows the internal organization and its sophistication—experienced in movement through the space— to be perceived. There is a seamless transition between internal and external organization, which puts the internal techniques and their mastery on display externally. This fine tuning between experience, form, and performance can be described as elegance in architecture. The projects in this book possess formal features and material articulations sufficiently rich to engage the realm of bodily sensation. Buildings that produce elegant sensations have formal characteristics including presence, balance, feature and surface refinement, and restrained opulence.

An elegant building needs to be situated such that its presence is perceived, and, at the same time, it must participate as an extension of the field in which it operates. Formal balance is created when the refinement of transformational spatial configurations produce forms that seemingly defy gravity. An exceptionally sophisticated integration of structure, building systems, and new materials may allow for forms to appear suspended or in possession of lightness. In terms of formal appearance, this lightness includes fine and delicate qualities within the multiple assemblies and individual elements that constitute the building design. The scale of each element in the building including storage, cavities and spaces needs to be attenuated and designed with precision in order to produce such desired effects. In Accumulated Surface, designed by Xiaoqing Guo, Hanning Liu, and Yingxin Zhang, the directionality of carefully attenuated surfaces is broken up by precisely designed misalignments where passenger and logistic areas create buoyancy, lightness, and balance. These qualities are usually achieved through continuity, yet, in this project, they are achieved through highly choreographed misalignments between disjunct surfaces.

If the scale of each element is too diminutive in relation to the greater building design, or if the building is constituted by too many smaller pieces, then the occupant may be overwhelmed, and the aesthetic potential is lost. When the relation of elements and systems to building is attuned, elegant sensations—rather than unresolved or chaotic sensations—may be achieved at points of juxtaposition.

Refined surfaces must be elaborated to develop juxtapositions between different formal features and are crucial to the production of elegant sensations. The formal opulence of a building is constituted by creating a genealogy of formal features that are at once distinctive yet interrelated. In an elegant composition, each feature is endowed with differences, and difference between features is gradual. Changes between features are mediated by surface modulation. These areas of change are constructed as deviations from a rule-generated surface, embedding geometrical characteristics within the perceptual and material circumstances of building. In Contort, by Hao Zheng and Meng Zhen, rectilinear floors are converge upon a circular geometry, which embeds geometrical characteristics within the perceptual and material circumstances of the building in terms of flow, view, and spatial organization. The structure or surface is key, as it provides a background from which features acquire legibility and, ultimately, a framework for their performance.

THE PRESENCE—AND FUTURE—OF AESTHETICS

While techniques are continually developed, updated, and changed, architects need to adapt and make changes in technique that are useful for their discipline. To return to the previous discussion of emergent technologies, artificial intelligence is a data-driven technique that is used to argue for dematerialization and efficiency in urbanism in service of autonomous vehicles. If a data-driven technology is used to affect the material world, we have a better chance of maintaining the exciting experiences that large cities offer today. Style transfer, for instance, uses recognition software and AI image banks to re-write images that are fed through its portal. This effectively hacks an existing software to generate images that are relevant to contemporary culture. If these images are materialized through an iterative design process, they can affect the material condition of the city. The aesthetics associated with projects that use such tools effectively are contemporary.

Aesthetics can guide and deepen implementation of technology in design processes. Digital techniques are powerful allies in distilling the aesthetics that can drive a

project and yield elegant architectural sensations. An increasingly prevalent trend is the development of digital models that integrate aspects of material quantities and cost. Here, design moves beyond effective use of CNC fabrication towards a highly integrated model that can compute costs dependent on factors such as material curvature and joinery. The customization of these parts as well as their modulation, fabrication, and assembly provide a bespoke quality to architecture. Thus, the formal attributes of architecture developed during the design process may integrate nuances of negotiation with fabrication industries, streamlining project workflows while enhancing the embedded custom qualities and intelligence of designs.

The pursuit of aesthetics in the MSD-Advanced Architecture Design program ultimately incorporates a wider range of technologies deployed narrowly in its quest to create aesthetics that manifest in built architecture. These are assemblies of different materials that come together to yield an aesthetic including structure, logistics, and surface. Mastery of technique remains important and underpins the use of digital technologies in the design and manufacturing of buildings. But, ultimately, a highly sophisticated formal language—including the driving force of aesthetic pleasure—propels these projects forward.

PROJECT DESCRIPTIONS FORM

Airports are developed as a series of layers that move material through them separating human and non-human spaces. The stratification of these layers is absolute, and a given. The projects form is derived from the vastness of the space necessary for the movement of human and non-human material. The area necessary is covered by a long-span truss that determines the form of the airport. Form in this sense is one determined by the most efficient routes that material takes through it. The most useful things in society are determined by their redundancy and not their efficiency. For example, the laptop contains different processors for calculation, writing papers, and surfing the internet for example. This redundancy is why cell phones have now turned into becoming minicomputers. In the same way the following projects take advantage of logistics and human spaces and nest them in one another to create forms that alter spatial perception and oscillate between human experience and storage.

PROJECT 10 **CONTORT**

JFK Airport New Terminal Hub, Queens, New York

Hao Zheng, Meng Zhen

CONTORT has two axes of articulation, the oblique and the
orthogonal. The combination of both axes results in spaces that
negotiate both and results in a third spatial condition one that
is neither on the oblique or orthogonal. The swelling of the form
develops tension and compression between the different cavities
whether large or small. The material moves through the project
in different ways, the logistics systems is sometimes contained
within the structure and at other times is compressed between
spaces that are open to human experience. This flickering
between logistics and human spaces contributes to the project
form. The overall form is also in between figure and ground
allowing for spaces around the figure to be occupied by humans
and no humans alike.

Right: Short Building Section

Bottom: Choisey Axonometric

01 Truck Dock
02 Passenger Drop-off
03 Cargo Lift
04 Cargo Storage
05 Departure Hall
06 Luggage Sorting System
07 Cargo Sorting Area
08 Skylight

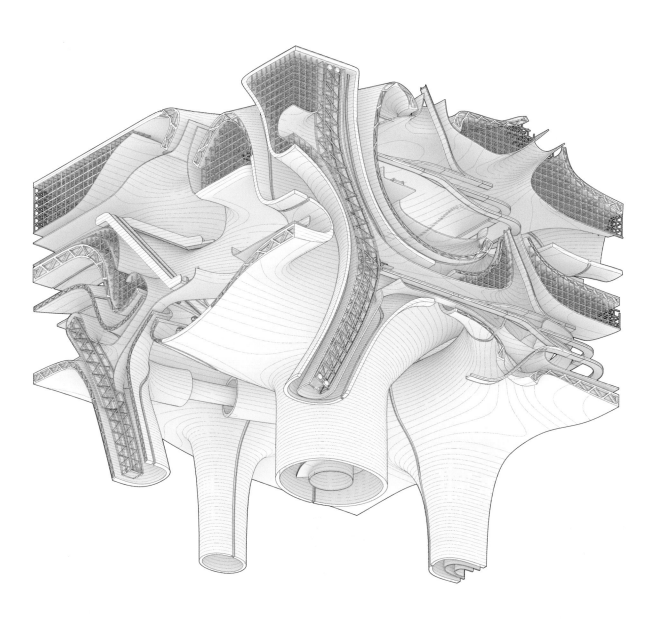

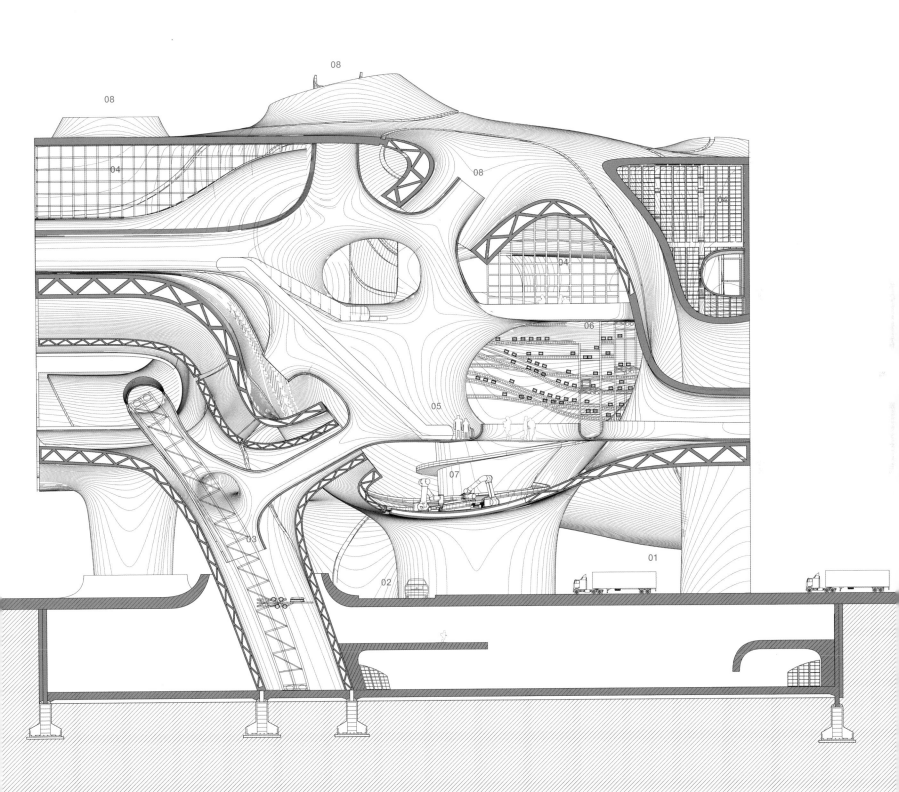

CONTORT, JFK AIRPORT NEW TERMINAL HUB, QUEENS, NEW YORK   **PROJECT 10**   FORM

Section Model Rendering

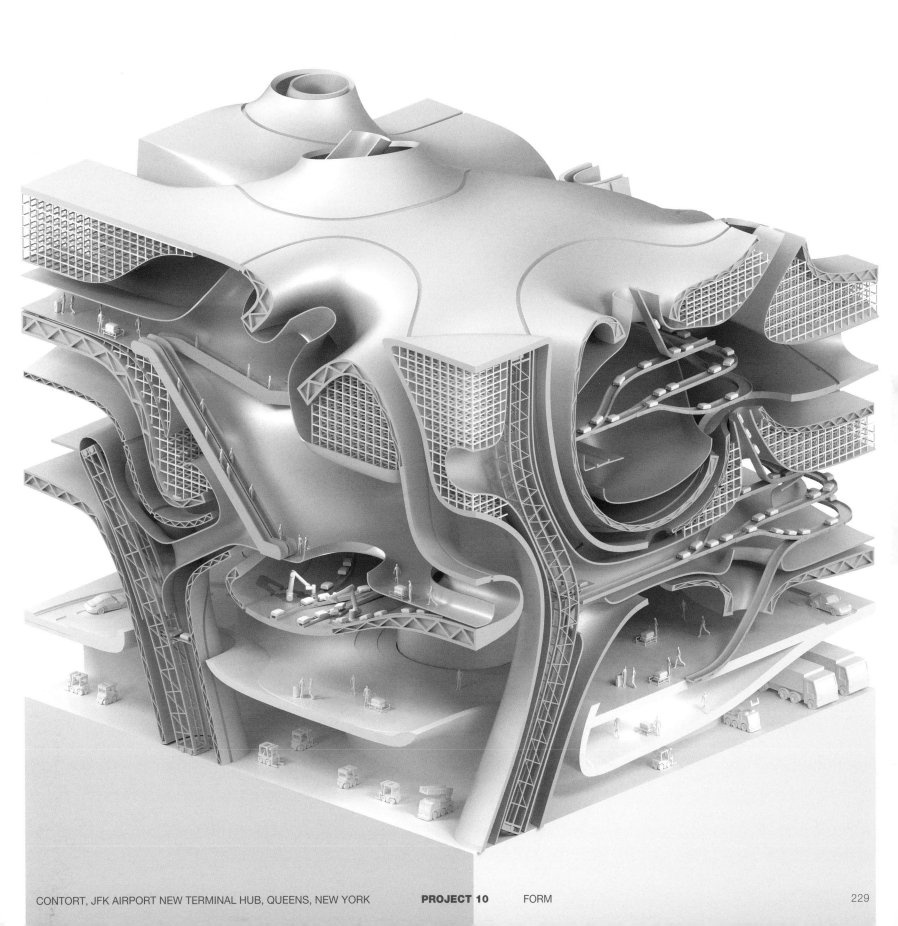

Right: Physical Section Model, 2'x2'x2', 3D Printed PLA

Bottom: Detail View of Physical Section Model

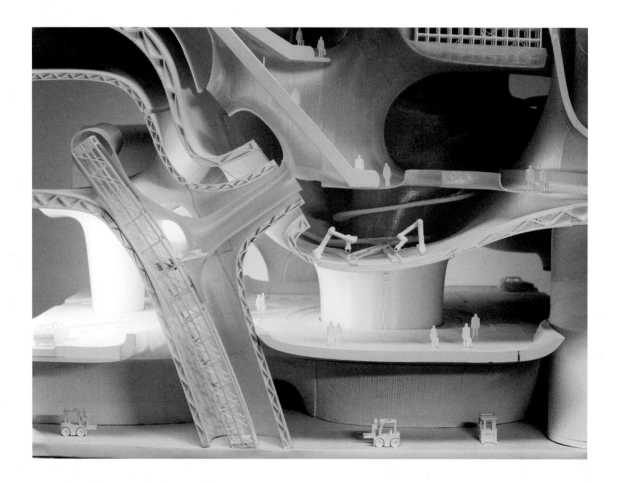

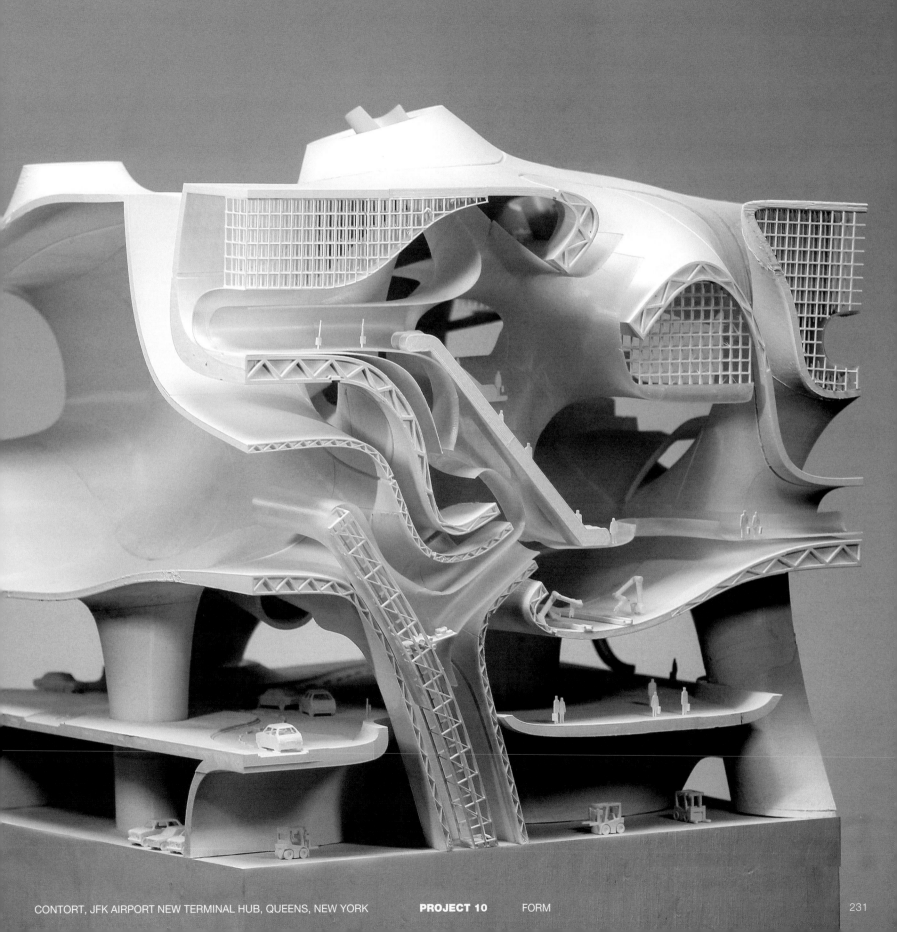

Physical Section Model, 2'x2'x2', 3D Printed PLA

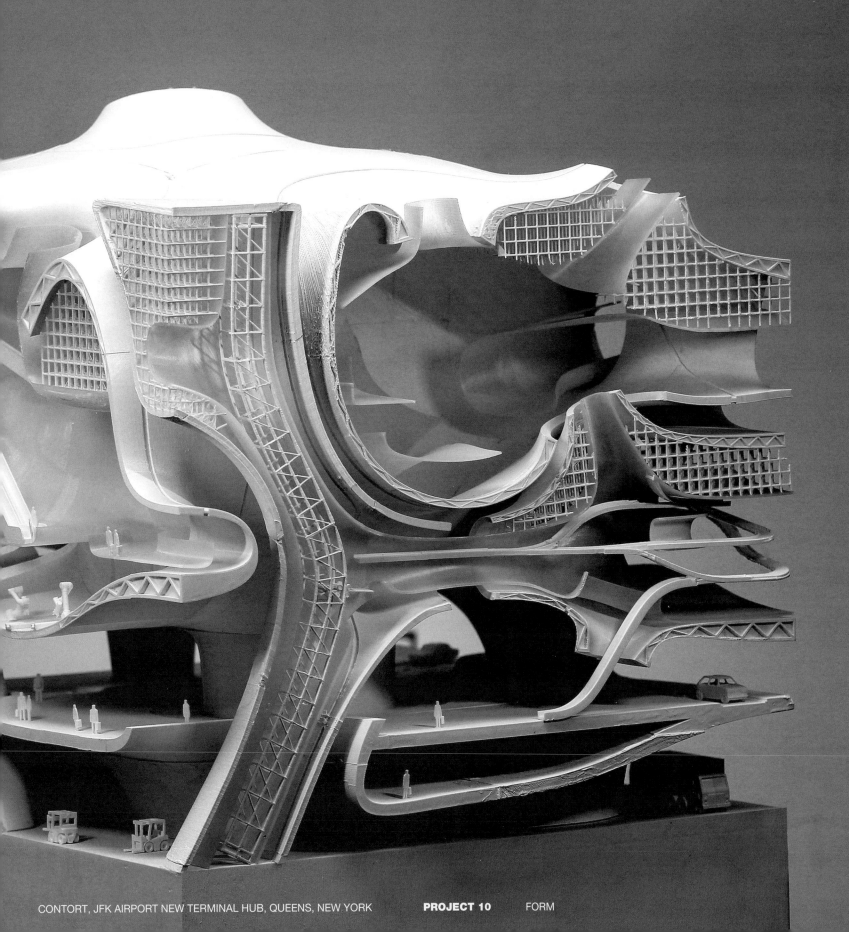

PROJECT 11 **MACHINE**

JFK Airport New Terminal Hub, Queens, New York

Zhuoqing Cai, Jounghwa Kim, Zehua Zhang

MACHINE utilizes the cargo and luggage sorting systems as
the façade of the building yielding a machine aesthetic. The
aesthetic arrives from the sorting mechanism of the logistics
system accumulating and making the enclosure of the building.
The process is revealed on the exterior of the building providing
a unique experience for passengers entering or using another
terminal. As the sorting mechanism penetrates the building
envelope it bundles into three-dimensional horizontal stacks
that organizes the spaces for passengers. On the interior of the
building, the layers of logistics equipment give way to a series of
linear spaces allowing the passengers the same experience as
cargo.

Top Left: Short Building Section

Bottom: Long Building Section

01   Baggage Claim
02   Restroom
03   Cargo Sorting Area
04   Cargo Pick-up Area
05   Cargo Transportation
06   Cargo Storage
07   Pedestrian Bridge
08   Offices
09   Lounge Space
10   Passenger Check Point
11   Atrium

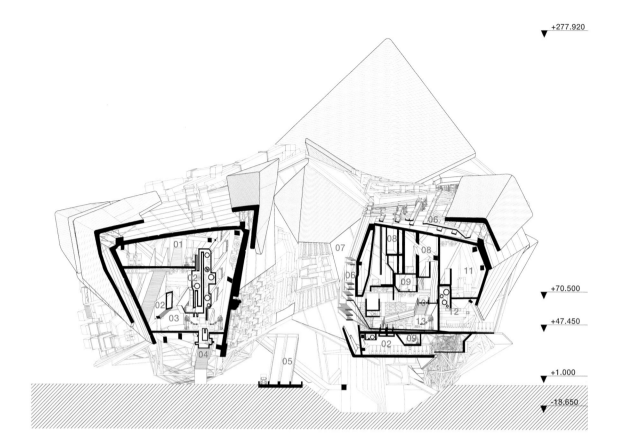

+277.920

+70.500

+47.450

+1.000

-18.650

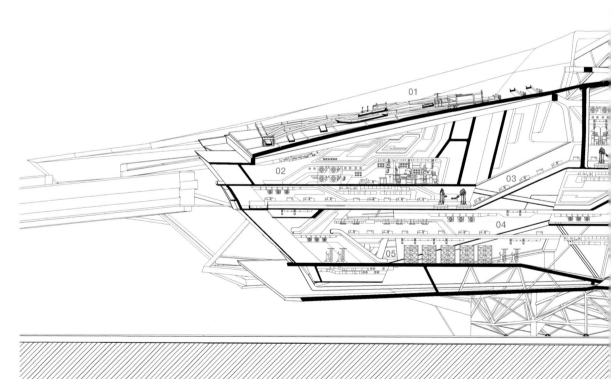

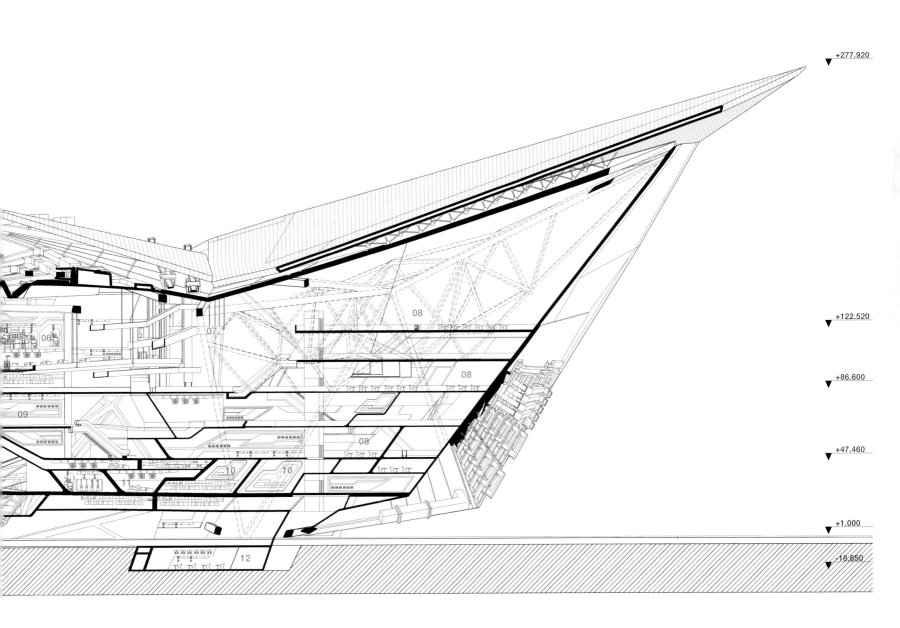

+277.920

+122.520

+86.600

+47.460

+1.000

-18.650

06

07

08

08

09

08

10   10

1

12

Section Model Rendering

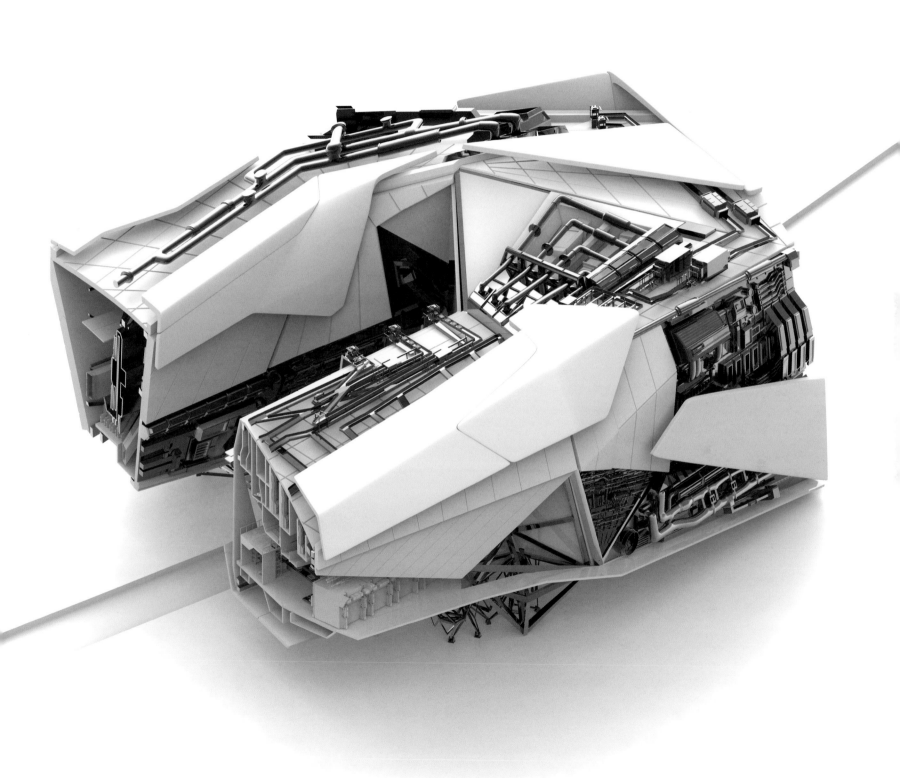

Right: Physical Section Model, 2'x2'x2', 3D Printed PLA

Bottom: Detail View of Physical Section Model

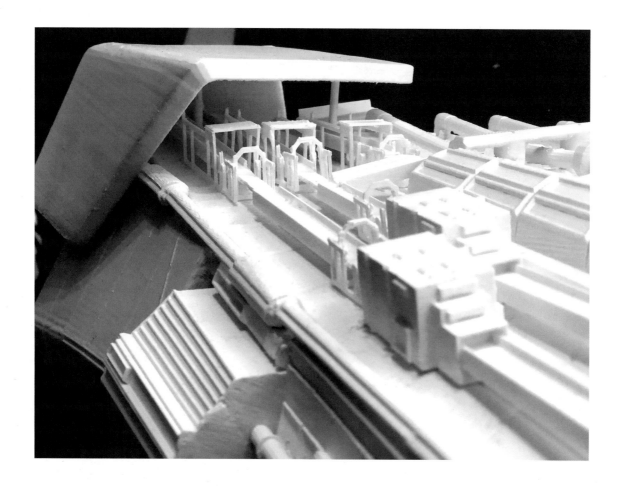

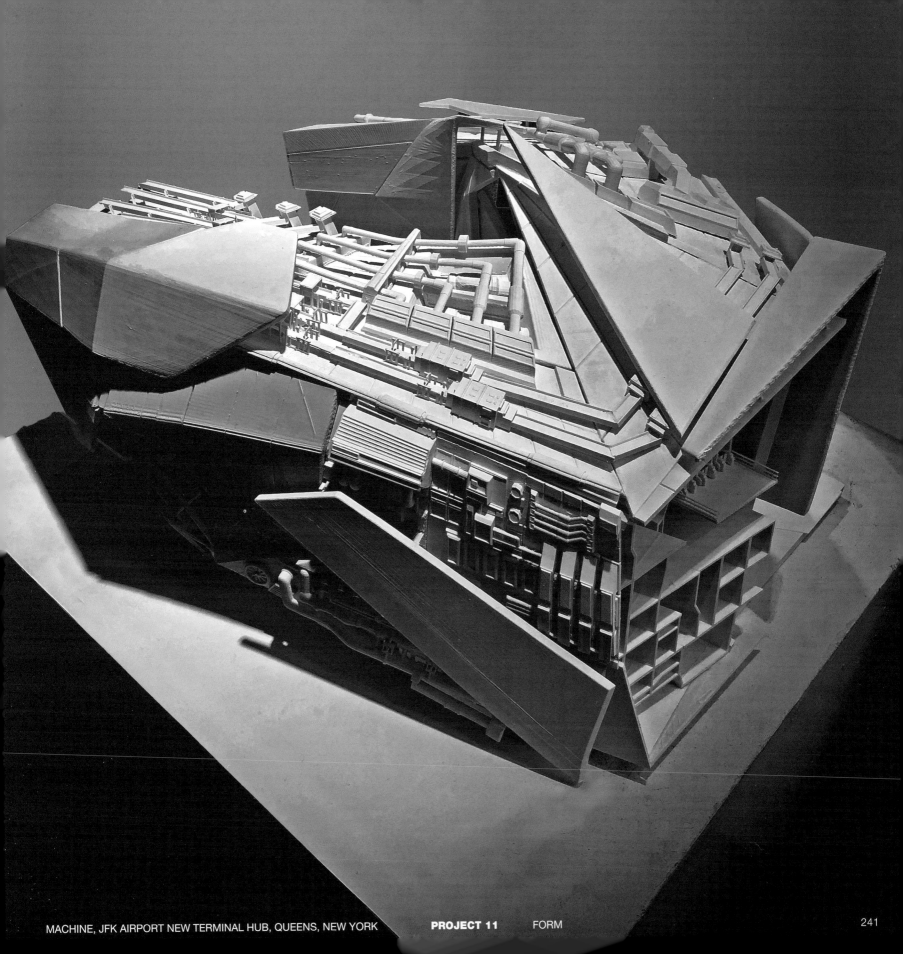

MACHINE, JFK AIRPORT NEW TERMINAL HUB, QUEENS, NEW YORK **PROJECT 11** FORM

PROJECT 12   **BLOCK**

JFK Airport New Terminal Hub, Queens, New York

Yu Mao, Wenhao Xu, Adriana Davis

BLOCK leverages the structural capacity of surface to develop a form that incorporates humans and logistics at different places within a mass that is hovering over the site. The heaviness of the form is in contrast with the structural surfaces that provide the stability for the project to be lifted in addition to the insides being used in novel ways. The compression of public space outside and on the interior articulates a desire to oscillate between human and non-human spaces, not relegating one function to one form. The structural elements in some cases are used by people and have logistics poke through them, and on the converse the program switches to mostly contain logistics and yet there are spaces for people that travers these areas.

Long Building Section

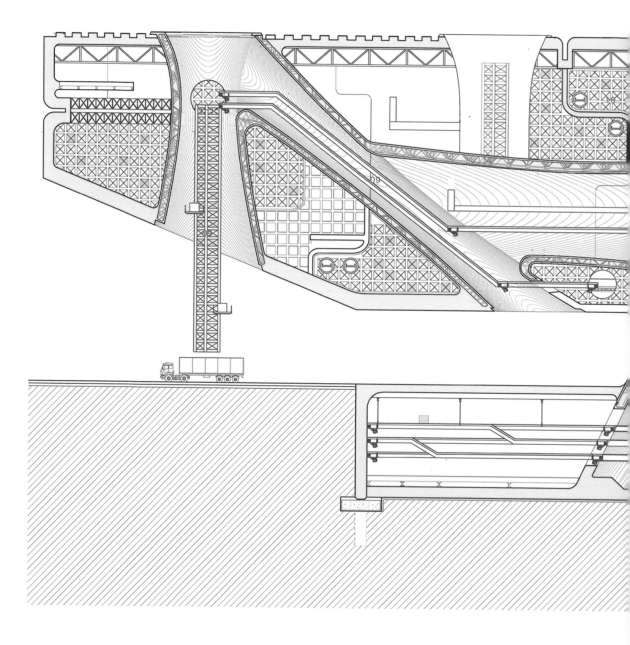

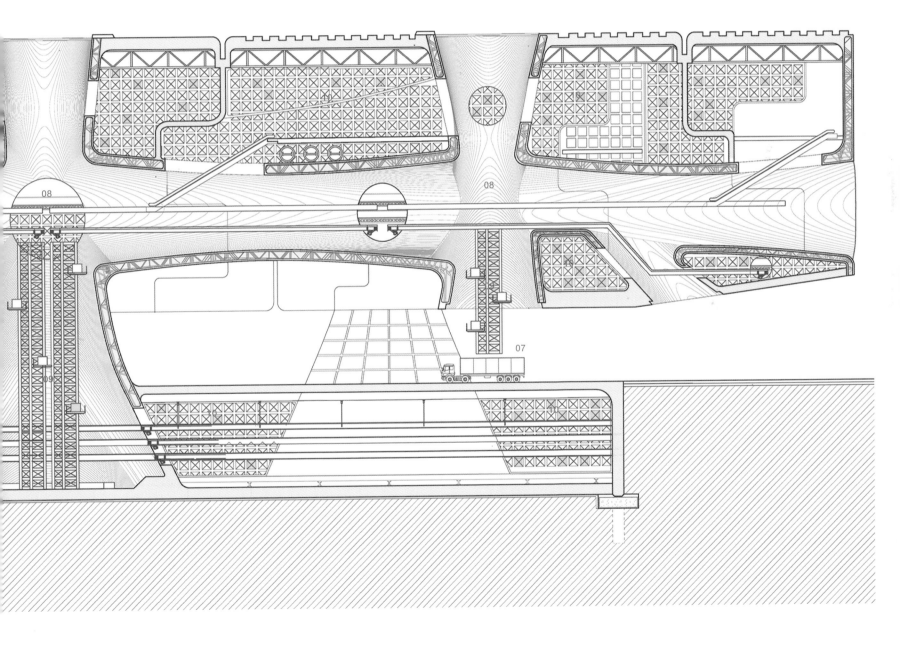

BLOCK, JFK AIRPORT NEW TERMINAL HUB, QUEENS, NEW YORK **PROJECT 12** FORM

Top Right: Floor Plan

Bottom: Long Building Elevation

01   Luggage Distribution System
02   Luggage Drop-off Area
03   Passenger Drop-off Area
04   Air Train
05   Air Train Station
06   Passenger Pick-up
07   Cargo Pick-up and Drop-off
08   Main Hall
09   Cargo Transportation System
10   Cargo Storage
11   Cargo Distribution System
12   Baggage Claim

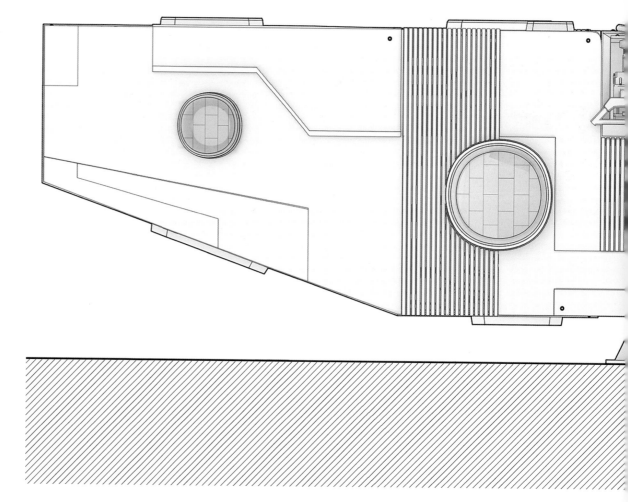

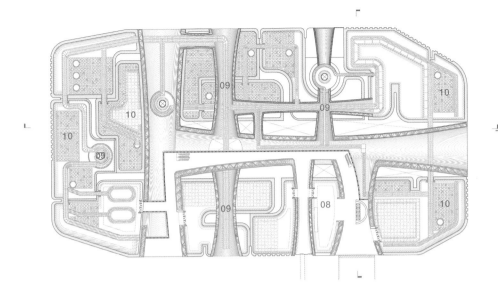

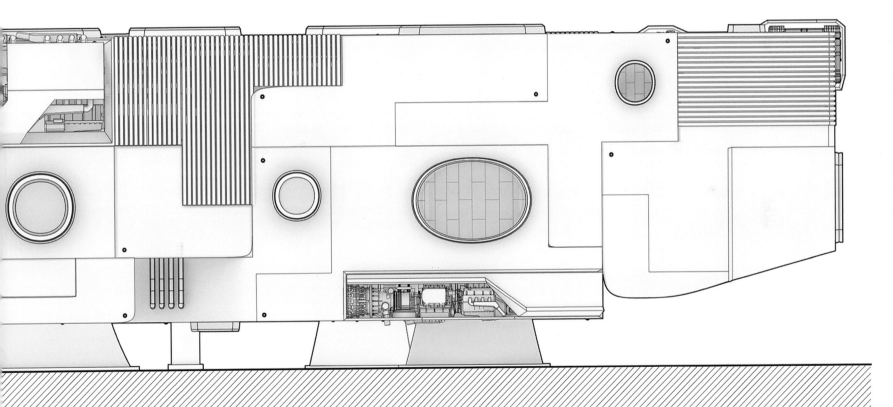

Right: Section Model Rendering

Left: Exploded Axonometric

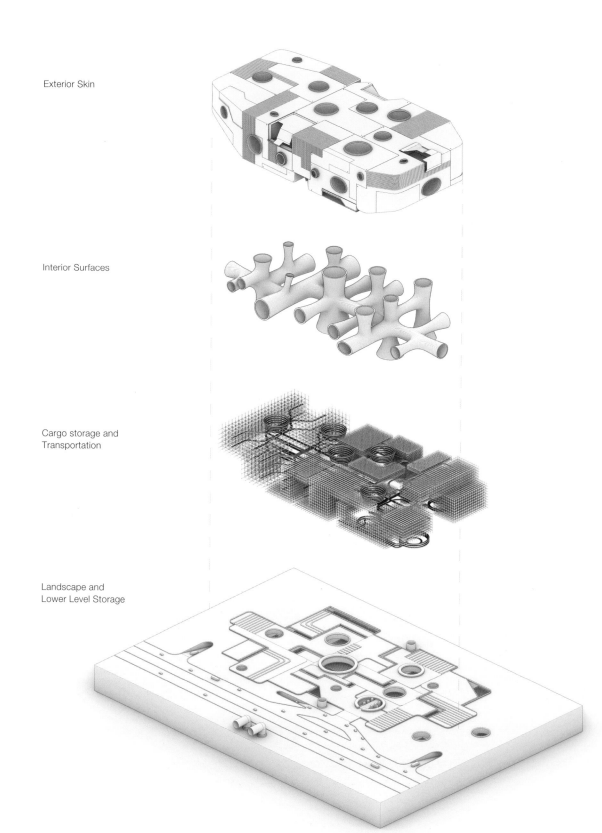

Exterior Skin

Interior Surfaces

Cargo storage and
Transportation

Landscape and
Lower Level Storage

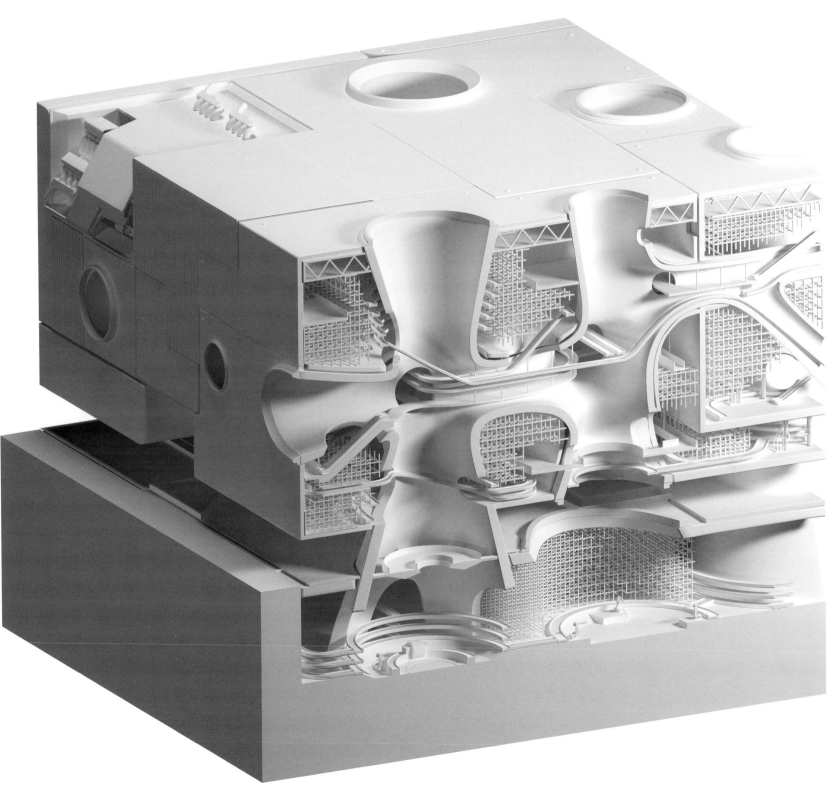

BLOCK, JFK AIRPORT NEW TERMINAL HUB, QUEENS, NEW YORK **PROJECT 12** FORM

Physical Section Model, 2'x2'x2', 3D Printed PLA

Physical Section Model, 2'x2'x2', 3D Printed PLA

PROJECT 13   **NEST**

JFK Airport New Terminal Hub, Queens, New York

Wenjia Guo, Qingyang Li, Yuanyi Zhou

NEST is designed as a repository for packages delivered by drones that are sorted by size and weight through the different compartments contained off of the main arteries of material flow. Material flow expands and contracts cavities around it for human experience. The building form negotiates the ground plane in a delicate manner increasing the tension between the packages, their flow and the human. The resulting series of drop offs and pick-ups allow the building to disengage the ground in areas. These systems of organization along with the movement of humans develop internal forms that push the co-existence of repository and human experience simultaneously. The redundancy in the surfaces allows for the careful calibration of human experience that is intersected with material flows developing an exciting experience for the human.

Ground Floor Plan

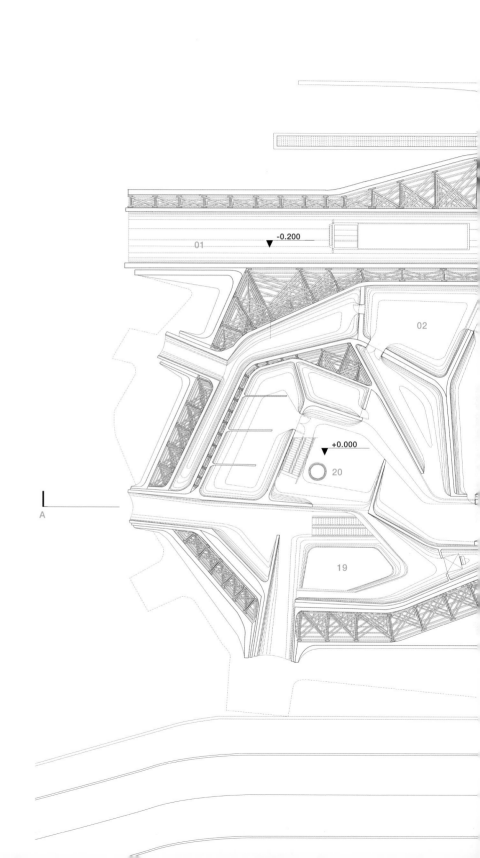

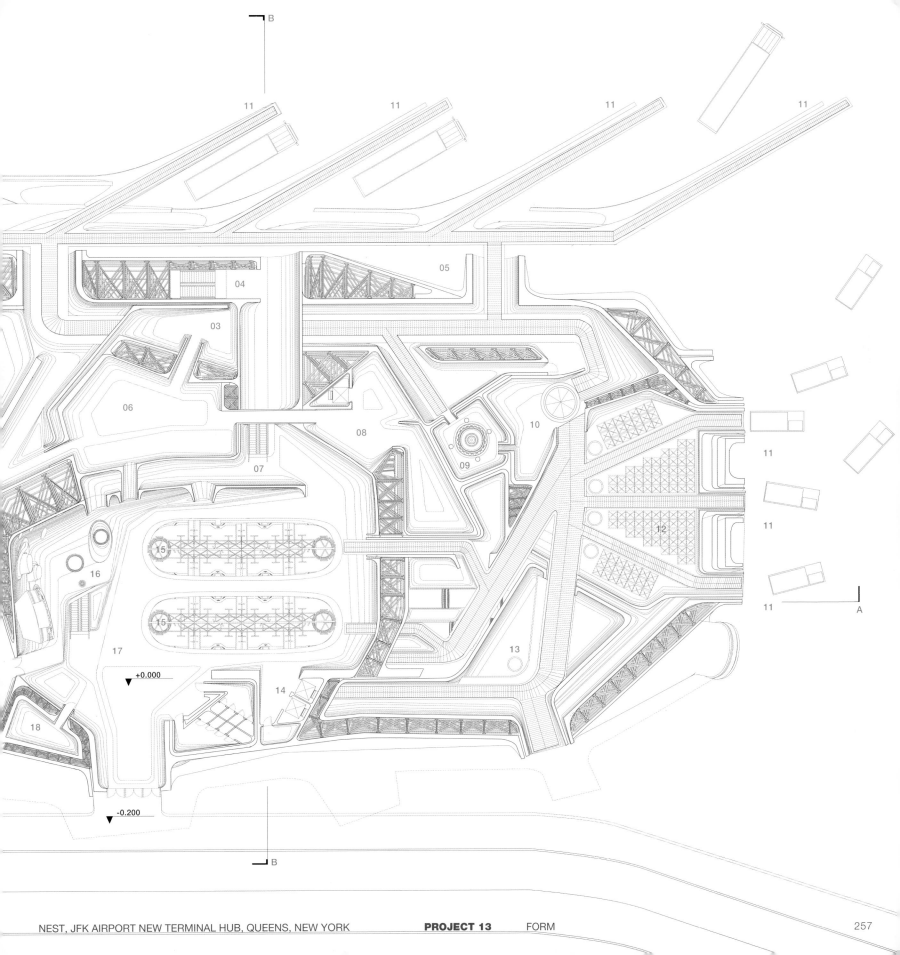

NEST, JFK AIRPORT NEW TERMINAL HUB, QUEENS, NEW YORK   **PROJECT 13**   FORM

Long Building Section

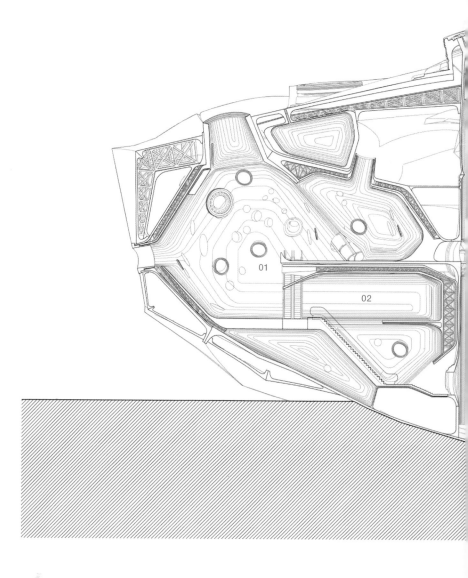

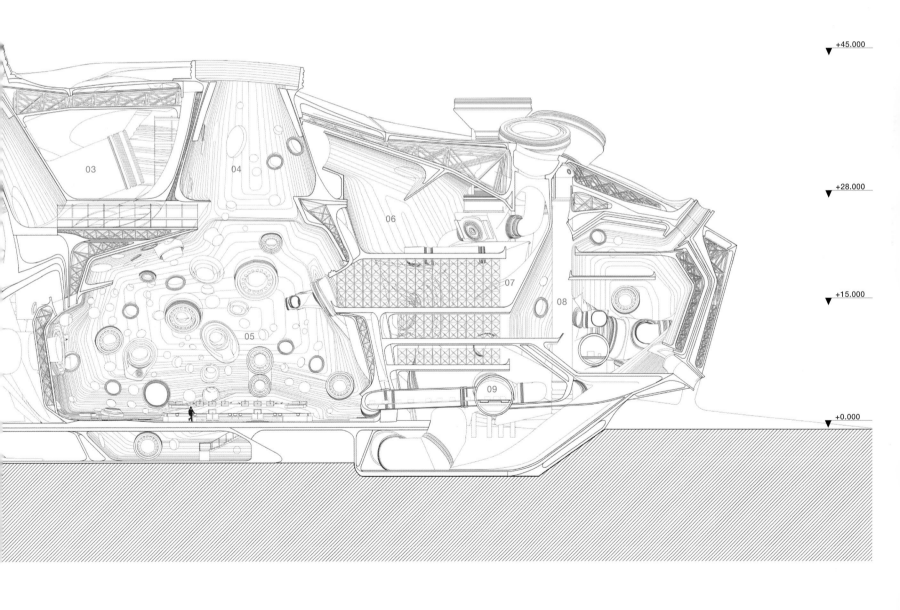

03

04

06

07

08

05

09

+45.000

+28.000

+15.000

+0.000

Section Model Rendering

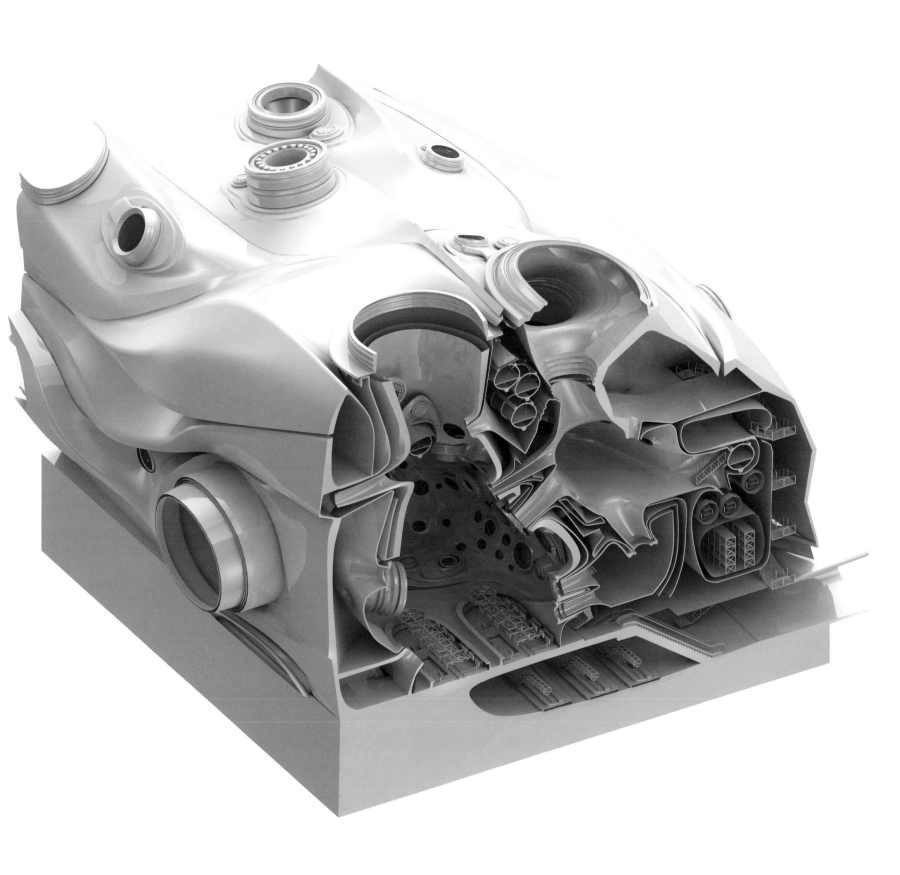

Right: Physical Section Model, 2'x2'x2', 3D Printed PLA

Bottom: Detail View of Physical Section Model

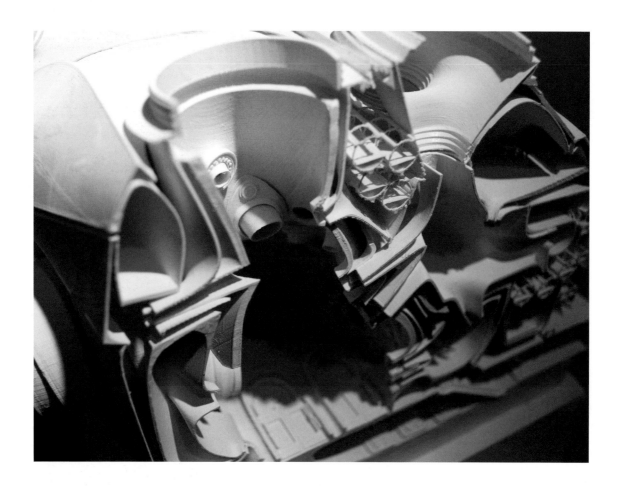

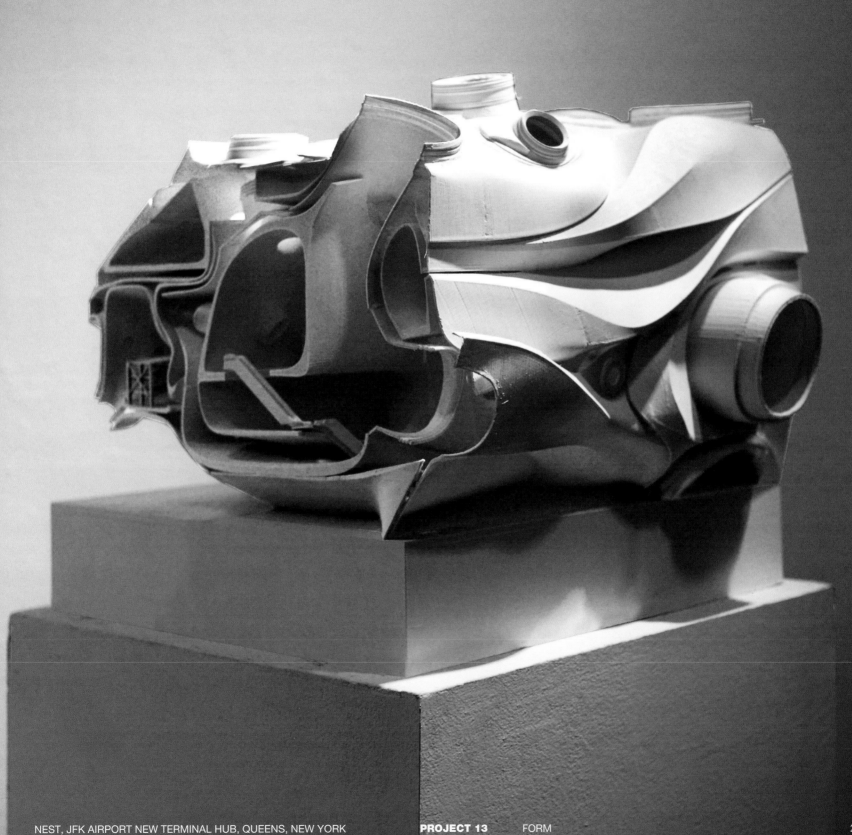

CONTRIBUTORS' BIOGRAPHIES

Ali Rahim

Professor of Architecture
Director MSD-AAD
Author

Ali Rahim is a Professor of Architecture at the Weitzman School, University of Pennsylvania where he directs the Master of Science in design, Advanced Architecture Design program. He received a Master of Architecture from Columbia University where he won the Award in Design Excellence and a BS in Architecture from the University of Michigan. He has served as the Studio Zaha Hadid Visiting Professor at the University of Applied Arts in Vienna, as the Louis I. Kahn Visiting Professor at Yale University, and as a Visiting Architecture Professor at Harvard University and Southern California Institute of Architecture (SCI-Arc). He is also Director of Contemporary Architecture Practice with Hina Jamelle in TriBeCa, New York City, and Shanghai, China. The firm is known for its award-winning and futuristic work that uses digital techniques for the design and manufacturing of architecture. His projects have been exhibited extensively, at such locations as the Museum of Modern Art (New York), the Serpentine Gallery (London), and the Tel Aviv Museum of Art. He has received many awards for his work including 50 under 50, Architectural Record Design Vanguard, Interiors and Products. His work has been published in over 200 domestic and international magazines, journals, and newspapers. His authored books include Catalytic Formations: Architecture and Digital Design (China Building Press, 2012), Catalytic Formations: Architecture and Digital Design (Routledge, 2006) and has co-edited Impact (2020) and Elegance (2007) for Architectural design, London and Contemporary Techniques in Architecture (2002) and Contemporary Processes in Architecture (2000) also for Architectural Design London.

Ezio Blasetti

Critic MSD-AAD

Ezio Blasetti is a Lecturer at the Weitzman School of Design, University of Pennsylvania. He has earned a Master of Science in advanced architectural design from Columbia University after having previously studied in Athens and Paris. In 2009 he co-founded ahylo, a design, research and construction practice as well as "apomechanes," an annual intensive summer studio on algorithmic processes and fabrication. Founder of algorithmicdesign.net, Ezio is 1/3 of Serge Studio and his recent collaborations include biothing, acconci studio, and a|Um studio. His recent work at Acconci Studio has received awards in international competitions – 2008 Annual Design Review I.D. / Perm Museum XXI / Kravi Hora Sculpture Park. He has taught generative design studios and seminars by means of computational geometry at Pratt Institute, the Architectural Association, Rensselaer Polytechnic Institute, and Columbia University. He is a registered architect in Greece, where in 2004 he co-founded otn studio, a young design-build practice. His work has been exhibited and published internationally.

Brian DeLuna

Critic MSD-AAD

Brian DeLuna is a Lecturer at the Weitzman School of Design, University of Pennsylvania and Visiting Assistant Professor at Pratt Institute. He received a Master of Science, Advanced Architecture Design from Columbia University and a Bachelor of Architecture from Southern California Institute of Architecture. His prior experience includes teaching at the New Jersey Institute of Technology, Princeton University as assistant to Hani Rashid, and conducting several workshops throughout the United States focusing on Digital Design and Visualization. He is the principal of Parabol, an interdisciplinary design firm operating in New York and Los Angeles. Prior work experience includes collaborating with international architecture firms including Xefirotarch, Los Angeles and Asymptote Architecture, New York where he supervised a wide range of high-profile projects as a senior designer.

Nathan Hume

Critic MSD-AAD
Author

Nathan Hume is a Lecturer at the University of Pennsylvania. He received a Master of Architecture from the Yale University School of Architecture and a Bachelor of Architecture from The Ohio State University. He is a licensed architect and partner at Hume Coover Studio with Abigail Hume in Brooklyn, New York. Hume Coover Studio strives to engage popular culture and contemporary architectural form through built and speculative projects, with an emphasis on experimenting with the organization of space through complex geometry, innovative materials, and counter-intuitive planning. Nathan and Abigail's work and writings have been published in the New York Times, Wired, Metropolis, Tarp, and Project and exhibited at the Yale University School of Architecture, the New York Center for Architecture and the Museum of Modern Art. Abigail and Nathan are also co-creators and editors of suckerPUNCHdaily.com a website that reviews the work of contemporary artists, architects, and designers who offer the stunningly unexpected and beautiful. Through suckerPUNCH they mounted the exhibition Fresh Punches at the Land of Tomorrow gallery and published the accompanying book.

Masoud Akbarzadeh

Author

Masoud Akbarzadeh is an Assistant Professor of Architecture in Structures and Advanced Technologies and the Director of the Polyhedral Structures Laboratory (PSL) at the Weitzman School, University of Pennsylvania. He holds a D.Sc. from the Institute of Technology in Architecture, ETH Zurich, where he was a Research Assistant in the Block Research Group. He holds two Masters degrees from MIT, a Master of Science in Architecture Studies (Computation) and a Master of Architecture, the thesis for which awarded him the SOM Prize. He also has a degree in Earthquake Engineering and Dynamics of Structures from the Iran University of Science and Technology and a BS in Civil and Environmental Engineering. His main research topic is Three-Dimensional Graphical Statics, which is a novel geometric method of structural design in three dimensions. In 2020, he has received the National Science Foundation CAREER Award to extend the methods of 3D/Polyhedral Graphic Statics for Education, Design, and Optimization of High-Performance Structures.

Arup Team

Author

Arup is a multinational professional services firm headquartered in London which provides engineering, architecture, design, planning, project management and consulting services for all aspects of the built environment. Founded by Sir Ove Arup in 1946, as the Ove N. Arup Consulting Engineers. He set out to build a firm where professionals of diverse disciplines could work together to produce projects of greater quality than was achievable by them working in isolation. In 1963, together with the architect Philip Dowson, Arup Associates was formed, this group continues to work under the banner of Arup Architecture following a streamlining of the Arup brand in 2018. Arup has over 14,000 staff based in 92 offices across 35 countries, and is present in Africa, the Americas, Australia, East Asia, Europe and the Middle East. Arup has participated in projects in over 160 countries. The article is co-authored by Susan Baer (Aviation, America's Leader), Pablo Lazo (Masterplanning, America's Leader), Justin Powell (Senior Aviation Expert), Jorge Valenzuela (Senior Transaction Advice Expert), Abigail Rolon (Senior Economic Expert), Jackie Coburn (Senior Airport Planner), Gabriela Antunes (Masterplanning and Urban Design), Alix Cocude (Transaction Advice Specialist).

Preetam Biswas

Author

Preetam Biswas is a Director of Structural Engineering at SOM. He has earned two Masters Degrees from the University of Illinois, a Master of Science in Civil Engineering, Construction Management and a Master of Architecture in Structural Engineering, Architectural Practice and Technology. He studied at the University of Bombay, Sir J.J. College, for his Undergraduate degree. He led the structural design of several award-winning towers, long-span structures such as airports, convention centers and stadiums, and specialty structures like cable wall systems. His notable work, Chhatrapati Shivaji International Airport in Mumbai (2014), features a long-span roof covering 70,000 square meters, making it one of the world's largest roofs without an expansion joint. Biswas has played a key role in establishing the Structural Engineering group in SOM's New York office. Within the SOM firmwide Structures Practice, his accomplishments include the initiation of new services as part of an integrated project delivery method for the construction phase of buildings. He has authored multiple technical papers. He is a voting member of the ASCE Tall Building Committee and serves as Chair of the Task Committee for Design and Performance of Tall Buildings for Wind. He is also member of the Structural Engineers Association of New York (SEoNY) Structural Engineering Licensure Committee.

Cristiano Ceccato

Author

Cristiano Ceccato is an Associate Director at Zaha Hadid Architects. He received a Master's degree in Computer Science from the Imperial College of Science and Technology and a Diploma in Architecture degree from the Architectural Association. His work entails a broad range of management, design and technology leadership responsibilities, leading large-scale public and private projects worldwide. Professional focus includes business development and client management; design and development of building infrastructure, including geometric rationalization & constructability resolution of structural & envelope systems; project governance and cost control through the introduction of Building Information Modelling (BIM) systems and associated practice methodologies across the firm. Previously he worked for Gehry Partners and was Director of Research & Consulting for Gehry Technologies. And He became an elected Fellow of the Royal Society of Arts in 2004. He has lectured widely about computational rule-based design systems and parametric form finding in digital building processes. He has also held academic faculty positions in London, Milan, Hong Kong, Los Angeles and Australia.

Christopher Hight

Author

Christopher Hight is a Professor of Architecture at Rice University School of Architecture. He has been a Fulbright Scholar and obtained a Ph.D. from the London Consortium at the University of London and a Master's degree in the Histories and Theories of Architecture from the Architectural Association. He is a designer and theorist who teaches graduate and undergraduate design studios and a theory seminar at Rice University School of Architecture. The design studios are organized as collaborative design research laboratories addressing the nexus of landscape, urbanism and emerging electronic and material assemblies. Previously he taught at the Architectural Association's Design Research Laboratory and has worked for the Renzo Piano Building Workshop. His books include one on cybernetics, formalism and post-World War Two architectural design (Routledge, 2007) and has co-edited an issue of Architectural Design on network design practices. He has published over 30 articles and has lectured internationally. At Rice he is the editor of the Architecture At Rice book series and organized the fourth Kennon symposium, Modulations.

Megan S. Ryerson

Author

Megan S. Ryerson is the UPS Chair of Transportation and an Associate Professor of City and Regional Planning and Electrical and Systems Engineering at the Weitzman School, University of Pennsylvania. She received her PhD from Civil and Environmental Engineering at the University of California, Berkeley an M.S. Civil and Environmental Engineering from the University of California, Berkeley and a B.S. Civil and Environmental Engineering from the University of Pennsylvania. She was appointed Associate Dean for Research of Weitzman School in 2018. She received her Ph.D. in Civil and Environmental Engineering from the University of California, Berkeley in 2010 and her B.Sc. in Systems Engineering from the University of Pennsylvania in 2003. Her major contributions are in the field of transportation infrastructure planning and demand forecasting. Her work has investigated how airports compete for air service across megaregions, how airlines can reconfigure their disaster planning to achieve more resilient outcomes, and how flights can be planned more proactive to reduce fuel consumption. She is a Governor-appointed member of the Pennsylvania Department of Transportation Aviation Advisory Committee, and is also a member of the Pennsylvania Department of Transportation State Transportation Innovation Council, the Board of Advisors for the Eno Center for Transportation, the Women's Transportation Seminar Philadelphia Chapter, and she was appointed by the U.S. Secretary of Transportation and the Governor of Pennsylvania to aviation-related advisory committees.

Tom Verebes

Author

Tom Verebes is Associate Dean of New York Institute of Technology. He received his Ph.D. from RMIT in Australia, a Research Certificate from the Laboratory of Primary Studies in Architecture in Paris, a Grad Dip (Design) from the Architectural Association in London and a Bachelor of Architecture and Bachelor of Science (Arch.) from McGill University in Canada. He has been the and the director of OCEAN CN, based in New York and Hong Kong. He has been Director of the AA Shanghai Summer School for eleven years (2007-2017) and AA Visiting School Xixinan (2017) in China. His former academic roles include Provost of Turenscape Academy in Beijing, the Associate Dean for Teaching & Learning (2011-2014), and Associate Professor at the University of Hong Kong (2009-2016), Co-Director of the Design Research Lab at the AA in London, where he had taught from 1996 to 2009. He was a guest professor at Akademie der Buildenden Künste ABK Stuttgart (2004-2006), and he has held visiting professor roles at University of Pennsylvania, Rensselaer Polytechnic Institute, Syracuse University, RMIT, Singapore University of Technology & Design SUTD, and University of Tokyo. He received his He has been published over 150 publications and he has lectured extensively in Asia, Europe, North America, Australia, Africa and the Middle East.

Caleb White

Author

Caleb White is Lecturer at the Weitzman School at the University of Pennsylvania. He received his Master of Architecture from the Weitzman School, University of Pennsylvania, and a Bachelors in Environmental Design from the University of Colorado where he was on the Deans List. He currently teaches a variety of courses ranging from digital modeling techniques and representation to emerging machine learning technology applied to architectural design. His interests are focused on the history of the autonomy of architecture in the city and the legacy of the urban object. He has also taught at Pratt Institute in Brooklyn New York. He is also Project Designer and Manager at the New York and Shanghai based firm Contemporary Architecture Practice. His projects include AMEC in Nanchang, China as well as Tencent, Xi'an, China and Mango TV, Changsha, China. His expertise is in the use of narrow technology that develops novel design and manufacturing techniques for architecture.

ACKNOWLEDGMENTS

Ali Rahim

Future Airports was made possible with funding from the University of Pennsylvania Weitzman School of Design and Weitzman Department of Architecture. I would like to personally thank Dean Frederick Steiner for his support.

I would also like to thank the Master of Science in Design, Advanced Architectural Design students and the team of faculty at the University of Pennsylvania. The students worked diligently to conceptualize and develop their work within the studio setting. My colleagues Brian Deluna, Nathan Hume, and Ezio Blasetti contributed greatly through our many discussions and their teaching of the students during desk critiques as well as reviews of student work. Our teaching assistants Caleb White, Angela Huang, Zachary Kile and Carrie Frattali contributed in their roles as teaching various software, drawings and physical model building. Finally I would like to thank all of the participants who contributed to the discussions during organized mid and final reviews: Preston Scott Cohen, Evan Douglis, Winka Dubbeldam, Hina

Jamelle, Ferda Kolatan, Rodolphe El Khoury, Jonathan Massey, Christopher Hight, Mariana Ibanez, Tom Verebes, Simon Kim, Andrew Saunders, Danielle Willems, Ed Gaskin, Marilyn Jordan Taylor, Marcelyn Gow, Mariana Ibañez, Viola Ago, Stan Dorin, Lisa Kenyon and Johannes Schafelner.

A special thanks to ARUP New York, Goldman Sachs New York and Zaha Hadid Architects, Kohn Pederson and Fox and Skidmore Owens and Merrill New York. Tom Kennedy of ARUP lectured brilliantly on logistics and the sustainability of an airport within a City and allowed ARUP's use of their space at 77 Water Street for Penn activities. Martha Kelley of Goldman Sachs lectured at 200 West Street and described private and public sector funded projects in great detail that are developed by Goldman Sachs in New York City. Patrik Schumacher lectured about Beijing Airport and the many challenges and revelations that occurred through the airport design and construction. Stan Dorin at KPF lectured about the intricate planning required in airports and their logistics and shared some of the work in their proposal for the Singapore Changde Airport. Peter Lefkovits at SOM gave us an overview of what it takes to design airports through three case studies of their own designs including their newly opened Mumbai International Airport.

This series of lectures and discussions elevated the discourse with the students but showed in the elevated the work of the students following these visits. All four of these lecture experiences were invaluable in the development of the criticality in thought and understanding of the complexity involved in the development of airports.

I would also like to thank the authors who contributed their time and effort to write articles for this book including Masoud Akbarzadeh, ARUP, Preetam Biswas, Cristiano Ceccato, Christopher Hight, Nate Hume, Megan Ryerson, Tom Verebes, and Caleb White,

Lastly, Caleb White, an architecture graduate of the Weitzman School of Design, has been heroic in his work on *Future Airports*. I would also like to thank Leon Yi-Liang Ko for his assistance in re-formatting parts of the book and Kirby Anderson at ORO Editions for her relentless work on editing the texts.

CR ARTICLES

AUTHORS

Masoud Akbarzadeh

Arup Team

Preetam Biswas

Cristiano Ceccato

Christopher Hight

Nathan Hume

Ali Rahim

Megan S. Ryerson

Tom Verebes

Caleb White

CR PROJECTS

CRITICS

Ali Rahim (Program Director)

Ezio Blasetti

Brian DeLuna

Nathan Hume

TEACHING ASSISTANTS

Carrie Frattali

Angela Huang

Ryosuke Imaeda

Zachary Kile

Angeliki Tzifa

Caleb White

2017 MSD-AAD STUDENTS

Mostafa Akbari	Mariana Righi
Zhuoqing Cai	Shatakshi Sharma
Xinyue Cao	Yingke Sun
Yifan Chu	Jiaqi Sun
Mengying Cui	Ziyi Tang
Wenna Dai	Shangzi Tu
Danni Dong	Hasan Caner Uretmen
Zihao Fang	Yuwei Wang
Wenjia Guo	Ruochen Wang
Yuting He	Daosheng Wang
Wenqi Huang	Di Xiao
Yuan Ji	Mengqi Xu
Hong Jiang	Haozhou Yang
Chae Young Kim	Xu Yao
Joung-Hwa Kim	Long Ye
Mikyung Lee	Dazhong Yi
Qingyang Li	Zehua Zhang
Yihan Li	Bei Zhang
Qiaoxi Liu	Xing Zhang
Chuqi Liu	Weimeng Zhang
Danyang Lou	Qishi Zhang
Yibo Ma	Weinan Zhao
Xiaoqing Meng	Shiling Zhong
Pu Pang	Yuanyi Zhou
Mu Qiao	Lei Zhou
Bowen Qin	Chengyao Zong
Khondaker Muhibur Rahman	